International Study on the Impact of Copyright Law on Digital Preservation

July 2008

A joint report of

The Library of Congress National Digital Information Infrastructure and Preservation Program

The Joint Information Systems Committee

The Open Access to Knowledge (OAK) Law Project

The SURFfoundation

The *International Study on the Impact of Copyright Law on Digital Preservation* is available in electronic form from each of the author organizations.

Cover image:
Digital Mercury by heyjoewhereyougoinwiththatguninyourhand available at http://www.flickr.com/photos/heyjoewhereyougoingwiththatguninyourhand/69725621/. This image is licensed under a Creative Commons Attribution 2.0 Generic License. To view a copy of this license go to http://creativecommons.org/licenses/by/2.0/ or send a letter to Creative Commons, 171 Second Street, Suite 300, San Francisco, California, 94105, USA.

ISBN: 978-0-9802988-9-5

Printed by QUT Printing Services, Brisbane, Australia

This study focuses on the copyright and related laws of Australia, the Netherlands, the United Kingdom and the United States and the impact of those laws on digital preservation of copyrighted works. It also addresses proposals for legislative reform and efforts to develop non-legislative solutions to the challenges that copyright law presents for digital preservation.

The International Study on the Impact of Copyright Law on Digital Preservation was written by:

The Library of Congress – National Digital Information Infrastructure and Preservation Program (NDIIPP) (U.S.):

June M. Besek – Executive Director, Kernochan Center for Law, Media and the Arts, Columbia Law School

William G. LeFurgy – Project Manager, Digital Initiatives, Office of Strategic Initiatives, Library of Congress

Christopher D. Weston – Attorney-Advisor, U.S. Copyright Office, Library of Congress

Joint Information Systems Committee (JISC) (U.K):

Adrienne Muir – Department of Information Science, Loughborough University

Open Access to Knowledge (OAK) Law Project* – Queensland University of Technology (QUT) Law Faculty (Australia).

Benedict Atkinson – Research Officer, OAK Law

Emma Carroll – Research Assistant, OAK Law

Jessica Coates – Project Manager, Creative Commons Clinic, ARC Centre of Excellence for Creative Industries and Innovation, QUT

Brian Fitzgerald – Professor of Intellectual Property and Innovation, QUT Law Faculty & Project Leader, OAK Law

*The OAK Law Project is funded by the Australian Department of Education, Employment and Workplace Relations

SURFfoundation (Netherlands):

Wilma Mossink – Legal Advisor, SURFfoundation

The introduction, summary and joint recommendations were jointly prepared. Each national group prepared its own country report.

The authors extend special thanks to:

Annemarie Beunen – Corporate Strategy Department, National Library of the Netherlands

Erin Driscoll – Legal Officer, National Film and Sound Archive, Australia

Michelle Gallinger – Digital Preservationist, Office of Strategic Initiatives, Library of Congress

Neil Grindley – Programme Manager, Digital Preservation, JISC London Office

Helen Hockx-Yu – Web Archiving Programme Manager, The British Library

Scott Kiel-Chisholm – Project Manager, OAK Law and Legal Framework for e-Research Project, QUT

Paul Koerbin – Manager, Web Archiving, the National Library of Australia

Abigail Potter – Digital Preservation Specialist, Library of Congress

Mary Rasenberger– former Senior Advisor for Public Policy and Programs, Office of Strategic Initiatives, Library of Congress

Sarah Waladan – Minter Ellison Lawyers

Table of Contents

A Note about Style

While the country reports are largely parallel, they are not entirely so, due to variations in the laws and practices relating to digital preservation in the participating countries. Also, each country report was created using the conventions for legal writing in the source country. Consequently there are differences among the country reports in citation style, spelling, punctuation, etc.

Part 1: Introduction

1.1 Purpose and Background of the Report

1.1.1 This Report was undertaken:

(1) to review the current state of copyright and related laws and their impact on digital preservation;
(2) to make recommendations for legislative reform and other solutions to ensure that libraries, archives and other preservation institutions can effectively preserve digital works and information in a manner consistent with international laws and norms of copyright and related rights; and
(3) to make recommendations for further study or activities to advance the recommendations in the Report.

1.1.2 Traditional works of authorship are increasingly created and disseminated to the public in digital form. Today, many radio and television programs, musical compositions, movies, maps, reports, stories, poems, letters, scholarly articles, newspapers and photographs are "born digital." There is also a growing trend to convert analog material to digital form ("digitization") so that it can be easily and efficiently stored, transmitted and accessed.

1.1.3 New forms of authorship, such as web sites, blogs and "user-generated content" of all kinds are flourishing in the dynamic environment of the Internet. These new works reflect the world's culture as much as their analog predecessors.

1.1.4 Embodying creative works in digital form has the unfortunate effect of potentially decreasing their usable lifespan. Digital information is ephemeral: it is easily deleted, written over or corrupted. Because information technology such as hardware, software and digital object formats evolves so rapidly, it can be difficult to access and use digital materials created only a few years ago. Countless born digital works are created every day, but countless born digital works are also lost every day as they are removed, replaced, superseded or left, forgotten, in obsolete formats and media. Digitized and born digital materials are an important part of the world's cultural heritage, but unless active steps are taken to preserve them, they will be lost.

1.1.5 Preservation is critical in the digital context to ensure continued long term access to historically, scientifically and socially valuable materials, so that future generations will be able to benefit from works created in the present day. Libraries, archives and other preservation institutions have been responsible for much of the preservation that has occurred in past centuries. Many books, musical compositions, drawings and other works are still available today for scholars and historians to read, hear and see because of the preservation efforts of these institutions. It is clear, however, that in many cases the digital equivalents of those analog works preserved in the past are not being preserved in any systematic way, in part because digital preservation triggers copyright concerns in a way that analog preservation does not.

1.1.6 There are significant technical, financial and legal obstacles to digital preservation. This Report focuses on the law – in particular, on copyright and related rights issues. Many of the activities involved in digital preservation, such as making multiple copies of a work, distributing copies among multiple institutions, and migrating works to new technological formats and media, involve the exercise of exclusive rights, including but not limited to the reproduction right. As the laws of the countries discussed in this report demonstrate, in many cases exceptions and limitations do not accommodate the actions required for digital preservation. The copyright and related rights issues, and various strategies to address them, are discussed further below.

1.2 The Participating Partners

1.2.1 This Report was prepared by the following organizations:

- *Australia*: Open Access to Knowledge Law Project;
- *The Netherlands*: The SURFfoundation;
- *The United Kingdom*: Joint Information Systems Committee; and
- *The United States*: Library of Congress, National Digital Information Infrastructure and Preservation Program.

1.2.2 The Open Access to Knowledge (OAK) Law Project (http://www.oaklaw.qut.edu.au) is led by the Faculty of Law of the Queensland University of Technology and funded by the Australian Government's Department of Education, Employment, and Workplace Relations. It is working towards facilitating optimal access to knowledge as a way of improving social, economic and cultural outcomes. With this in mind, the project is developing practical and effective copyright management resources and protocols for removing barriers to the reuse of information within the Australian and international academic and research sector. As part of these activities, in 2007 the project launched its OAK List website (http://www.oaklist.qut.edu.au/), which categorises the publishing agreements of key Australian and other relevant publishers, to assist repository managers, funding organizations, universities, authors and members of the public in better understanding the operation of these agreements. The OAK Law project also regularly publishes reports and guidelines, including: *OAK Law Project Report No. 1: Creating a legal framework for copyright management of open access within the Australian academic and research sectors* (2006), *Building the Infrastructure for Data Access and Reuse In Collaborative Research: An Analysis of the Legal Context* (2007) and *A Guide to Developing Open Access Through Your Digital Repository* (2007).

1.2.3 The SURFfoundation is a partner in SURF, the collaborative organisation for higher education institutions and research institutes aimed at breakthrough innovations in information and communication technologies. SURF provides the foundation for the excellence of higher education and research in the Netherlands. Collaboration has resulted in services and products that could not have been achieved by the institutions in isolation. SURF initiatives have an impact through the combination of high-quality knowledge, advantages of scale, and a demanding user group. SURF collaborates with a number of partners abroad to share knowledge and to profit from advantages of scale. The results that SURF achieves are also guiding examples in an international setting.

1.2.4 The Joint Information Systems Committee (JISC) supports tertiary education and research in the United Kingdom through technology innovation programs and by the central support of information and communication technologies services. The JISC Board and its sub-committees are senior managers, academics and technology experts working in UK further and higher education. The JISC is funded by the UK tertiary education funding bodies and works with the UK research councils. The JISC also works internationally with organizations in support of the global infrastructure to ensure appropriate and sustainable information and communication technologies provision for the UK education and research communities. The JISC has supported the development of digital preservation through its Digital Preservation and Records Management and predecessor programmes and collaboratively supports services such as the Digital Curation Centre. The JISC legal service provides the tertiary education sector with legal information in order to prevent legal issues from becoming a barrier to the adoption of information and communications technologies in learning, teaching and administration.

1.2.5 The National Digital Information Infrastructure and Preservation Program (NDIIPP) is a program led by the U.S. Library of Congress. The goal of NDIIPP is to develop a national strategy to collect, preserve and make available the growing volume of digital content, especially materials that are created only in digital formats, for current and future generations. The program is working with over 130 partners from universities, libraries, archives, government agencies at all levels, and commercial content and technology organizations. NDIIPP is principally concerned with three areas: 1) capturing, preserving, and making available significant digital content; 2) building and strengthening a national network of partners; and 3) developing a technical infrastructure of tools and services.

1.3 Description of the Study Process

1.3.1 The participating organizations began by developing a joint outline of the topics relevant to digital preservation and copyright, and related rights, and of the legal and factual subject areas to be addressed in each individual country report.

1.3.2 Each participating organization produced its own section of the joint report and formulated recommendations with respect to its own country's laws. They worked together on the introductory sections.

1.3.3 After the individual country reports were completed, the participating organizations worked together to develop the summary of findings and joint recommendations discussed in section 6, below.

1.4 Digital Preservation Overview

1.4.1 The term "preservation" has different meanings. In general terms, preservation refers to a series of activities (managerial, financial, technical) undertaken to prevent deterioration of a document or artifact and to ensure that it will continue to be usable. It may also refer to activities taken to ensure the integrity and long-term availability of information contained in rare or fragile documents or artifacts through the creation of surrogates for access purposes. Traditional preservation strategies, such as providing appropriate storage and environmental conditions, are still necessary in the digital environment, but they are not enough to ensure that digital information is preserved.

1.4.2 "Digital preservation" refers broadly to the series of managed activities necessary to ensure continued access to digital materials for as long as necessary, such as collection, description, migration and redundant storage. The materials subject to digital preservation may be born digital or be the products of digitization projects. Digital preservation activities are undertaken by a range of preservation institutions, including for example by libraries, archives and museums. Such institutions may operate independently or may be located within other bodies such as educational institutions or government entities.

1.4.3 Works in digital form present significant challenges for preservation that most analog works do not. Many analog materials remain stable for long periods of time and require only intermittent interventions for purposes of preservation. Moreover, degradation of an analog work is usually gradual enough to provide advance warning that preservation efforts are required. For example, one can perform a fold test to determine if the paper on which a book was printed has become brittle, or smell the vinegar that signals degradation of films. Digital materials, in contrast, cannot be unattended for long: their preservation requires regular intervention. They may suffer from "bit rot," a degradation that usually cannot be discerned by the naked eye and therefore may not be discovered until someone tries to use the work. Bit rot often renders the entire digital copy useless. Technological obsolescence is another problem for digital works. Even if their bits remain intact, the hardware and software required to access them may be difficult or impossible to obtain. Because of these characteristics, preservation of digital materials must begin at or shortly after production or acquisition.

1.4.4 Long term management of a digital work usually requires that multiple copies of the work be made over the course of its lifetime. One purpose for making copies is for security and disaster preparedness. Since it is always possible that digital works can be destroyed due to fire, flood, or other calamity, it is necessary to retain one or more redundant copies in different locations. Another purpose is to migrate information content from an old to a new technology, such as copying works from a floppy disk to a server. Access to content – either by users or by institution staff to verify its integrity – also may entail making a copy on a screen and in computer memory.

1.5 Challenges that Copyright Laws Present for Digital Preservation

1.5.1 Digital preservation necessarily involves the exercise of one or more of the exclusive rights of the author or other right holder. For example, reproduction is a fundamental activity of digital preservation. The right of distribution may be implicated by disseminating digital copies to multiple institutions to protect against catastrophic loss. And, to the extent access is required for digital preservation best practices, that access may implicate the right of "making available," or of public performance or display.

1.5.2 Digital technologies have also changed the manner in which works are distributed and acquired in ways that create tension between long term preservation needs and copyright laws. Previously, copyrighted works were marketed in tangible "hard copy" form, and libraries, archives and other preservation institutions could acquire them on the market (or, in some cases, pursuant to legal deposit laws) for current use and long term preservation. But now, many works are never produced in hard copy. Some works – such as web sites and various types of "user-generated content" available on the Internet – are not made available for acquisition, but only for listening or viewing. Those works cannot be preserved unless they can be copied or otherwise acquired by a digital archive or other preservation institution. Other types of works such as e-journals are available on the market, but the terms of use may not permit the creation or retention of archival copies.

1.5.3 The unauthorized exercise of the rights in a work may result in infringement of copyright under the law of the various jurisdictions unless:

(1) the material is not protected by copyright (i.e., it is in the public domain);
(2) the copying is permitted under an exception in the copyright law or related legislation (e.g., pursuant to an exception for libraries, archives or other preservation institutions or legal deposit); or
(3) digital preservation is undertaken by the owner of copyright in the work or with the permission of the owner.

1.6 The International Legal Context for Digital Preservation

1.6.1 The Berne Convention for the Protection of Literary and Artistic Works[1] provides the foundation for governance of copyright law internationally. All of the countries discussed in this report are members of this treaty. In addition, all have joined, or have indicated that they intend to join, the treaties that provide the principal modern updates to the Berne Convention – the World Intellectual Property Organization (WIPO) Copyright Treaty (WCT) and the WIPO Performances and Phonograms Treaty (WPPT), as well as the World Trade Organization's Agreement on Trade-Related Aspects of Intellectual Property Rights (TRIPs).

1.6.2 Together, these agreements require members to provide authors of literary and artistic works with a number of exclusive rights with respect to their works, including the rights of reproduction, adaptation, broadcasting, public performance, communication to the public and distribution to the public, subject to certain limitations and exceptions. In addition, performers of phonograms (also referred to in this report as sound recordings) are provided with a right of fixation, and performers and producers of phonograms are granted rights of reproduction, distribution, rental, and making available their fixed performances. All of these rights are subject to limitations and exceptions.

1.6.3 The Berne Convention allows exceptions to the right of reproduction under certain conditions, known as the "three-step test":

> It shall be a matter for legislation in the countries of the Union to permit the reproduction of [literary and artistic works] in certain special cases, provided that such reproduction does not conflict with a normal exploitation of the work and does not unreasonably prejudice the legitimate interests of the author. Berne art. 9(2).

1.6.4 The WIPO Copyright Treaty builds upon Berne's three-step test by providing that contracting parties may provide for limitations or exceptions to the rights granted under that treaty or under the Berne Convention in "certain special cases that do not conflict with a normal exploitation of the work and do not unreasonably prejudice the legitimate interests of the author." Art. 10. In other words, the WIPO Copyright Treaty makes the three-step test applicable to exceptions and limitations with respect to any of the

---

[1] Berne Convention for the Protection of Literary and Artistic Works, opened for signature September 9, 1886, 1 B.D.I.E.L. 715, http://www.wipo.int/treaties/en/ip/berne/trtdocs_wo001.html.

rights granted to authors under either that Treaty or the Berne Convention. The WPPT similarly makes the three-step test applicable to rights granted under that treaty.

1.6.5 Thus, while these treaties do not mandate any exceptions or limitations specific to preservation activities or preservation institutions, the treaties do permit such exceptions or limitations, provided they comport with the three-step test.

1.6.6 The EU Information Society Directive (Directive 2001/29/EC of the European Parliament and of the Council of 22 May 2001 on the harmonization of certain aspects of copyright and related rights in the information society) permits, but does not require, members of the European Union to provide exceptions and limitations for certain activities of publicly accessible libraries, educational establishments or museums, or by archives. The permitted exceptions and limitations are: (1) for specific acts of reproduction of copyrighted works which are not for direct or indirect economic or commercial advantage, art. 5(2)(c); and (2) for use by communication or making available of copyrighted works in their collections, for the purpose of research or private study, to individual members of the public by dedicated terminals on the premises of such establishments, provided those works are not subject to purchase or licensing terms to the contrary, art. 5(3)(n).

1.6.7 All of the countries discussed in this report have specific exceptions for libraries and archives (and sometimes also for other preservation institutions) in their copyright laws. There are some similarities among jurisdictions, but also some significant variations. Some variations are due to unique characteristics of a particular country's legal system. Other variations reflect the rapid pace of technological change and the fact that some countries have updated their laws more recently than others to try to accommodate library and archives and other preservation institution activities in the digital environment.

1.7 Roadmap to the Report

1.7.1 The following sections discuss, for each of the jurisdictions represented in this report:

- Major digital preservation activities currently ongoing;
- The copyright and related rights laws that bear on preservation, and relevant exceptions and limitations;
- Areas where there is tension between the laws and digital preservation activities;

- Current efforts within existing law to undertake digital preservation, either through exceptions and limitations or pursuant to agreements with right holders; and
- Recommendations for change.

1.7.2 The final section of the report consists of a summary of the report's major findings and a series of joint recommendations agreed to by all of the organizations that participated in the study and the preparation of this report.

Part 2: Country Report for Australia

Benedict Atkinson,[2] Emma Carroll,[3] Jessica Coates[4]
and Brian Fitzgerald[5]

2.1 Major Digital Preservation Activities in Australia

2.1.1 Although Australian copyright law sets out a number of exceptions designed to facilitate preservation of cultural collections, as well as a scheme requiring publishers to deposit copies of published printed material with the National Library of Australia (NLA), due to a number of significant gaps Australian federal law does not currently support compulsory collection and preservation of digital material.[6] Digital preservation activities in Australia are thus not governed by uniform standards and requirements. However, a number of voluntary (permission based) digital archiving schemes have been in operation since the 1990s. Led by the NLA, libraries, including the libraries of educational institutions, play a primary role in digital preservation.

Cultural Heritage Institutions

National Library of Australia – PANDORA

2.1.2 The NLA's PANDORA (Preserving and Accessing Networked Documentary Resources of Australia) web archiving project is the

---

2 Research Officer, OAK Law, Queensland University of Technology (QUT).

3 Research Assistant, OAK Law, QUT.

4 Project Manager, Creative Commons Clinic, ARC Centre of Excellence for Creative Industries and Innovation, QUT.

5 Professor of Intellectual Property and Innovation, QUT Law Faculty & Project Leader, OAK Law.

6 Tasmania and the Northern Territory are the only Australian jurisdictions to have passed laws requiring compulsory deposit of electronic material: *Libraries Act 1984* (Tas), s 22; *Publications (Legal Deposit) Act 2004* (NT), ss7 and 13.

most significant digital preservation initiative implemented in Australia. Established in 1996, the PANDORA digital archive consists of records collected by 10 institutions, seven of which are public libraries and all of which are government funded.[7] PANDORA selectively archives and provides long-term access to online publications and websites that are of cultural significance or long-term research value to Australia.

2.1.3 Each participating institution focuses on a different category of materials, with the NLA and state libraries focusing on archiving resources published from their jurisdictions; the National Film and Sound Archive responsible for film and music related publications; the Australian War Memorial for military history; and the Australian Institution for Aboriginal and Torres Strait Islander Studies (AIATSIS) for publications and websites relating to Australian indigenous peoples. Materials are manually selected by institution officers, with each institution maintaining their own selection guidelines.[8] For example, the NLA collects material located on Australian or overseas servers, where the content of that material is:

- about Australia;
- on a subject of social, political, cultural, religious, scientific or economic significance and relevance to Australia and written by an Australian author; or
- written by an Australian of recognised authority and constitutes a contribution to international knowledge.[9]

2.1.4 Participating institutions ask selected owners and publishers for permission to archive, and make accessible online, relevant digital content.[10] Generally publishers grant permission to:

- copy their material into the PANDORA archive for retention;
- communicate the material to the public in perpetuity; and

---

[7] National Library of Australia, Northern Territory Library, State Library of New South Wales, State Library of Queensland, State Library of South Australia, State Library of Victoria, State Library of Western Australia, Australian Institute of Aboriginal and Torres Strait Islander Studies, Australian War Memorial, and National Film and Sound Archive.

[8] See http://pandora.nla.gov.au/selectionguidelinesallpartners.html.

[9] See http://pandora.nla.gov.au/selectionguidelines.html#auscontent.

[10] The NLA's criteria for selection is that a work must be: about Australia; or by an Australian author; or on a subject of social, political, cultural, religious, scientific or economic significance and relevance to Australia; or by an Australian author of recognised authority and make a contribution to international knowledge. See http://pandora.nla.gov.au/overview.html#factsheet.

- make any further reproductions or communications that are reasonably necessary to preserve the material and make it available to the public.

2.1.5 In addition to its selective archiving practices, during 2005, 2006 and 2007 PANDORA undertook three large scale harvests of the entire .au domain using HTTrack (www.httrack.com), a free offline browsing software.[11] It hopes to continue to conduct such harvests annually for several years (at a minimum) in order to build expertise in this method of archiving; however, this is subject to funding and policy decisions.

2.1.6 The NLA is currently conducting a review of its web archiving scope, methods and practices, including investigating the legal and technical obstacles to these domain harvests. In the meantime, it is limiting the risk associated with the whole of domain harvests by:

- not providing public access to the material;
- collecting content only where it is permitted by the robots.txt exclusion standard;[12]
- automatically providing a notification to each server harvested; and
- discontinuing harvesting in response to requests to do so.

In the future, the NLA hopes to provide public access to this material. If this should become the case, policies will be put in place to disable access to archived material upon request.

2.1.7 The NLA manages PANDORA using a web based digital curatorial system called PANDAS (PANDORA Digital Archiving System). This purpose-built software assists the automatic recording, description and (where appropriate) provision of access to the archive. To keep up with technological developments, both preservation master copies and a display copy of the material in appropriate formats are maintained. Metadata is also kept to assist with the long term preservation strategies and processes. Many titles are regularly re-harvested to take into account updated content.[13] Access to the archive is gained via the PANDORA website at (http://pandora.nla.gov.au).

---

[11] See http://pandora.nla.gov.au/documents/auscrawls.pdf.

[12] See http://www.robotstxt.org/.

[13] PANDORA Australia's Web Archive, *PANDORA Overview,* available at http://pandora.nla.gov.au/overview.html#factsheet..

State Library of Tasmania

2.1.8 Assisted by State compulsory deposit legislation that applies to digital publications (see further at 2.2.31 below), the State Library of Tasmania (SLT) has undertaken two significant digital preservation projects:

- Our Digital Island – Preserved Tasmanian Websites; and
- STORS (Stable Tasmanian Open Repository Service) – Long-term storage of Tasmanian electronic documents

2.1.9 The Our Digital Island project (http://odi.statelibrary.tas.gov.au), launched in 1998, allows access to over 2000 archived Tasmanian websites. The collection can be browsed by subject or title, with accessibility determined by administrators.

2.1.10 STORS (http://www.stors.tas.gov.au/logon.do) facilitates publisher compliance with Tasmania's legal deposit requirements. Publishers upload documents each of which is allocated a permanent URL (web address). Publishers can apply metadata to the document providing publication information such as history, superseded versions and versions in alternate formats. They can also restrict access. Over 2750 electronic publications have been submitted.

Other Cultural Institutions

2.1.11 Three non-library cultural institutions participate in PANDORA.[14] Other than these activities, there appear to be no coordinated digital preservation activities currently being undertaken by the Australian museums and galleries sector, with preservation projects primarily being undertaken on an ad hoc -basis by individual institutions.[15]

2.1.12 Australia's largest museum, the NSW Powerhouse Museum (http://www.powerhousemuseum.com), selectively preserves its digital holdings, including audiovisual material and computer software and hardware. The museum's collection includes objects relating to Australian and world history, science, technology, design, industry, decorative arts, music, transport and space exploration. An Electronic Resource Management Group is responsible for developing the museum's digital preservation

[14] The Australian Institute of Aboriginal and Torres Strait Islander Studies, the Australian War Memorial, and the National Film and Sound Archive.

[15] Some museums and galleries, such as Museum Victoria, digitize hardcopy works to make them more accessible to the public. The principal purpose of such digitization is not preservation.

strategy.[16] Uniform digital preservation standards are yet to be adopted.

2.1.13 Museum Victoria, the body established in 1983 to oversee Victoria's State cultural institutions,[17] archives digital photographic images and digital copies of collection documents, including analogue images, manuscripts and maps. The organisation began saving copies of deteriorating photographs on digital media (initially CD-ROMs) in 1990.[18] Digital holdings are stored on a server and backed up to tape in the multimedia repository as part of the general collection management system.[19] Museum Victoria is currently in the process of developing a Digital Asset Management system which will become its primary digital preservation system.

Government Archives

2.1.14 The National Archives of Australia[20] (NAA) and relevant State archives[21] are responsible for archiving federal government records and materials.[22] The NAA is working towards implementing standards for permanent storage of government digital records. To allow for storage of the growing volume of digital records, the NAA has adopted an open source document conversion and preservation system called XENA (XML Electronic Normalising for Archives). XENA converts digital records from file

---

[16] The committee is considering: shelf lives of objects stored in digital formats; how to retain equipment to access/play these objects; equipment obsolescence; standards for archiving including international standards; managing the selection process; future interoperability issues; costs involved with developing and maintaining preservation technology and necessary funding; and the extent of the role of digital technology in future museum curating.

[17] The institutions managed by Museum Victoria include the Melbourne Museum, Immigration Museum, Scienceworks and the Royal Exhibition Building.

[18] National Library of Australia, *Museum Victoria Image Capture Project*, available at http://www.nla.gov.au/libraries/digitisation/dfo16.html.

[19] Thus primarily items are preserved digitally, with analogue back-ups. Some audio and audio-visual works are being added to the repository or stored on the server also.

[20] *Archives Act 1983.*

[21] *Territory Records Act 2002* (ACT); *State Records Act 1998* (NSW); *Information Act 2002* (NT); *Public Records Act 2002* (Qld); *State Records Act 1997* (SA); *Archives Act 1983* (Tas); *Public Records Act 1973* (Vic); *State Records Act 2000* (WA).

[22] Storage formats include paper, negatives, prints, sound, film and video. The NAA recognises that most records are now created digitally – see 'Open Standards Key to Digital Preservation' (2006) ZdNet, March 31, available at http://wwwzdnet.com.au/news/software/soa/Open-standards-key-to-digital-preservation/0,130061733,139248913,00.htm.

formats that may become obsolete into open source file formats that are permanently accessible. XENA allows stored converted data to be accessed in its original format. To safeguard against obsolescence, XENA software utilises 'plug-in' architecture that enables it to be updated as technology progresses and file formats advance.[23]

Educational and Research Institutions

2.1.15 A large number of Australian educational institutions maintain digital collections of material produced by students and staff.[24] However, most institutions have developed these archives independently, and no standard collection or preservation activities operate across the sector. Nevertheless, in an effort to develop uniform interoperability standards, a number of Australian institutions participate in the worldwide Open Archive Initiative,[25] which aims to facilitate access to digital archives.

2.1.16 For example, the Queensland University of Technology (QUT), a participant in this initiative, maintains an ePrint repository that archives and provides online access to university research literature in digital format.[26] QUT requires its researchers to deposit in the repository copyright works produced in the course of their QUT employment, where those works can be classified as "material which represents the total publicly available research and scholarly output of the University".[27] Material excepted from this category includes material which is to be commercialised, material which contains confidential material, and material which

[23] The NAA's digital archiving policy using XENA is 'recognised nationally and internationally as a sustainable, scaleable and innovative answer to the complexities of digital preservation and access.' (Council of Australasian Archives and Records Authorities 'Digital Archiving in the 21st Century' *Archives Domain Discussion Paper* (2006)).

[24] For a full list of Australian educational institutions maintaining archive collections, see Appendix One of *A Guide to Developing Open Access through your Digital Repository*, (Open Access to Knowledge Law Project, Queensland University of Technology, 2007) http://eprints.qut.edu.au/archive/00009671/01/9671.pdf.

[25] See http://www.openarchives.org/.

[26] Queensland University of Technology, *ePrints Archive,* available at http://eprints.qut.edu.au.

[27] 1.3.2 'F/1.3 E-print repository for research output at QUT', *Queensland University of Technology Manual of Policy and Procedures* (Queensland University of Technology) http://www.mopp.qut.edu.au/F/F_01_03.jsp. See also 'E-Print Archive', *Copyright Guide* (Queensland University of Technology), http://www.tils.qut.edu.au/copyrightguide/publishingan/eprintarchi.jsp.

is subject to a contrary legal agreement.[28] Researchers are encouraged to negotiate contracts that permit archiving and dissemination of works produced. Post-graduate students are also encouraged to deposit their work in the repository.

2.1.17 The grant of a perpetual non-exclusive access licence to QUT is a condition of deposit, as is the grant of a licence to archive users to print and save electronic copies of whole papers for individual, non-commercial use.[29] Other copyright management decisions are left up to the individual researcher, although QUT management copyright guidelines endorse the use of open content licensing schemes such as Creative Commons and AESharenet.[30]

2.2 Overview of Copyright, Related Rights, and Legal Deposit Laws of Australia as Applied to Digital Preservation

Copyright

2.2.1 The Federal *Copyright Act 1968 (Cth)*, which regulates the use of copyright material, is the principal instrument governing digital preservation in Australia. (Relevant provisions of the *Copyright Act 1968 (Cth)* are attached as Appendix B.) Australian copyright law implements the provisions of all major international copyright treaties, beginning with the Berne Convention and extending to the World Intellectual Property Organisation's (WIPO) Copyright Treaty and Performances and Phonograms Treaty of 1996. The *Copyright Act* also implements a bilateral treaty agreed with the United States in 2004.[31]

2.2.2 Copyright in Australia applies to two categories of material: original literary, dramatic, musical and artistic *works*;[32] and subject

[28] 1.3.2 'F/1.3 E-print repository for research output at QUT', *Queensland University of Technology Manual of Policy and Procedures* (Queensland University of Technology), http://www.mopp.qut.edu.au/F/F_01_03.jsp.

[29] See *QUT E-Prints – Copyright Matters* (Queensland University of Technology), http://eprints.qut.edu.au/copyright.html.

[30] See, for example, 'Managing Your Copyright', *Copyright Guide* (Queensland University of Technology), http://www.tils.qut.edu.au/copyrightguide/publishingan/managingyour.jsp.

[31] Australia-United States Free Trade Agreement, http://www.dfat.gov.au/trade/negotiations/us_fta/index.html. See the implementing *USFTA Implementation Act 2004* Act and recent amendments from the *Copyright Amendment Bill 2006.* The *Copyright Regulations 1969, the Copyright Tribunal (Procedure) Regulations 1969* and the *Copyright (International Protection) Regulations 1969* also govern copyright practice and procedure.

[32] *Copyright Act 1968* (Cth), Part III.

matter other than works (sound recordings, films, sound and television broadcasts and published editions).[33] Copyright works are protected for the life of the author and a posthumous period of 70 years. Other subject matter is generally protected for 70 years from first publication, the exceptions being broadcasts and crown copyright, which are protected for 50 years from the date of first publication, and published editions, which are protected for 25 years.

Exclusive Rights

2.2.3 The exact nature of the economic rights granted to copyright owners by the Australian *Copyright Act* varies between subject matter; however, in general they give copyright owners the exclusive right to control the following uses of their works:

- reproduction - including digitising an analogue work;
- communication – including electronically transmitting (eg broadcasting) material and making it available online (eg on a website or via a peer-to-peer service);
- publication;
- performance in public; and
- making an adaptation of the work – eg translating the work.

2.2.4 Copyright infringement occurs directly or by authorisation. Infringement normally occurs when a person exercises any of the exclusive rights without permission of the owner;[34] however, infringement may also occur when a person (including a corporation) authorises someone else to infringe copyright.[35]

---

[33] *Copyright Act 1968* (Cth), Part IV. The principle of territoriality applies to copyright protection - material created or first published in Australia or in a country with which Australia has a reciprocal agreement, or by a person who is a citizen or resident of Australia, is protected.

[34] *Copyright Act 1968* (Cth), ss 36(1) and 101(1). Direct infringement occurs where a person, who is not the copyright owner, performs in Australia any of the exclusive acts in relation to the whole or a 'substantial part' of a work, without licence or consent of the copyright owner (whether express or implied), and where no defence or exception to infringement is applicable.

[35] *Copyright Act 1968* (Cth), ss 36(1A) and 101(1A). In determining whether a person (or organisation) has authorised an infringement the following matters must be taken into account: the extent of the person's power to prevent the act (ie their level of control), the nature of any relationship between the person and the infringer who performed the act and whether the person took reasonable steps to avoid the act (including complying with any relevant industry codes of practice).

2.2.5 The *Copyright Act* specifies a number of exceptions that exempt copyright users from infringement liability. These are discussed further below.

Moral Rights

2.2.6 In addition to the economic rights discussed above, Australian copyright law provides the creators of certain works with three moral rights:

- the right of integrity;[36]
- the right of attribution;[37] and
- the right not to be falsely attributed.[38]

2.2.7 These rights are personal rights which vest automatically in the creators of works and films, but not sound recordings, broadcasts or published editions. The rights generally last for the same term as copyright[39] and cannot be assigned, transferred or waived. Authors or performers may, however, consent to uses that would otherwise breach moral rights.[40]

2.2.8 The *Copyright Act* provides a defence against an action for infringement of the moral rights of integrity and attribution where the act or omission in question is 'reasonable in all the circumstances'.[41] In determining what is 'reasonable' the purpose, manner and context in which the material is used can be taken into account, as well as (in the case of the right of attribution) the difficulty or expense involved in identifying the creator.

Database Rights

2.2.9 Unlike some other jurisdictions, Australia has not legislated to extend specific copyright rights to databases or protect them sui generis. Instead, Australian common law authority suggests that courts would consider most databases to be protected as a

[36] *Copyright Act 1968* (Cth), s 195AQ. Infringing the right of integrity of authorship involves subjecting the work, or authorising the work to be subjected, to derogatory treatment.

[37] *Copyright Act 1968* (Cth), s 193.

[38] *Copyright Act 1968* (Cth), s 195AC.

[39] See *Copyright Act 1968* (Cth) s195AM. The exception is the author's right of integrity in a cinematograph film, which lasts for the author's lifetime only.

[40] See *Copyright Act 1968* (Cth), ss 195AW, 195AWA and 195AXJ.

[41] *Copyright Act 1968* (Cth), ss 195AR and 195AS.

compilation or literary work - the Australian Federal Court has held that both telephone directories[42] and television program guides[43] are sufficiently original in character to be protected by copyright.

Performance Rights

2.2.10 Australian copyright law grants performers both economic[44] and personal rights over audio (but not audiovisual) recordings of their performances. These rights consist of:

- the right to authorise the recording and communication of live performances (and distributions of recordings of live performances);[45]
- copyright in sound recordings;[46] and
- moral rights in performances.[47]

2.2.11 The first two of these rights only apply to performances that took place after 1 October 1989. A performer's rights to authorise recording and communication of their performances or the reproduction or performance of recordings last for 50 years from the date of the performance. Rights to authorise communication of recordings or the use of a recording in a soundtrack last for 20 years from the date of recording.[48]

[42] See *Desktop Marketing Systems Pty Ltd v Telstra Corporation Limited* [2002] FCAFC 112. Cf *Feist Publications Inc v Rural Telephone Services Co Inc* 499 US 340 (1991) where the alphabetical arrangement of a telephone directory did not satisfy the requirements for originality under US law. Section 10(1) of *Copyright Act* defines a 'literary work' to include 'a table, or compilation, expressed in words, figures or symbols'.

[43] *Nine Network Australia Pty Limited v IceTV Pty Limited* [2008] FCAFC 71 (8 May 2008).

[44] The economic rights for performers in sound recordings became effective from 1 January 2005. Section 22(3A) of the Act provides that the performer and the owner of any sound recording of the performance own the copyright jointly, subject to any agreement to the contrary. Commissioned sound recordings for which the the performer is paid a fee, or those made under an employment contract, are owned by the commissioner or employer (section 97(3)).

[45] See *Copyright Act 1968* (Cth), pt XIA.

[46] *Copyright Act 1968* (Cth) s22(3A). This right is subject to any agreement to the contrary, and does not apply to commissioned performances or performances conducted in the course of employment - s 97(3).

[47] *Copyright Act 1968* (Cth), ss 195AXA, 195AXB and 195AXC.

[48] *Copyright Act* sections 248CA(3), 248G(1) and (2)).

2.2.12 The moral rights granted to performers mirror the moral rights in traditional works. Generally, they will last for the duration of the copyright in the sound recording, although the right of integrity in a recorded performance only lasts until the performer's death.[49] The same reasonableness exemptions that apply to traditional moral rights also apply to performers' moral rights.[50] Furthermore, to make the authorisation process efficient for performances involving multiple performers, the *Copyright Act* permits an agent acting for a group of performers to grant permission to reproduce etc any sound recordings.[51]

Relevant Exceptions and Limitations

2.2.13 The Act contains three categories of exceptions to copyright infringement:

- general exceptions;
- statutory licences; and
- user and purpose-specific exceptions.

2.2.14 The most commonly used of the general exceptions are the 'fair dealing' provisions (sections 40 and 103C). Unlike their US equivalent, the fair use exception, Australia's fair dealing provisions are strictly limited to activities undertaken for one of the following purposes:

- research and study;
- criticism or review;
- reporting the news;
- parody or satire; and
- judicial proceedings and legal advice.

2.2.15 As none of these prescribed purposes appear to encompass preservation activities, it is unlikely that the fair dealing provisions would be held to permit institution-based digital preservation activities. Similarly, while a number of specific use exceptions exist which permit device and format shifting, these apply only to actions undertaken by individuals for private and domestic purposes and hence would not permit institutional preservation schemes.[52]

[49] *Copyright Act 1968* (Cth), s 195ANA.

[50] *Copyright Act 1968* (Cth), ss 195AXD and 195AXE.

[51] See *Copyright Act 1968* (Cth), ss 113A and 191B.

[52] *Copyright Act 1968* (Cth) ss 43C, 47J, 109A and 110AA.

2.2.16 Other exceptions in the *Copyright Act*, such as the statutory licensing schemes for educational institutions,[53] could in theory be interpreted to permit various types of digital preservation.[54] However, as these exceptions require payment and do not provide the certainty or breadth of application required for most large scale or ongoing preservation activities, they are not generally relied upon for such purposes.

2.2.17 The most important exceptions with respect to digital preservation, and the only exceptions likely to provide sufficient certainty to support large-scale archive projects, are therefore the specific exceptions for libraries and archives.

Libraries and Archives Exceptions

2.2.18 Division 5 of Part III of the Copyright Act sets out a number of exceptions to permit specific activities by libraries and archives. The Act defines 'archives' to include all bodies (whether incorporated or unincorporated) in custody of a collection of documents or other material of historical significance or public interest, which is maintained for the purpose of conserving and preserving those documents or other material, and not for the purpose of deriving a profit.[55] This definition embraces non-profit libraries, archives, museums and galleries, collections maintained by non-profit institutions (such as universities and schools), and collections held by for-profit organisations where the collection itself is not operated for a profit.

2.2.19 Sections 49(9) and 50(10) restrict the definition of 'library' for the purpose of these two exceptions to institutions whose collections are accessible (in whole or in part) to the public or other library users directly or via inter-library loans. This in effect serves to prohibit the application of these exceptions to private collections (eg maintained by corporate entities) that do not permit public access either directly or through an inter-library loan service.

---

[53] *Copyright Act 1968* (Cth) Part VB.

[54] See Hudson, E. and Kenyon, A. "Without Walls: Copyright Law and Digital Collections in Australian Cultural Institutions" (2007) 4(2) SCRIPT-ed 197 at footnote 54, available at http://papers.ssrn.com/sol3/papers.cfm?abstract_id=1007391.

[55] *Copyright Act 1968* (Cth) s10(4). In addition, section 10(1) specifies that 'archives' includes archival material in the custody of the Australian Archives, the Archives Office of New South Wales, the Public Record Office of Victoria and the Archives Office of Tasmania.

Preservation by Libraries and Archives of Copies of Works and Other Subject Matter

2.2.20 Section 51A of the *Copyright Act* permits libraries and archives to reproduce and communicate a work for preservation purposes if it has been damaged, deteriorated, lost or stolen[56]. An almost identical exception in s110B allows preservation copies and communications to be made of sound recordings or cinematograph films, with the one difference that these materials may be preserved *against* damage, deterioration, loss or theft. Anecdotally, collecting institutions make little differentiation between preservation activities undertaken against or in response to damage, deterioration, loss and theft.

2.2.21 In addition, since 1 January 2007 key cultural institutions have had the right to make up to three copies[57] of works, sound recordings and films of 'historical or cultural significance' for the purpose of preserving it against loss or deterioration.[58] This exception, which is set out in ss51B, 110BA and 112AA, was introduced to ensure that the Australian *Copyright Act* permitted best practice preservation practices.[59] 'Key cultural institutions' include the National and State libraries and archives, as well as any other institution prescribed by the regulations.[60]

2.2.22 With respect to published materials (as opposed to manuscripts or original works of art) both these exceptions are limited by the additional condition that preservation copies may only be made where the material cannot be obtained within a reasonable time at an ordinary commercial price – the 'commercial availability' test. With respect to the key cultural institution exceptions, the exception specifically notes that electronic copies must be taken into account in deciding whether the material is commercially

---

[56] *Copyright Act 1968* (Cth) ss51A and 110B.

[57] *Copyright Act 1968* (Cth) s51B allows for triplicate preservation copying of manuscripts, original artistic works and published works. Section 110BA allows the same for unpublished and published sound recordings and films, and section 112AA for published editions (and the works therein).

[58] An 'authorized officer' of the library or archives determines whether (ie, must be 'satisfied that') material is of historical or cultural significance (*Copyright Act 1968* (Cth) ss 51B, 110BA and 112AA).

[59] Copyright Amendment Bill 2006 Supplementary Explanatory Memorandum, para. 95, available at
http://parlinfoweb.aph.gov.au/piweb//view_document.aspx?TABLE=OLDEMS&ID=2419.

[60] Section 51B(1)(a). No additional institutions have so far been specified under the Copyright Regulations 1969.

available.[61] In practice, this is also likely to be the case for ss51A and s110B.

Subsequent Use of Preservation Copies

2.2.23 Although the s51A and s110B preservation exceptions permit 'communication' of copyright material, this is limited to communications made for preservation purposes (eg internal emailing and transferring of preservation files) and does not extend to making the material generally available online to the public (eg as part of a library website). Preservation copies made by a library may therefore only be accessed by the public under the same terms as other material held in the library's collection (see below). The exceptions to this rule are preservation copies of original artistic works, sound recordings and cinematograph films, which may be made available for viewing or listening on dedicated computer terminals within the library premises.[62]

The Special Case or 'Flexible Dealing' Exception

2.2.24 On 1 January 2007 a new category of exceptions set out in s200AB of the *Copyright Act* came into effect. These new exceptions, which are based on the 'three-step' test incorporated into the main international copyright treaties,[63] are intended to introduce more flexibility into the uses certain key user groups (including libraries) can make of copyright material.

2.2.25 With respect to libraries and archives, s200AB allows for certain uses of material that would normally infringe copyright, where those uses are:

- made by or on behalf of the body administering the library or archives;

[61] The Act requires the authorized library officer to declare that after reasonable investigation the officer ascertained that:

(i) a copy (not second-hand) could not be obtained within a reasonable time at an ordinary commercial price; or

(ii) if a copy of another edition of the work (not second-hand) could be obtained within a reasonable time at an ordinary commercial price, the library was nonetheless justified in making a reproduction from the library copy.

[62] Sections 51A(3A) and 110B(2A) and (2B). Only library or archive officers may communicate material to the public. In practice, information is supplied by secure access, eg password protected. In relation to original artistic works, the act further specifies that they may only be made available on dedicated terminals which do not allow further reproductions or communications eg by printing or emailing.

[63] See, for example, Berne Convention for the Protection of Literary and Artistic Works Art 9, Agreement on Trade-Related Aspects of Intellectual Property (TRIPs Agreement) Art 13 and WIPO Copyright Treaty Art 10.

- for the purpose of maintaining or operating the library or archives; and
- not being made partly for the purpose of obtaining a commercial advantage or profit.[64]

2.2.26 Additionally, in accordance the three step test, the use must:

- be a 'special case';
- not conflict with a normal exploitation of the work; and
- not unreasonably prejudice the legitimate interests of the right holder.[65]

2.2.27 No court cases have so far been brought involving s200AB and the scope of the section is therefore uncertain. At first glance, the exception appears to operate in a similar fashion to the US style 'fair use' defence and could be argued to embrace a broad range of uses. The purpose of *maintaining* or *operating* a library or archive, for example, could include format shifting to allow libraries and archives to maintain access to works published in an obsolete digital format.

2.2.28 Nevertheless, the 'three-step test' limitations placed on the scope of the provision, and the administrative requirements necessary to apply these limitations, may considerably circumscribe its practical effect. It is not yet clear, for example, what the terms 'normal exploitation' or 'unreasonably prejudice' might mean in the context of Australia domestic law. It also seems unlikely that copying that takes place as part of any large-scale or systematic preservation project would be held to be a 'special case'.[66] Most importantly, from a practical point of view, it is unclear how a library or its officers are expected to apply the various elements of the test on a day-to-day basis.

---

[64] *Copyright Act 1968* (Cth), s 200AB(2).

[65] *Copyright Act 1968* (Cth), s 200AB(1). The meaning of 'special case' is in accordance with Article 13 of the TRIPS Agreement. This is also satisfies the 'three-step' test outlined in Articles 1(4) and 10 of the WIPO Copyright Treaty; see Article 9 Berne Convention, Article 13 TRIPS, and Art. 17.1.4 AUSFTA containing a covenant to join the WIPO Copyright Treaty.

[66] Section 200AB(7) ascribes to 'special case' the same meaning as Article 13 of the TRIPS Agreement *Limitations and Exceptions*: 'Members shall confine limitations or exceptions to exclusive rights to certain special cases which do not conflict with a normal exploitation of the work and do not unreasonably prejudice the legitimate interests of the right holder.

Further Applicable Exceptions

2.2.29 The table below sets out other exceptions to copyright in the Australian *Copyright Act* which are potentially relevant to digital preservation by libraries and archives.

s 49	Reproduction and communication of works in response to a user request for the purposes of research or study	Allows direct public access to works by authorising the library or archives to provide users with a single copy of the work for the purpose of research or study following a request in writing (or orally if the user is in a remote location)
s 50	Reproduction and communication of works by libraries or archives for other libraries or archives	Facilitates copies made for inter-library loan schemes in relation to requests made by Parliamentary libraries or under s 49
ss 51 and 110A	Reproducing and communicating unpublished works, sound recordings and films in libraries or archives	Allows copies to be made of: - unpublished material for research, study or publication, where the author has been dead more than 50 years; or - theses kept in university library collections or archives, for the purposes of research or study.
s 51AA	Reproducing and communicating works in the Australian Archives	Allows the Australian Archives to make and supply reference or replacement copies of works to regional offices for users who for reason of location are unable to inspect the work in the central archives.
s 52	Publication of unpublished works kept in libraries or archives	Facilitates publication of unpublished works housed in libraries or archives within the scope of s 51 (only where prescribed notice of publication was given and the identity of the unpublished work's copyright owner was unknown ie orphan works)
s 53	Application to illustrations accompanying articles and other works	Allows the aforementioned provisions to apply in relation to artistic illustrations accompanying works.

Legal Deposit

2.2.30 Section 201 of the Federal *Copyright Act* requires publishers to deposit one copy of all library materials published in Australia with the National Library of Australia. 'Library materials' is narrowly defined to only include materials such as books, periodicals and newspapers and is widely regarded as not currently applying to digital material.[67] Publishers are obliged by law to deposit materials at their own expense, and libraries therefore *receive* rather than actively collect or *capture* material preserved.

2.2.31 Similar provisions are enacted by the State legislatures to require the deposit of published material with the relevant State library.[68] In general, these provisions echo their Federal counterpart in that they are limited to deposit by the publisher of printed materials. The notable exceptions are the legal deposit statutes of Tasmania and the Northern Territory, which are both couched in broad terms that include electronic and online materials.[69] In practice, these broader deposit provisions are not generally enforced, due primarily to the impracticality of identifying and storing the enormous amounts of digital material 'published' in the internet era. Both the Tasmanian and Northern Territory Acts, for instance, would appear on their face to require the deposit not only of software, CDs and DVDs, but also of all websites, blogs, chatroom transcripts, and comments published in any webspace. The 'Our Digital Island' initiative of the State Library of Tasmania,

[67] Section 201(5): '...a book, periodical, newspaper, pamphlet, sheet of letter-press, sheet of music, map, plan, chart or table, being a literary, dramatic, musical or artistic work or an edition of such a work, but does not include a second or later edition of any material unless that edition contains additions or alterations in the letter-press or in the illustrations.' For interpretation of this provision, see *2007 Discussion Paper on the Extension of Legal Deposit* (Department of Broadband, Communication and Digital Economy, 2007), pp. 4-5, available at http://www.arts.gov.au/__data/assets/pdf_file/80928/legal_deposit_discussion_paper_2007.pdf.

[68] *New South Wales Copyright Act 1879-1952* (NSW), ss 5-7, *Publications (Legal Deposit) Act 2004* (NT), *Libraries Act 1988* (Qld), *South Australian Libraries Act 1982* (SA) s35, *Tasmanian Libraries Act 1984* (Tas) s 22, *Victorian Libraries Act 1988* (Vic) s49, *Western Australian Copyright Act 1895* (WA) ss 4, 7-9.

[69] The Tasmanian *Libraries Act 1984* requires the deposit of 'any book, periodical, newspaper, printed matter, map, plan, music, manuscript, picture, print, motion picture, sound recording, photographic negative or print, microphotograph, video recording, and *any other matter* or thing whereby words, sounds, or images are recorded or reproduced'. (italics added) The Northern Territory's *Publications (Legal Deposit) Act 2004* applies to any document available to the public including books, newspapers, magazines, periodicals, reports, newsletters, calendars, directories, handbooks, guides, sheet music, maps, pamphlets, audio cassettes, video cassettes, films, multimedia kits, computer magnetic tape, computer optical discs, floppy discs, compact discs, CD-ROMs, DVDs, websites and PDF files (s4).

has sought to address this issue by interpreting its state legal deposit provisions to permit it to selectively harvest websites and electronic publications without seeking copyright owner permission.[70]

2.2.32 In late 2007 the Federal Government released a discussion paper and call for submissions addressing the viability of expanding the Commonwealth scheme for legal deposit to include the deposit of electronic and audiovisual material.[71] This paper is discussed further at 2.4.7-2.4.9 below.

Technological Protection Measures Provisions

2.2.33 Technological Protection Measures (TPMs) are used by many copyright owners to control access to, reproduction of and communication of digital objects. The Australian *Copyright Act* prohibits in most cases the manufacture, supply and use of devices that circumvent TPMs.[72] The Act also specifies certain exceptions to this prohibition, including where the copyright owner gives permission to allow circumvention;[73] circumvention for the purpose of interoperability;[74] and circumvention for the purpose of security testing.[75]

2.2.34 The only exceptions listed in the Act which are relevant to libraries and archives are ss116AN(8) and 132APC(8), which permit non-profit libraries, archives and educational institutions to circumvent a TPM for the sole purpose of making acquisition decisions.[76] These exceptions are narrowly framed to apply solely to institutional purchasing decisions, thereby protecting the

[70] The State Library of Tasmania is conscious of commercial sensitivities involved in legal deposit of digital material and is actively developing cooperative relationships with commercial online publishers. Lloyd Sokvitne, 'Our Digital Island: Web Preservation Issues and Solutions at the State Library of Tasmania' available at http://ausweb.scu.edu.au/aw99/papers/sokvitne/paper.html.

[71] *2007 Discussion Paper on the Extension of Legal Deposit* (Department of Broadband, Communication and Digital Economy, 2007), available at http://www.arts.gov.au/__data/assets/pdf_file/80928/legal_deposit_discussion_paper_2007.pdf.

[72] *Copyright Act 1968* (Cth); civil infringement provisions sections: 116AK – 116AQ; criminal: sections 132APC-132APE.

[73] *Copyright Act 1968* (Cth) ss 116AN(2) and 132APC(2).

[74] *Copyright Act 1968* (Cth) ss 116AN(3) and 132APC(3).

[75] *Copyright Act 1968* (Cth) ss 116AN(5) and 132APC(5).

[76] *Copyright Act 1968* (Cth) ss 116AN(8), 132APC(8), 132APD(7) and 132APE(7).

commercial interests of copyright owners but offering non-profit institutions little scope to carry out preservation activities.

2.2.35 In addition to these defined exceptions, the *Copyright Act* also empowers the Minister to prescribe certain acts of circumvention as permitted by listing them in the Copyright Regulations. These prescribed acts currently include the reproduction or communication of copyright materials under the libraries and archives exceptions set out in the *Copyright Act*.[77] These entities can thus rely on the Regulations to perform, without owner authorisation, a range of circumvention activities necessary for effective preservation.

2.2.36 Unfortunately, however, these prescribed exceptions only apply to the act of circumvention, and do not allow the manufacture or supply of circumvention devices. While it is likely that they would permit individual libraries and archives to hire personnel to create one-off circumvention programs for them, it is clear that they would not permit the acquisition of circumvention programs from external sources or the sharing of programs between libraries. As many TPMs are virtually impossible for even the most skilled of technicians to circumvent, particularly where obsolete technologies are involved, most institutions will lack the ability to circumvent TPMs themselves. This means that in effect, the TPM exceptions provided by the Act have very few practical applications and the 'digital lock-out' created by the current TPM laws persists.

Copyright Law and Contracts

2.2.37 Although the issue is regarded as a legal grey area, currently the *Copyright Act* does not prohibit contracting out of the statutory exceptions.[78]

2.2.38 The 2002 *Copyright and Contract*[79] report by the Copyright Law Review Committee (CLRC) found that in Australia, copyright owners (principally publishers) frequently supply digital material to

[77] *Copyright Act 1968* (Cth) ss 116AN(9) and 132APC(9) exempt from liability circumvention acts prescribed under the *Copyright Regulations 1969* (Cth). The prescribed acts are listed in Schedule 10A of the *Regulations* and they apply to purposes authorized under sections 49, 50, 51A, 110A and 110B of the Act.

[78] It could be argued that the statutory exceptions are intended to apply absolutely – ie, prohibition of contracting-out is implied in the exceptions – but the more orthodox interpretation is that contract can exclude exceptions.

[79] *Copyright and Contract* (Copyright Law Review Committee, 2002), http://www.clrc.gov.au/www/agd/agd.nsf/Page/Copyright_CopyrightLawReviewCommittee_CLRCReports_CopyrightandContract_CopyrightandContract.

libraries and other users under licences that specifically limit or exclude acts permitted by the *Copyright Act*. In particular, restrictions are often placed on the right of institutions to:

- copy works for preservation purposes under section 51A (or to make inter-library loans under sections 49 and 50);
- make 'fair dealings' for research or study (section 40); and
- make copies of works available online on library premises (section 49(5A)).

2.2.39 The CLRC report recommended that the *Copyright Act* be amended to make it clear that agreements purporting to modify the operation of certain exceptions to infringement (including the library and archive exceptions) should have no effect.[80] This recommendation has since been echoed in the House of Representatives, Legal and Constitutional Affairs Committee's *Inquiry into Technological Protection Measures Exceptions*,[81] as well as submissions prior to the implementation of the *Copyright Amendment Bill 2006*.[82]

2.2.40 The Government is yet to respond to the CLRC report.

2.3 The Impact of Copyright and Related Laws on Digital Preservation Activities in Australia

Effect of Copyright and Related Laws on Digital Preservation

2.3.1 Compared to other jurisdictions internationally, Australian copyright law currently provides libraries and archives with relatively advanced rights for the preservation of digital material held within their collection. Nevertheless, a number of legal barriers to the effective preservation of digital heritage within Australia still exist.[83] These barriers undermine the practicality of many preservation activities undertaken by libraries and archives,

---

[80] Copyright Law Review Committee, Parliament of Australia, *Copyright and Contract* (2002), 274.

[81] See also, recommendation 33 House of Representatives, Legal and Constitutional Affairs Committee, *Review of Technological Protection Measures Exceptions,* Parliamentary Paper 54/2006 (Feb 2006), http://www.aph.gov.au/house/committee/laca/protection/report.htm.

[82] See eg, submissions made in 2006 to the Senate Legal and Constitutional Affairs Committee in relation to provisions of the *Copyright Amendment Bill 2006.*

[83] For further discussion of the limits of the Australian Copyright Act's provisions dealing with preservation, see Kenyon, Andrew T. and Hudson, Emily, "Copyright, Digitisation, and Cultural Institutions" Australian Journal of Communication, Vol. 31, No. 1, pp. 89-105, 2004 http://ssrn.com/abstract=603861.

and create conflicts with the collection, preservation and access functions mandated by the archives' founding legislation.[84]

2.3.2 The main areas in which legal reform is still needed are discussed below.

Legal Deposit

2.3.3 Over the last ten years the principal production and distribution of copyright material has without question moved to electronic media. Materials of major cultural significance – from political party campaign statements to popular entertainment products – are increasingly being produced in digital and audiovisual formats or released exclusively online. A legal deposit scheme which focuses exclusively on printed materials can, therefore, no longer be said to provide an accurate record of a country's culture, knowledge and heritage.[85]

2.3.4 Nevertheless, due to the relative ease with which digital material is created and adapted, and the real problems involved in maintaining material (especially through format changes), and the sheer quantities of material posted online, compulsory deposit of all 'published' digital material with a single institution via procedures similar to those currently in place for print materials is clearly impractical. For this reason, the most effective legislative reform is likely to be a hybrid system, which combines compulsory deposit of hardcopy digital materials such as CDs and DVDs with permitting cultural institutions to harvest material consistent with the statutory preservation purposes of the institution and any agreed related purpose.

2.3.5 At present, most Australian State and Federal laws do not require publishers to deposit digital objects with the relevant collecting institution, nor do they permit collecting institutions to, without consent, capture digital objects for preservation purposes. Although the legal deposit laws of Tasmania and Northern Territory do encompass digital materials, they similarly do not support active collection of digital material.

2.3.6 To obtain digital materials for preservation, projects such as PANDORA and Our Digital Island therefore are forced to rely on

[84] See, for example s6 *National Library Act 1960*, http://scaletext.law.gov.au/html/pasteact/1/761/0/PA000100.htm.

[85] For discussion of the historical and policy rationale of legal deposit law in Australia, see John Gilchrist, *Copyright Deposit, Legal Deposit or Library Deposit? The Government's Role as Preserver of Copyright Material* [2005] Queensland University of Technology Law and Justice Journal 12.

an ad hoc system of voluntary agreements and legally 'grey' harvesting schemes that is inefficient and costly. By requiring officers of the relevant institution to actively seek out and negotiate rights in relation to non-print materials, this system results in incomplete and inadequate collection of culturally significant material whilst expending unnecessary manpower and time and exposing the collecting institutions to potential legal risk.

Commercial Availability and the Three-Step Test

2.3.7 In the digital environment format obsolescence means that materials must be regularly and routinely reproduced to ensure continued access, even while those materials are still commercially available. This differs from the analogue environment, in which libraries may rely on the same copy of a book for decades, generally long after it has left the commercial market. In this environment, the application of the commercial availability test and the three-step test conditions to the *Copyright Act*'s preservation exceptions for published materials creates significant problems. Based on anecdotal evidence, it appears that many library officers do not understand or feel confident in applying these tests, and are therefore forced to either ignore their requirements or make very little, if any, use of the exceptions to which they apply.

2.3.8 For example, the commercial availability test, if interpreted broadly, would appear to require libraries to purchase copies of expensive computer programs each time they are released in a new platform, rather than merely format-shifting the copy to which they already have access. It also prevents libraries from undertaking pro-active preservation by format shifting material into new and better formats as they become available, rather than waiting for old formats to disappear from the market entirely.

2.3.9 Meanwhile, the application of the three-step test, which was designed for international treaty law, to domestic law is extremely unclear. This is particularly the case due to the Australian parliament's incorporation of the 'special case' requirement into the new s200AB provisions, which would seem to preclude these provisions from applying to any ongoing or systematic preservation of digital materials.

2.3.10 The premise underlying the inclusion of these conditions in Australia's preservation provisions is the protection of copyright owner markets. That is, that each unauthorised act of copying and/or communication, even where it is conducted by a collecting institution, represents a potential commercial detriment to the copyright owner. The International Publishers' Association has expressed concern that the *Copyright Act*'s preservation provisions do not, like s200AB, require cultural institutions to satisfy the three-step test before undertaking digital preservation.[86] According to publishers, digital preservation reform proposals are a 'trojan horse' that could, if implemented, result in real damage to digital publication markets. This is because, say the publishers, permissive legislation could result in institutions creating digital repositories *and* making material in the repositories available to the public – thus undermining the digital market.

2.3.11 To persuade copyright owners that legislative reform to support digital preservation would not undermine commercial markets, reform proponents might be advised to investigate the commercial consequences of digital preservation. Would digital preservation reform, allowing, for instance, institutions to harvest digital objects, to format-shift and make multiple copies, *actually* undermine commercial markets? That is, does it interfere with the owner's *normal exploitation* of copyright material or *unreasonably prejudice* the owner's *legitimate interests*? This is particularly unlikely to be the case where prohibitions, or at least strict limitations, are placed on cultural institutions' ability to provide access to digital material to the public outside the library.[87]

Contracts and Technological Protection Measures

2.3.12 Currently Australian law places great power in the hands of copyright owners to override the provisions of the *Copyright Act* through the use of private agreements and technological measures. As almost all digital materials currently held by collecting institutions are subject to licensing agreements and locked behind TPMs, this results in private initiatives presenting a significant barrier to the practical preservation of digital material in Australia.

2.3.13 Although it is not clear that private agreements can be used to exclude the user exceptions provided by the *Copyright Act*, the legal uncertainty in this area means that collecting institutions must, in practice, assume that this is the case. The failure of the Federal Government to clarify the situation, despite repeated recommendations by its own advisory committees in favour of enshrining user rights, suggests that this will remain the case for the foreseeable future.

---

[86] IPA submission to the Senate Legal and Constitutional Affairs Committee inquiry into the *Copyright Amendment Bill 2006.*

[87] Andrew F Christie, *Cultural Institutions, Digitisation and Copyright Reform,* Intellectual Property Research Institute of Australia, 2007.

2.3.14 The situation with relation to TPMs is far more certain, but no less detrimental to digital preservation projects. Due to the lack of exceptions to permit the manufacture and supply of circumvention devices, Australia's current TPM laws fail to provide libraries with the practical ability to circumvent TPMs for the purpose of preserving their collection. This is particularly important for digital materials, due to the need to regularly migrate them as hardware and software formats become outdated. Furthermore, as time passes and TPMs attached to current storage formats become obsolete, it will only become more difficult or even impossible to disable the measures to allow adequate preservation or access, even with the original publisher's cooperation.

2.3.15 Unfortunately, this limitation on exceptions to allow the manufacture and supply of circumvention devices is imposed upon Australia by the Free Trade Agreement into which it entered with the United States in 2004. In the absence of changes to this Agreement, it is highly unlikely that exceptions permitting more effective access to circumvention devices will be provided.

2.3.16 Australia may therefore wish to explore alternative measures to ensure deposit institutions are able to effectively preserve and provide access to the legal deposit materials in their collections. Publishers could, for example, be required to provide materials free of TPMs as part of the legal deposit process, or to provide (on request) an effective means to disable or circumvent any TPMs necessary to access the material.

Moral and Performers' Rights

2.3.17 Certain preservation activities could constitute an infringement of moral rights (eg where the format of the material was being changed or the author or performer was unknown and therefore could not be attributed). However, it is likely that any such activities, if undertaken with due care by a collecting institution in the course of maintaining its collection, would be held to be reasonable and hence permitted by the *Copyright Act*.

2.3.18 However, performers' economic rights (as joint copyright owners) to authorise reproductions and communications of their recordings are not subject to these same reasonableness standards. Due to the difficulty of identifying and locating performers after the performance, these rights could significantly compromise any digital preservation activities which fall outside of the exceptions provided for by the *Copyright Act* and for which negotiated permissions must therefore be obtained. Even if a recognised system for negotiating generic authorisations by performers were introduced, the administrative and other costs of agreements could be prohibitive.

Access to Digital Material

2.3.19 Although not strictly required for preservation purposes, providing adequate access to digital materials held within institutions collections is a vital part of any effective collection management strategy. While Australian law currently provides a number of exceptions for the preservation of digital material, it is still extremely limited in the rights it provides for libraries to allow access to these materials. Reproduction and communication exceptions for libraries and archives allow limited one-off copying and communication of digital material for researchers and between libraries and archives.[88] But they fail to provide more general access to material, even where it is rare or no longer commercially available. This is a particular problem for digital materials due to their ephemeral nature, short commercial lifespan, and the rapid obsolescence of the hard and software tools required to access them.

Government Material

2.3.20 As an important aside, it should also be noted that while private copyright owners may raise concerns with providing greater preservation and access rights to libraries and archives, at the very minimum such rights should be provided in relation to government owned and publicly funded material. The question of access to and re-use of materials produced by government and other publicly-funded bodies has emerged as an important issue in recent years.[89] This interest has been driven not only by technological advances but also by a growing appreciation of the economic advantages to be gained by states which enable access to and re-use of public sector information.[90]

2.3.21 In most countries, the government sector is one of the primary producers and owners of intellectual property. Industry, artists and researchers, as well as the general public and other government

---

[88] *Copyright Act 1968* (Cth) ss49 and 50.

[89] See, for example, Directive 2003/98/EC, 17 November 2003, OJ L345/90, 31 December 2003 http://europa.eu.int/information_society/policy/psi/docs/pdfs/directive/psi_directive_en.pdf; the New Zealand National Digital Strategy (2007), http://www.digitalstrategy.govt.nz/Parts-of-the-Digital-Strategy/Content/New-Zealand-Digital-Content-Strategy/; and *Public Access Policy* (National Institute of Health, 2007), http://publicaccess.nih.gov.

[90] See for example, Peter N. Weiss, *Borders in Cyberspace: Conflicting Public Sector Information Policies and their Economic Impacts* (2002), US Department of Commerce, National Oceanic and Atmospheric Administration, National Weather Service, http://www.weather.gov/sp/Borders_report.pdf at 11 April 2007.

bodies, are increasingly demanding the ability to re-use this material for creative, educational and scientific purposes. Libraries and archives have the potential to play an important role in disseminating and preserving this material for the use of current and future generations. However, in order to do so, they must be granted greater rights to work with the material, beyond the traditional rights conferred upon National and State Archives. This could be achieved by amending Australian copyright law to apply separate preservation and access rights to Crown copyright material. Alternatively, uniform open access licensing policies that apply across both State and Federal governments could potentially be used to achieve the same result.[91]

Orphaned Works

2.3.22 Although not discussed at length in this report, another area in which copyright presents significant legal barriers to the preservation of digital materials is in relation to 'orphaned works' (ie works for which copyright owners cannot be identified). Where an institution's right to undertake preservation activities is unclear, the most legally and practically efficient response is often to simply ask the copyright owner for the required permission. This, however, is impossible to do where the copyright owner or their heirs are unable to be located. Worse, still, is where the copyright owner cannot even be identified, as this often makes it difficult to determine whether the material is still within copyright.

2.3.23 The issue of orphaned works is particularly relevant in relation to digital preservation, as digital-born works are by their nature prone to becoming 'orphaned'. Many (such as blogs and web pages) are informally created, with no real indicator as to who is the original creator. Others (such as wikis) can be the result of the collaboration of dozens or even hundreds of authors, many of whom may not be locatable. Finally, many digital works (such as software) are created and owned by companies that have a far

[91] See, for example, 'Government Information and Open Content Licensing: An Access and Use Strategy' (2006) Queensland Spatial Information Council, http://www.qsic.qld.gov.au/QSIC/QSIC.nsf/0/F82522D9F23F6F1C4A2572EA007D57A6/$FILE/Stage%202%20Final%20Report%20-%20PDF%20Format.pdf?openelement; Intrallect Ltd (E. Barker, C. Duncan) and AHRC Research Centre (A. Guadamuz, J. Hatcher and C. Waelde), *The Common Information Environment and Creative Commons: Final Report to the Common Information Environment Members of a study on the applicability of Creative Commons Licenses* (2005), http://www.intrallect.com/index.php/intrallect/knowledge_base/general_articles/creative_commons_licensing_solutions_for_the_common_information_environment__1/; and Mireille van Eechoud and Brenda van der Wal, *Creative Commons licensing for public sector information: Opportunities and pitfalls* (2007) Institute for Information Law, University of Amsterdam http://www.ivir.nl/publications/eechoud/CC_PublicSectorInformation_report_v3.pdf.

shorter lifespan than the copyright period of the works, meaning that there simply is no one able to seek permission from.[92]

2.3.24 The new s51B and s200AB provisions, which provide a broad right for libraries and archives to reproduce works for preservation and other purposes, have the potential to assist with the one-off preservation of orphaned works. However, due to the limited nature of these provisions – in particular s200AB's requirement that it only apply to 'special cases' and s51B's restriction to activities by only a few cultural institutions – they do not provide a solution for large-scale preservation projects seeking to deal with orphaned works.[93]

2.4 Overview of Responses to the Issue of Copyright and Digital Preservation in the Australia

Copyright Law Reform

2.4.1 Over the past decade a number of reports and reviews have been published by the Australian government in relation to copyright policy and reform. The majority of reviews have been conducted either by the relevant parliamentary committee charged with overseeing the introduction of proposed legislation (eg the Senate Standing Committee on Legal and Constitutional Affairs[94]) or the Copyright Law Review Committee[95] (CLRC), an independent committee appointed by the Attorney-General to report on Australian copyright law and policy from time to time. More recently, a number of reviews have also been conducted by the Attorney-General's Department, as the government department in charge of copyright policy.

2.4.2 Although none of these reports have focused on the issue of preservation of digital objects specifically, a number have dealt with issues or made recommendations of relevance to the topic. The most significant of these reports are discussed below.

---

92 See, for example, Graham Greenleaf, *Unlocking IP to stimulate Australian innovation: An Issues Paper A submission to the Review of the National Innovation System* (30 April 2007) at 37-41, http://www.innovation.gov.au/innovationreview/Documents/504(R)-Graham_Greenleaf.pdf.

93 Hudson, E. and Kenyon, A. "Without Walls: Copyright Law and Digital Collections in Australian Cultural Institutions" (2007) 4(2) SCRIPT-ed 197 at 212, http://papers.ssrn.com/sol3/papers.cfm?abstract_id=1007391.

94 See http://www.aph.gov.au/senate/committee/legcon_ctte/index.htm.

95 See http://www.clrc.gov.au/.

Copyright and Contract

2.4.3 As is discussed above, in this 2002 report the CLRC recommended that the *Copyright Act* be amended to ensure that contracts purporting to modify the operation of the library and archive exceptions have no effect.[96] The Government is yet to respond to the CLRC report.

Review of Digital Agenda Act Reforms

2.4.4 In 2003 Law firm Phillips Fox was commissioned by the Attorney-General to conduct a review of the amendments introduced by the *Copyright Amendment (Digital Agenda) Act 2000*, including a substantial public consultation process.[97] In its final report,[98] Philips Fox devoted two chapters to issues relating to libraries and archives, and made a number of recommendations of relevance to the preservation and dissemination of digital objects, including:

- libraries should be permitted to make public access copies from a preservation copy of a fragile work;[99]
- it should be clarified that different editions of works are treated as different publications for preservation purposes;[100]
- that libraries and archives be permitted to communicate low resolution reproductions of the whole of an artistic work both within and external to the institution;[101]
- that further consideration be given to the effects of digital copying by libraries and archives, and the extent to which those copies are further copied or communicated;[102] and
- that the TPM provisions be amended to allow supply or use of a circumvention device or service for any exception allowed under the Act, including the library and archive provisions.[103]

96 Copyright Law Review Committee, Parliament of Australia, *Copyright and Contract* (2002), 274.

97 See *Review of Digital Agenda Act reforms – April 2003* (Australian Government Attorney-General's Department, 2003), http://www.ag.gov.au/www/agd/agd.nsf/Page/Publications_ReviewofDigitalAgendaActreforms-April2003.

98 *Digital Agenda Review: Report and recommendations* (Philips Fox, January 2004) http://www.ag.gov.au/www/agd/agd.nsf/Page/Publications_PhillipsFoxreportDigitalAgendareview-January2004.

99 *Id.* at 67.

100 *Id.*

101 *Id.* at 70.

102 *Id.* at 69.

2.4.5 The Australian Government implemented the first two recommendations as part of the *Copyright Amendment Act 2006*; the third and fourth were regarded as being fulfilled by the *Fair Use Review 2005*; and the final was effectively superseded by Australia's US Free Trade Agreement obligations (which prohibited any such exception).[104]

Fair Use and Other Copyright Exceptions Review

2.4.6 In 2005, the Attorney-General's Department conducted a review on whether the Australia should introduce a US-style 'fair use' exception, which included a detail review of the existing exceptions of the *Copyright Act*.[105] Although no final report was released, and the review's initial issues paper[106] did not specifically reference the library and archive provisions, a number of the public submissions in response to this paper did touch upon issues of relevance to this report, including the preservation exceptions, TPMs and orphaned works.[107] Furthermore, the *Copyright Amendment Act 2006*, which was introduced in part in response to this review, included amendments relating to library and archive copying, including the s200AB 'three-step test'

[103] *Id.* at 107.

[104] See Digital Agenda Review - Government responses to Phillips Fox recommendations and related matters (Australian Government Attorney-General's Department, 2006), http://www.ag.gov.au/www/agd/rwpattach.nsf/VAP/(CFD7369FCAE9B8F32F341DBE097801FF)~BGOVTRESPONSEDIGITAL.doc/$file/BGOVTRESPONSEDIGITAL.doc.

[105] See *Fair Use* (Australian Government Attorney-General's Department, 2006) http://www.ag.gov.au/www/agd/agd.nsf/Page/Copyright_IssuesandReviews_Fairuse.

[106] *Fair Use and Other Copyright Exceptions: An examination of fair use, fair dealing and other exceptions in the Digital Age* (Australian Government Attorney-General's Department, May 2005), http://www.ag.gov.au/www/agd/rwpattach.nsf/VAP/(CFD7369FCAE9B8F32F341DBE097801FF)~FairUseIssuesPaper050505.pdf/$file/FairUseIssuesPaper050505.pdf.

[107] See, for example, *Fair Use and Other Copyright Exceptions: An examination of fair use, fair dealing and other exceptions in the Digital Age Submission of the Australian Digital Alliance* (Australian Government Attorney-General's Department, July 2005), http://www.ag.gov.au/www/agd/rwpattach.nsf/VAP/(AEEBC4E05675B564D2489B776B8B056A)~p137+ADA.PDF/$file/p137+ADA.PDF; *Fair Use and Other Copyright Exceptions: An examination of fair use, fair dealing and other exceptions in the Digital Age Submission of the Copyright in Cultural Institutions (CICI) group* (Australian Government Attorney-General's Department, July 2005), http://www.ag.gov.au/agd/WWW/rwpattach.nsf/VAP/(AEEBC4E05675B564D2489B776B8B056A)~p144+Cultural+institutions+group.PDF/$file/p144+Cultural+institutions+group.PDF; and Kimberlee Weatherall, *Fair use, fair dealing: The Copyright Exceptions Review and the Future of Copyright Exceptions in Australia Background Paper to Oral Presentation* (SNAPSHOT 3, 20 May 2005), http://www.ipria.net/publications/Occasional%20Papers/Occasional%20Paper%203.05.pdf.

exception for library and archives and several exceptions permitting key cultural institutions to make up to three preservation copies of material of historical or cultural significance to Australia.[108]

Legal Deposit

2.4.7 In its 2004 election policy Strengthening Australian Arts the former Coalition Government committed to consider the viability of expanding the Commonwealth scheme for legal deposit to include the deposit of electronic and audiovisual material.[109] This commitment can, in part, be attributed to direct campaigning by the NLA and other library institutions.[110]

2.4.8 In response to this commitment, the Federal Government released a discussion paper and call for public submissions on the issue in late 2007.[111] This paper set out the arguments for and against legal deposit of electronic and audiovisual material, and sought comments on how any extension to the current provisions may be implemented. Specific topics raised in the issues paper include:

- the definition of material to be deposited;
- whether any legal deposit scheme should permit active harvesting by libraries;
- whether any specific exceptions or limitations should apply to deposited material; and
- what, if any, provisions should be introduced to deal with TPMs.

2.4.9 Submissions in response to the issues paper were due by 11 January 2008. The government response to the paper is still forthcoming. In the meantime, activities such as PANDORA and the Our Digital Island project represent the ongoing efforts of the

---

108 *Copyright Act 1968* (Cth) s51B allows for triplicate preservation copying of manuscripts, original artistic works and published works. Section 110BA allows the same for unpublished and published sound recordings and films, and section 112AA for published editions (and the works therein).

109 *The Coalition Government Election Policy 2004 Strengthening Australian Arts* (The Nationals, 2004), http://www.nationals.org.au/downloads/australian_arts_policy_document.pdf, p.13.

110 PANDORA, *Legal Deposit*, available at http://pandora.nla.gov.au/legaldeposit.html.

111 *2007 Discussion Paper on the Extension of Legal Deposit* (Department of Broadband, Communication and Digital Economy, 2007), http://www.arts.gov.au/__data/assets/pdf_file/80928/legal_deposit_discussion_paper_2007.pdf.

library community to circumvent this weakness in current digital preservation practices.

Activities to Develop Non-Legislative Solutions

Handbooks and Guidelines

The NLA and PADI

2.4.10 The NLA maintain an online 'subject gateway' to digital preservation guideline resources. The *Preserving Access to Digital Information* (PADI) initiative aims to:

- facilitate the development of strategies and guidelines for the preservation of access to digital information;
- develop and maintain a website for information and promotion purposes;
- actively identify and promote relevant activities; and
- provide a forum for cross-sectoral cooperation on activities promoting the preservation of access to digital information.[112]

2.4.11 A multinational advisory group made up of members from the international library community was established to provide guidance and advice to the PADI initiative. The NLA announced in 2002 that PADI had signed a Memorandum of Understanding with the (UK) Digital Preservation Coalition. PADI continues to form partnerships to remain an internationally reputable service to digital preservation.

The NLA and the APA

2.4.12 In 2002 the Australian Publishers' Association (APA) and the NLA developed and released a code of practice for providing long-term access to Australian online publications. This code recognised the combined responsibility of both organisations in ensuring the availability in posterity of Australian online publications. The code outlines the conditions and responsibilities that each partner agrees to observe in order to give effect to this. For example, the code addresses such issues as standards for circumvention of TPMs when archiving electronic publications and the restriction of access to publications (such as through reading rooms of partner

[112] Preserving Access to Digital Information, *About PADI,* available at http://www.nla.gov.au/padi/about.html.

institutions) where necessary to preserve publishers' commercial interests.[113]

Awareness Raising, Sharing Knowledge and Training

ADRI

2.4.13 In 2004 the NAA developed the Australasian Digital Recordkeeping Initiative (ADRI) in association with all ten national, state and territory public record institutions in Australia and New Zealand.[114] The initiative seeks to facilitate collaboration on the "development, articulation and implementation of a common set of strategies for enabling the making, keeping and using of the digital records of governments".[115] The ADRI operates to pool resources and expertise in order to develop and facilitate a single Australasian approach to digital preservation of government records. The initiative aims to provide common standards and specifications, guidelines and best practice manuals, case studies, marketing and promotional material as well as strategic documents designed to guide the work of ADRI.[116] In 2007 the ADRI released a model plan for use by archiving authorities implementing digital archiving procedures.[117] It offers guidance across the Australasian government sector and addresses standards required to realize a digital archives repository, as well as associated business rules and tools.

ALIA

2.4.14 The Australian Libraries and Information Association (ALIA) is a professional organisation that acts as a collective voice for libraries and information services. ALIA are therefore ideally

---

[113] National Library of Australia, *Nurturing Our Digital Memory: Digital Archiving and Preservation at the National Library of Australia,* available at http://www.nla.gov.au/nla/staffpaper/2002/berthon1.html.

[114] The ADRI is essentially an undertaking of the CAARA (Council of Australasian Archives and Records Authorities) comprising of the heads of the government archives authorities of the Commonwealth of Australia, New Zealand and each of the Australian States and Territories.

[115] Australasian Digital Recordkeeping Initiative, *About ADRI,* available at http://www.adri.gov.au/content.asp?cID=14.

[116] Australasian Digital Recordkeeping Initiative, *Research and Development,* available at http://www.adri.gov.au/content.asp?cID=2.

[117] Australian Digital Recordkeeping Initiative, *Model Plan for an Archive Authority Implementing Digital Recordkeeping and Archiving, v1.0, 2 March 2007*, available at http://www.adri.gov.au/model-plan.doc.

placed to report on conflicts between digital preservation and copyright and assist in the development of best practice for digital preservation.

2.4.15 ALIA policies include a commitment to the preservation of (and enduring access to) published and documentary records in all formats.[118] To meet this commitment, ALIA have extended their traditional role of fostering and supporting collaborations among libraries and information services to include ensuring preservation of digital records. The association encourages preservation activities through:

- education in relation to preservation skills and promoting awareness of preservation issues among public policy makers;
- research in the field of preservation, in particular where it relates to technological developments;
- development of authoritative standards, specifications and benchmarks in the field of preservation (and encouraging compliance with these); and
- development of national preservation program.[119]

APSR

2.4.16 The Australian Partnership for Sustainable Repositories (APSR) project aims to establish a centre of excellence to develop best practice in Australia in the management of scholarly assets in the digital format.[120] Funded by the Federal government, the partnership assists researchers in creating systems to manage electronic research data through educational programmes and collaborative system (eg software and tools) development projects. The operation of the APSR is limited to material sourced from educational and research institutions.

The ARROW Project

2.4.17 The Australian Research Repositories Online to the World (ARROW) project aims to identify and test software or solutions to support best practice institutional digital repositories, such as e-prints (see earlier discussion of QUT ePrint at 2.1.16), electronic publications, e-research and electronic theses. ARROW links in

[118] Australian Library and Information Association, *ALIA Policies,* available at http://www.alia.org.au/policies/preservation.html.

[119] Australian Library and Information Association, *ALIA Policies,* available at http://www.alia.org.au/policies/preservation.html.

[120] Australian Partnership for Sustainable Repositories, *About,* available at http://www.apsr.edu.au/about.html.

with digital preservation activities undertaken by educational and research institutions and focuses around the development, management and implementation of technology in relation to digital research material.[121] The NLA is currently, through ARROW, developing and testing a national resource discovery service using metadata harvested from various institutional repositories.[122]

2.5 Recommendations for Legal Reforms or Practical Solutions in Australia to Facilitate Digital Preservation

2.5.1 Australian federal copyright law does not facilitate digital preservation for two main reasons:

- the legislation does not require publishers to deposit copies of digital objects with the NLA, nor does it permit the NLA to 'harvest' objects without consent; and
- lawmakers have not recognised that effective digital preservation depends on regular format-shifting and multiple copying that is not supported by the current provisions of the Australian *Copyright Act*.

2.5.2 Amending the *Copyright Act* to make digital collection compulsory, whether on a comprehensive deposit or a selective harvesting basis, is technically simple and, if the Tasmanian legislative precedent is taken as a yardstick, politically feasible. A more permissive legislative approach to the preservation provisions in relation to copyright material generally is unlikely, however, until legislators are convinced that allowing for format-shifting and multiple copying will not undermine the copyright owner's commercial market. Nevertheless, there is a strong argument that at a minimum libraries and archives should be granted greater rights to reproduce government and publicly funded material, whether through amendments to the *Copyright Act* or the institution of effective, government-wide open access schemes.

---

[121] Australian Research Repositories Online to the World, *About ARROW,* available at http://arrow.edu.au/about/.

[122] Australian Research Repositories Online to the World, *About ARROW,* available at http://arrow.edu.au/about/.

2.5.3 Any legislative amendments to facilitate digital preservation, whether for all or only certain copyright materials, would also need to:

- clarify the application of the commercial availability and three-step tests to digital materials so as to enable adequate format-shifting of aging digital material;
- provide for practical circumvention or disabling of TPMs for preservation purposes;
- protect cultural institutions against liability for infringement of moral and performers rights; and
- invalidate any contractual provisions that seek to exclude libraries' rights to undertake preservation activities.

2.5.4 Ideally, the amendments would also loosen current provisions restricting access to obscure digital material.

2.5.5 Another consideration relevant to reform proposals is the fragmentary character of current digital preservation initiatives in Australia. Reform of the Federal copyright law would ideally be accompanied by uniform legislative or policy reforms to create consistency in digital deposit and preservation activities in the Australian jurisdictions.

2.5.6 The recommendations below for digital preservation reform are intended to accommodate copyright owners' concerns and the preservation purposes of cultural institutions.

Recommendations

1 The Australian Federal government should commission an independent study to determine the effect of digital preservation on commercial markets for digital publications.

2 All Australian jurisdictions should reform their digital deposit laws and practices on a consultative and, so far as possible, complementary and uniform basis.

3 Preservation institutions should be encouraged to agree on uniform principles or guidelines for digital preservation to ensure effective conservation of Australia's cultural heritage.

4 Preservation institutions should, at a minimum, be granted rights to reproduce government and publicly funded material for preservation and dissemination purposes, either legislatively or via the use of uniform open access licensing schemes.

5 The Australian Federal *Copyright Act* should be amended to:

a) extend the current legal deposit laws to digital materials, including granting the right for deposit institutions (notably the NLA) to actively harvest online material;

b) explicitly permit format-shifting and multiple copying of digital holdings for preservation purposes;

c) clarify that agreements purporting to modify the operation of certain exceptions to infringement (including the library and archive exceptions) have no effect;

d) provide libraries with the ability to effectively preserve material that is subject to TPMs, whether by extending the current exceptions to the TPM provisions or by requiring legal deposit material to be TPM free; and

e) permit the communication of digital holdings, particularly where they are no longer commercially available, in and outside institutional premises to facilitate access as per the institutions' fundamental role.

Part 3: Country Report for the Netherlands

Wilma Mossink[123]

3.1 Major Digital Preservation Activities in the Netherlands

3.1.1 Major digital preservation initiatives in the Netherlands involve different types of works. The first digitisation projects started in the late 1990's. Those first initiatives were taken to rescue Dutch heritage but other initiatives followed. The Koninklijke Bibliotheek, the National Library of the Netherlands (National Library or KB) plays an important role in many of the digitisation projects, as discussed throughout this report

3.1.2 Launched in 1997, Metamorfoze[124] was the first national preservation project in the Netherlands. Funded by the Ministry of Education, Cultural Affairs and Science, Metamorfoze was set up to rescue important parts of the Dutch paper heritage that were decaying due to acidification.

3.1.3 Since 1997 two phases of the Metamorfoze programme have been completed. The third phase of the project started in 2005 and will run until 2008. It is expected that after 2008 the programme will continue for eight more years. So far, around 60 institutions have carried out approximately three hundred preservation projects.

3.1.4 A number of public organisations whose remit includes long-term preservation of digital data have joined forces to establish the Netherlands Coalition for Digital Preservation (NCDD)[125]. The

[123] Legal Advisor, SURFfoundation, the Netherlands. The contribution of Annemarie Beunen, Corporate Strategy Department, National Library of the Netherlands, who wrote the material concerning database rights, is gratefully acknowledged.

[124] Metamorfoze Programma, http://www.metamorfoze.nl/programma/programme.html.

[125] Netherlands Coalition for Digital Preservation, http://www.ncdd.nl/en.

Coalition aims to deal with both the technical and the organisational challenges of digital preservation. First on the agenda is a national survey of the current state of digital preservation in the Netherlands, which is being funded by the Ministry of Education and Culture. The study will reveal which organisations preserve specific categories of data, and in what manner. Next, the Coalition will develop a strategic action plan to realise a sustainable technical and organisational infrastructure.

3.1.5 Members of the Coalition include 3TU.Federation[126], with the Data Centre of the three Dutch universities of technology, Dutch Institute for Sound and Vision[127], Statistics Netherlands (CBS)[128], Data Archiving and Networked Services (DANS)[129], Royal Netherlands Academy of Arts and Sciences (KNAW)[130], National Library of the Netherlands[131], the Ministry of the Interior and Kingdom Relations[132], the National Archives of the Netherlands[133], Netherlands Organisation for Scientific Research (NWO)[134], and SURFfoundation[135], a Netherlands collaborative organ-isation for higher education and research.

3.1.6 The NCDD's office is based at the National Library of the Netherlands.

Cultural Heritage Institutions

3.1.7 An important initiative that preserves electronic publications such as scientific articles and CD-ROMs is the e-Depot of the National Library. As the Netherlands does not have legal deposit

126 3TU.Federation, http://www.tudelft.nl/live/pagina.jsp?id=998c2980-ae4a-4268-a14a-a2add4f82682&lang=en.

127 Beeld en Geluid, http://portal.beeldengeluid.nl/.

128 CBS, http://www.cbs.nl/en-GB/default.htm?Languageswitch=on.

129 Data Archiving and Networked Services, DANS, http://www.dans.knaw.nl/en/.

130 Koninklijke Nederlandse Akademie van Wetenschappen (KNAW) (Royal Netherlands Academy of Arts and Sciences), http://www.knaw.nl/.

131 Koninklijke Bibliotheek (National Library of the Netherlands), http://www.kb.nl/index-en.html.

132 Ministerie van Binnenlandse Zaken en Koninkrijksrelaties, http://www.minbzk.nl/bzk2006uk/.

133 Het Nationaal Archief, http://www.en.nationaalarchief.nl/default.asp.

134 NWO, http://www.nwo.nl/nwohome.nsf/pages/SPPD_5R2QE7_Eng.

135 SURFfoundation, http://www.surffoundation.nl/smartsite.dws?id=5289&ch=ENG.

legislation, deposit of analogue and digital material is based on the cooperation of publishers. The e-Depot is a logical extension of the task of the National Library to collect and preserve all publications printed in the Netherlands, and the strategy to preserve electronic publications stems largely from this role. E-Depot is discussed further below.

3.1.8 The National Library not only preserves e-journals but also other electronic objects. It recently started a research project to preserve and keep accessible Dutch web sites for the future. In this project the National Library archives selected web sites in as detailed a manner as possible. For long-term accessibility the KB thinks that emulation is the most viable strategy. This should enable scientists to use the archive for future research.

3.1.9 This is the first website preservation project in which the digital endurance of the web sites takes a central role. The first phase of the project ended in May 2007. The second phase is focused on extending the selection of web sites to be archived, preservation research and incorporating the work processes which were set up in the project into the structural processes of the National Library.

Beelden voor de Toekomst

3.1.10 A major project for preservation of Dutch cultural audiovisual heritage is Beelden voor de Toekomst (Images for the Future) [136]. The project aims at the conservation, digitisation and making available of 137,200 hours of video material, 22,510 hours of film, 123,900 hours of audio material and 2.9 million pictures. The project also intends to place the audiovisual material in a context so that it can be searched easily. This is not only done for educational use but also for use by the general public and the creative industry.

3.1.11 The serious decay of the Dutch audiovisual collections at the archival institutions and the rather limited availability and searchability of the collections were the reasons for initiating this large-scale project. A basic collection of digital film and audio should be made available either under a Creative Commons licence or should be available with no copyright restrictions.

3.1.12 The project Beelden voor de Toekomst is run by a consortium consisting of six partners: Stichting Nederlands Filmmuseum (Dutch Film Museum)[137], Nederlands Instituut voor Beeld en

[136] Beelden voor de Toekomst, http://www.beeldenvoordetoekomst.nl/.

[137] Filmmuseum, http://www.filmmuseum.nl/website/exec/frontpageread/page.html?id=722-6e6c2e66696c6d6d757365756d2e50616765.

Geluid (Dutch Institute for Sound and Vision)[138], Centrale Discotheek Rotterdam (Central Discotheque)[139], Nationaal Archief (National Archives)[140], Vereniging Openbare Bibliotheken (Dutch Public Libraries Association)[141] and Stichting Nederland Kennisland (Netherlands Knowledgeland)[142].

3.1.13 The starting point for digitising the audiovisual material of the members of the consortium is that the digitised material should be made available very broadly. The availability should lead to services developed by either public or private parties. Getting access to the material does not mean that the material always will be free of charge. Remuneration for the material depends on the nature of the user. It is the intention to make the material available for educational purposes for a relatively low price. Private parties could be asked to pay a price according to market prices.

Databank of Digital Daily Newspapers

3.1.14 In 2006 the National Library initiated the Databank of Digital Daily newspapers project. The project involves the large-scale digitisation of Dutch national, regional, local and colonial newspapers and makes these freely available on the internet. After finishing the project the Databank will contain eight million pages of newspapers, from 1618 to the twentieth century.

Dutch Parliamentary Papers

3.1.15 In cooperation with the House of Parliament, the National Library digitises all records and supplements of the House of Representatives and the Senate from the period 1814 through 1995. The total collection contains about 2.5 million pages.

Geheugen van Nederland

3.1.16 Geheugen van Nederland[143] (Memory of the Netherlands) is the national programme regarding the digitisation of the Dutch cultural

---

[138] See note 127, *supra*.

[139] MuziekWeb - Centrale Discotheek Rotterdam, http://www.muziekweb.nl.

[140] See note 133, *supra*.

[141] Vereniging van Openbare Bibliotheken, http://www.debibliotheken.nl/index.jsp?objectid=11736.

[142] Kennisland : KnowledgeLand, http://www.kennisland.nl/en/index.html.

[143] Het Geheugen van Nederland, http://www.geheugenvannederland.nl.

heritage. Through this programme collections of archives, museums and libraries are digitised and made available on the internet. The collection not only contains texts but also sound and moving images. The coordination is done by the National Library and financed by The Ministry of Education, Culture and Science.

Digitaal Erfgoed Nederland Digital Heritage Netherlands (DEN)

3.1.17 DEN is a national knowledge centre for ICT and cultural heritage that works in close collaboration with cultural heritage institutions. Commissioned by the Dutch Ministry of Education, Cultural Affairs and Science, DEN collects and distributes information about IT standards and other quality instruments. DEN maintains an IT register and project bank, investigates how cultural heritage institutions are actually using the existing IT knowledge, and organises meetings about innovation.

3.1.18 The project bank contains examples of different kinds of digitisation projects in the cultural sector.

Archives Task Force

3.1.19 A very important digital curation project is the Digital Accessibility of Archives Task Force (Taskforce Digitale Toegankelijkheid Archieven) – usually known simply as the Archives Task Force[144]. This Task Force has been formed for the period 2004-2008. It serves the archives sector and works in close cooperation with it. The lead institution is the National Archive of the Netherlands, in close collaboration with the Association for Records Management and Archives (DIVA). It also maintains contacts with the Dutch Digital Heritage Association (DEN).

3.1.20 The mission of the Task Force is not strictly the preservation of archives itself but the development of a self-regulating and dynamic quality system for digital accessibility, for use by the entire Dutch archives sector. The system defines quality standards for digital accessibility within the archives sector and enables the sector to define, control and improve continuously the quality of the digital services of the sector. It also collects and records information and experiences, as well as best and worst practices, in the field of digital services.

[144] Taskforce Archieven, http://www.taskforce-archieven.nl/.

Government Archives

3.1.21 The country report for the Netherlands does not include information about major digital preservation activities undertaken by the government.

Educational and Research Institutions

DANS

3.1.22 Data Archiving and Networked Services (DANS) is an institute under the auspices of Royal Netherlands Academy of Arts and Sciences (KNAW), which is also supported by the Netherlands Organisation for Scientific Research (NWO) [145].

3.1.23 According to its web site DANS has been storing and making permanently accessible research data in social sciences and the arts and humanities since its establishment in 2005. DANS intends to ensure free availability of as much data as possible for use in scientific research. DANS manages and improves a user-friendly Electronic Archiving System (EASY). This system is open to all researchers in social sciences and the arts and humanities and allows them to search data and permanently store their data themselves. It is the objective of EASY to become the electronic repository for data from the social sciences and the arts and humanities in the Netherlands.

3.1.24 In March 2008 DANS introduced a hallmark (seal of approval) for use by researchers in social sciences and humanities.[146] The hallmark contains seventeen guidelines which data producers, data consumers and data archives must meet to receive the qualification 'future sustainable' or 'future proof'. The hallmark, which builds upon international attempts to develop criteria for trusted digital repositories, is the first of its kind.

3.1.25 DANS takes part in numerous projects aimed at preserving and permanent archiving of data for scientific research. A large international project which DANS coordinates with a series of foreign partners is DARIAH (Digital Research Infrastructure for the Arts and Humanities).[147] Its aim is to set up a European data infrastructure.

---

[145] About DANS, http://www.dans.knaw.nl/en/over_dans.

[146] Data Seal of Approval, www.datasealofapproval.org.

[147] DARIAH – Digital Research Infrastructure for the Arts and Humanities, http://www.dariah.eu/?q=node/28.

3TU.Datacentre

3.1.26 The libraries of the three Dutch universities of technology (Delft, Eindhoven and Twente) joined forces to provide for long term storage for technical-science data and opened their own data centre for digital data sets. The 3TU.Datacentre will ensure well-documented storage and long-term access to technical-science study data. This will guarantee the long-term availability of the entire Dutch technical-science heritage. The data centre was set up because the data sets which form the basis for a scientific publication, were not being preserved for the long term.

University Projects

3.1.27 Recently the libraries of Leiden University and University of Amsterdam, together with the National Library of the Netherlands, launched a project entitled Dutch Prints on Line, which in the long run aims at the digitization of all (150,000) works that are listed in the Short Title Catalogue of the Netherlands (STCN). STCN represents a complete overview of all works printed in the Netherlands between 1540 and 1800. The project will copy and digitise some 1.3 million pages, covering 5,000 to 7,000 works from the last two decades of the 18th century.

3.2 Overview of Copyright, Related Rights, and Legal Deposit Laws of The Netherlands as Applied to Digital Preservation

Copyright

3.2.1 Who and what are covered by copyright can be found in the Copyright Act (Auteurswet). (Relevant provisions of the Dutch Copyright Act are attached as Appendix C.) Article 1 of the Act stipulates that the author of a literary, scientific or artistic work or his successors in title have the exclusive right to communicate that work to the public and to reproduce it, subject to the limitations in the law.

3.2.2 Unless there is proof to the contrary, the person who is named as author in or on the work is deemed the owner of the work. Where there is no indication of the name of the author, the person who communicated the work to the public is viewed as the author.

3.2.3 There are a few exceptions to the principle that the creator or author of a work is the owner of the work. These exceptions are incorporated in articles 6, 7 and 8 of the Copyright Act. Article 7 is a work for hire/work made in the course of employment provision. Unless otherwise agreed between the parties, the employer is deemed by law to be the author of certain literary, scientific or artistic works created through the labour of an employee.

3.2.4 The Dutch Copyright Act protects a range of works. Generally, any creation in the literary, scientific or artistic areas, whatever the mode or form of its expression, is protected. Article 10 gives a non-limitative enumeration of possible copyright protected works. Literary, scientific or artistic works include, for instance, books, newspapers and all other writings but also musical and choreographic works, with or without words. Furthermore drawings, paintings, works of architecture and sculpture, lithographs, engravings and the like can be protected. In addition article 10 includes geographical maps, cinematographic works, works of applied art and industrial designs and models. Computer programs and the preparatory material and databases also fall within the range of works.

3.2.5 Reproductions of a literary, scientific or artistic work in a modified form, such as translations, arrangements of music, cinematographic and other adaptations and collections of different works are also protected as separate works, without prejudice to the copyright in the original work.

3.2.6 Under the Dutch Copyright Act an author has two kinds of rights: exploitation or economic rights and moral rights. Exploitation rights make it possible for an author to communicate his work to the public. The economic rights consist of the right of communication to the public and the reproduction right. Both rights are broadly defined.

3.2.7 The right of communication to the public includes:

the communication to the public of a reproduction of the whole or part of a work;

the distribution of the whole or part of a work or of a reproduction thereof, as long as the work has not appeared in print;

the rental or lending of the whole or part of a work, or of a reproduction thereof which has been brought into circulation by or with the consent of the right holder;

the recitation, performance or presentation in public of the whole or part of a work or a reproduction thereof;

the broadcasting of a work incorporated in a radio or television programme by satellite or other transmitter or by a closed-circuit system.

3.2.8 The reproduction right includes two different kinds of acts: the reproduction itself and the translation or adaptation of a work. Reproduction of a literary, scientific or artistic work includes the translation, arrangement of music, cinematographic adaptation or dramatization and generally any partial or total adaptation or imitation in a modified form, which cannot be regarded as a new, original work.

Secondary Infringement/Authorising Infringement

3.2.9 Article 29a(3) states that those who provide services or make, import, distribute, sell, hire out, advertise or possess equipment, products or components for commercial purposes will be acting unlawfully if those items are:

> offered, recommended, or traded with the intention of circumventing the protected operation of purposive technical provisions, or
>
> of only limited commercial purpose or use, apart from the circumvention of the protected operation of purposive technical provisions, or
>
> primarily designed, manufactured or adapted with the purpose of circumventing the protected operation of purposive technical provisions.

Moral Rights

3.2.10 Besides his exploitation rights an author has moral rights. The moral rights protect the personal bond between the author and his work and protect the integrity of the work. The Dutch Copyright Act does not use the terminology "moral rights": article 25 merely describes the rights an author has. The rest of the Act refers to those as the provisions of article 25. According to article 25 an author has the right to oppose the communication to the public of the work without acknowledgement of his name or other indication of authorship, or under a name other than his own. Furthermore he has the right to oppose to any other alteration and any distortion, mutilation or other impairment of the work that could be prejudicial to the name or reputation of the author or to his dignity.

3.2.11 The rights under article 25 cannot be transferred. An author can waive his rights, though, except for the right to oppose to the distortion or other impairment of the work that could be prejudicial to his name or reputation or to his dignity.

Database Rights

3.2.12 The Dutch implementation of the European Database Directive entered into force on 21 July 1999, one and a half years later than the Directive prescribed.[148] This delay was due to the extensive parliamentary debates on the implementation, which produced interesting considerations on key concepts in the Directive. The Dutch transposition, called the Databases Act, exclusively deals with the new sui generis right for database producers – or "database right" as it is called in the Netherlands.

3.2.13 The copyright chapter of the Directive has been implemented in the Dutch Copyright Act (DCA), which already acknowledged that collections may be protected by copyright. Moreover, the DCA contains a peculiarity in that it also affords copyright protection to non-original writings. In Dutch, this is called the geschriftenbescherming, which resembles the Scandinavian copyright protection for catalogues. While transposing the Database Directive, the Dutch government had to consider whether to abolish the geschriftenbescherming for non-original written databases. Although the Directive states that an original selection or arrangement is the sole criterion for meriting copyright, the government still decided to maintain the geschriftenbescherming for databases which neither meet this threshold nor qualify for the sui generis right. The Dutch status quo for non-original written databases was thus kept alive. This could, however, well be contrary to the harmonisation purposes of the Directive.

3.2.14 The Databases Act adopted the database definition from the Directive, and added that a database must also represent a substantial investment. This requirement for protection by the sui generis right has generated abundant literature and case law in the Netherlands. It gave rise to the "spin-off" theory, which provides that the substantial investment should primarily be aimed at the production of the database at issue. Consequently, costs incurred in the creation of information generated merely as a spin-off or by-product of a main activity may not be taken into account.

3.2.15 The Dutch spin-off theory applies to the situation where a company already collects the data necessary for the database as a result of its main activities, but the production of the database arguably is an additional activity, e.g. telephone directories or listings of TV programming information. The spin-off theory had many supporters but also some opponents among lawyers. Dutch

[148] Wet van 8 juli 1999, houdende aanpassing van de Nederlandse wetgeving aan richtlijn 96/9/EG van het Europees Parlement en de Raad van 11 maart 1996 betreffende de rechtsbescherming van databanken, *Staatsblad* 1999, 303.

courts reacted diversely to the spin-off theory; the judgments in which it was sustained roughly balance out those in which this theory was rejected. The Dutch Supreme Court also seems to have rejected it in a case concerning a database with listings of properties for sale maintained among estate agents.

3.2.16 Interestingly, in 2004 the European Court of Justice has adopted a stance related to the spin-off theory. As for investments in obtaining contents, the Court decided that costs incurred for creating new information may not count towards the substantial investment, only costs incurred for collecting already existing information. It would seem that this approach is to be applied to databases produced as main products and spin-offs alike, contrary to the Dutch spin-off theory. Since the European Court's 2004 judgment, Dutch courts generally appear to have replaced the spin-off theory with the Court's approach. For example, a court decided that property databases maintained by estate agents lacked sui generis protection because this mainly involved the creation of new data, while the subsequent verifying and updating gave no evidence of a substantial enough investment.[149]

3.2.17 Dutch courts have also produced interesting although diverse case law on search engines that provide deep links to other parties' databases. There is discussion on whether offering an alternative access to another's database amounts to extracting the whole database (functional approach), or whether extraction is only at issue when data are actually being transmitted to users via the server of the search engine (technical approach). A similar discussion is about the reutilisation right: does this require a copy on the search engine's server or not? Does a search engine itself actively and on its own initiative perform acts of reutilisation, or do users exclusively effectuate these acts by feeding a query into the search engine? Should the liability rules for service providers in the European E-commerce Directive also apply to search engines? Moreover, it may be justified to distinguish between the activities of a general search engine like Google – which may be legal unless the database producer applies technical protection measures against indexing – and specialised search engines which provide access to only a limited number of databases.

[149] The Dutch implementation and case law is extensively discussed in the Ph.D. thesis of A.C. Beunen, *Protection for databases. The European Database Directive and its effects in the Netherlands, France and the United Kingdom*, Nijmegen: Wolf Legal Publishers 2007, available at https://openaccess.leidenuniv.nl/dspace/handle/1887/12038.

Performance Rights

3.2.18 Performance rights are covered by the Neighbouring Rights Act (1993). Under this Act a performer has the exclusive right to authorise several acts. A performer can allow:

the recording of a performance;

the reproduction of a recording of a performance;

the sale, rental, lending, supply or otherwise bringing into circulation, or the importing, offering or having in stock for such purposes of a recording of a performance or a reproduction thereof;

the (repeated) broadcast, making available to the public or other form of publication of a performance or a recording of a performance or a reproduction thereof.

3.2.19 A performer is defined as an actor, singer, musician, dancer or any other person who acts, sings, delivers or otherwise performs a literary or artistic work. Artists who perform a variety or circus act or a puppet show are named as performers as well.

3.2.20 The moral rights of a performer are defined in article 5 of the Neighbouring Rights Act. It is stated there that a performer has the right to oppose the communication to the public of a performance without any acknowledgement of his name or other designation as a performer within reasonable grounds. A performer can also oppose the communication to the public of a performance not under his name and any alteration in the way in which he is designated. As in article 25 of the Copyright Act, a performer also has the right to oppose any alteration to the performance and any distortion, mutilation or other impairment of the performance that could be prejudicial to his name or reputation or his dignity as a performer.

Relevant Exceptions and Limitations

3.2.21 In 2004 the Directive 2001/29/EC on the harmonisation of certain aspects of copyright and related rights in the information society[150] (InfoSoc Directive) was implemented in the Dutch Copyright Act. This introduced a new provision for libraries, museums and archives regarding preservation, which was made possible by article 5c (2) of the InfoSoc Directive. A reproduction of a literary, scientific or artistic work for preservation purposes

[150] See http://eur-lex.europa.eu/LexUriServ/LexUriServ.do?uri=CELEX:32001L0029:EN:HTML.

will not be regarded as an infringement of copyright if the reproduction is made accordingly to the provisions in article 16n of the Copyright Act.

3.2.22 This exception to the exclusive right of the author is only permitted provided that the sole purpose of the reproduction is:

the restoration of the specimen of the work; or

retention of a reproduction of the work for the institution if the specimen is threatening to fall into disrepair; or to keep the work in a condition in which it can be consulted if there is no technology available to render it accessible[151].

3.2.23 Another condition is that this reproduction shall only be authorised if the specimen of the work forms part of the collection of the institution. Furthermore the provisions regarding the moral rights must be taken into account.

3.2.24 It was the intention of the legislature to make clear the intent of the exception by pinpointing the actions and describing the circumstances allowing reproduction for preservation. Regarding the stipulation that a specimen is threatening to fall into disrepair, the explanatory note to the implementation bill explains that an institution that wants to preserve a work does not need to prove that the work is falling into disrepair. It is sufficient to prove that it is likely that the specimen will no longer be usable[152].

3.2.25 The provision regarding preservation only addresses the reproduction of copyright protected material and not the making available of the works. That right needs to be negotiated between the institutions and the right holders.

3.2.26 The provision does not address the preservation of databases. For this purpose permission of the producer of a database is necessary.

3.2.27 Before 2004 the Dutch Copyright Act did not contain a provision for the preservation of literary, artistic or scientific works. Making a reproduction for preservation purposes was first discussed during the implementation bill of the Database Act in 1996. At the instigation of the FOBID Legal Committee, a committee of the Dutch Library Forum, an amendment regarding the safekeeping of cultural and artistic copyright protected material was debated in

[151] Article 16n.

[152] Nota naar aanleiding van het verslag, 28 482 nr. 5 p. 34.

Parliament[153]. It was stressed that preserving the public heritage was of great importance and therefore obstacles to preservation in the Copyright Act, Related Rights Act and Database Act should be removed.

3.2.28 The preservation exception is justified by the fact that archiving and preservation of copyright protected material is a core task of libraries, museums and archives. The government recognised that the rise and growth of the information society introduced several problems regarding the safekeeping of cultural heritage in the long term. The Parliament was aware that legal certainty should exist regarding the keeping of cultural heritage. It was understood that migration of copyright protected material to a new format or carrier is an action that involves acts for which permission of the right holder is required and for which a new exception had to be introduced. However the introduction of a new exception needs good reasons to justify a shift in the balance between right holder and user. The public interest was thought enough justification for this exception, which keeps cultural, artistic works and cultural heritage accessible in the long term.

3.2.29 Article 16n of the Copyright Act addresses literary, artistic and scientific works. The definition of those works can be found in article 10 of the Copyright Act, discussed earlier. The Dutch Copyright Act is medium neutral, which means that there is no distinction between analogue and digital material. No distinction is made between print and non-print material in Dutch copyright law. Neither is there a distinction between published or unpublished works. The work that is going to be preserved must be part of the collection of the institution.

3.2.30 The Neighbouring Rights Act has a corresponding provision about permitting digital preservation. Article 10 (f) states that a reproduction of a recording of a performance, phonogram, first print of a film or recording of a programme or a reproduction thereof, by libraries, educational institutions or museums accessible to the public, or by archives which are not attempting to achieve a direct or indirect economic or commercial benefit is not an infringement to the exclusive right of a performer, if the reproduction occurs with the sole aim of preserving those works of demonstrable threat of falling into disrepair or to keep the work in a condition in which it can be consulted if there is no technology available to render it accessible.

[153] Amendement Scheltema-De Nie en Wagenaar, 26 108 nr. 8

Who May Take Advantage of The Netherlands' Digital Preservation Exceptions

3.2.31 Only libraries, educational institutions, museums or archives which are accessible to the public and whose purpose does not include the attainment of a direct or indirect economic or commercial benefit may take advantage of this digital preservation exception. The condition that the institution must be accessible to the public does not mean that the general public needs to have access, so that an institution with a more specialised public like school libraries or research libraries may take advantage of the provision as well. For archives, the condition of public accessibility does not apply.

3.2.32 Lawful users of computer programs may undertake certain acts that could be relevant to preservation, but under strict conditions. Lawful users may make a backup copy, decompile the software for certain restricted purposes, or copy or adapt it.

Legal Deposit

3.2.33 The Netherlands does not have an act or provisions in law concerning depositing works.

Provisions Dealing with Deposit of Digital Works in National Libraries or Archives

3.2.34 Deposit in the e-Depot of the National Library is done on a voluntary basis. The National Library of the Netherlands offers long-term preservation facilities for electronic publications under a framework agreement with the Dutch Publishers Association (NUV). The agreement was concluded by mutual agreement between the NUV and the National Library and accepted on 10 June 1999 by the general meeting of NUV.

3.2.35 According to the agreement, the members of NUV agree to deposit all electronic publications with a Dutch imprint at the National Library, both the first editions and, in principle, subsequent updates. The publications are to be delivered in the way they are marketed, i.e. – in so far as applicable – in the original packing and including the accompanying retrieval software and manual or documentation in printed or electronic form.

3.2.36 Making deposited electronic publications available is governed by stringent restrictions. Deposited electronic publications may exclusively be consulted by authorised users via technical measures that operationally separate the publications from the publicly accessible network. Authorised users are the staff members employed by the National Library and authorised by the National Library to make use of the deposited electronic publications, and individual persons registered with the National Library by name and authorised by the Library to use the deposited electronic publications.

3.2.37 Deposited material is not lent out. It is, however, permitted to print a small part of the work or of some articles for one's own use. The present arrangement does not allow the use of deposited electronic publications for document delivery, unless the publisher concerned has explicitly given his approval.

Technological Protection Measures Provisions

3.2.38 Article 29a(2) of the Act deals with the circumvention of technical protection measures. It states that those who circumvent purposive technical provisions knowingly, or who should reasonably know they are doing so, shall be acting unlawfully.

3.2.39 Technical provisions refer to technology, equipment or components whose normal use would include the prevention or limitation of actions in relation to works which the author has not permitted. Technical provisions are purposive if the use of a work protected by the author is managed by means of control of access or by application of a protective procedure such as encryption, encoding or some other transformation of the work or a copy protection that achieves the intended protection.

3.2.40 Government orders may establish rules obliging the author to provide the user of a work, for specified purposes, with the means necessary to profit from limitations given to him in the Act. In this case a user must have lawful access to the work protected by the technical provisions. However an author will not have to supply access to a work that is made available to users under contractual conditions at a time and a place selected by the users individually.

3.2.41 Article 29a(4) rounds off the provisions regarding technical protection measures. It states that under certain circumstances the right holder must provide the means for users to benefit from specific exceptions. The government orders might range from measures that make it possible to copy for private purposes, to a provision to deposit a copy of the work at a central place to the obligation to provide a key to unlock the technical measure. There is no need to seek a government order, however, if the right holder within a reasonable time provides the user with the means to benefit from the exception. A government order is the ultimate remedy.

Copyright Law and Contracts

3.2.42 Article 29a (4) states that government orders may establish rules obliging the author or his successor in title to provide the user of a literary, scientific or artistic work for purposes specified in the preservation provision with the means necessary to profit from that limitation, provided that the user has lawful access to the work protected by the technical measures. The provisions in the previous sentence will not apply to works made available to users under contractual conditions at a time and a place selected by the users individually. From provisions in the Copyright Act it cannot be deduced if the exceptions in the Copyright Act can be overrriden by contract. However article 29a (4) implies that contractual arrangements can override these.

3.3 The Impact of Copyright and Related Laws on Digital Preservation Activities in the Netherlands

Effect of Copyright and Related Laws on Digital Preservation

3.3.1 As explained earlier, the preservation exception in the Dutch Copyright Act does not encompass the making available of the work. It is explicitly stated in the explanatory note of the Act that for that purpose, permission must be sought from the right holders.

3.3.2 As digital preservation and making available to the public are more or less connected, it might be imaginable that the digital preservation of orphan works will be hindered by copyright law. Although the right holder cannot be found or located to ask permission, the making available to the public of the orphaned work remains an infringement. This will deter many cultural and educational institutions.

Necessity of Obtaining Licences

3.3.3 When digital preservation is not allowed because the criteria mentioned in article 16n are not met, a licence needs to be obtained. Furthermore licences need to be obtained in case the preserved copyright protected works are going to be made available to the public.

Legal Deposit

3.3.4 The Netherlands does not have legal deposit laws that can be used to facilitate digital preservation.

Archival Agreements

3.3.5 In this context, the Dutch Institute for Sound and Images (NIBG) concluded an Archival Agreement with a number of collective societies of right holders to secure the Dutch cultural heritage. Both NIBG and the collective societies subscribed to the viewpoint that it was necessary to make arrangements for preservation and making available the works collected by NIBG. NIBG has an important function in collecting and preserving audiovisual material, which has national importance from a historical or cultural historical point of view.

3.3.6 NIBG not only has a role in archiving audiovisual material, it also has a task to make available and promote the use of this material and its documentation to scientific and educational institutions for research, teaching and cultural purposes. The Archival Agreement describes those various functions of NIBG extensively.

3.3.7 The collective societies have given permission to perform the functions as described in the Agreement within the strict borders of the Agreement. Furthermore NIBG is obliged to stipulate that the material will not be embodied in another production or work. Neither can the work be re-used nor reproduced and/or made available other than within the strictly defined use which must be made known to NIBG in advance. In addition NIBG will take precautions to prevent illegal distribution of the material made available to users.

3.3.8 As discussed earlier in this report, libraries not only want to preserve and digitise their collections, but they also would like to make those digitised collections available to the public, which is not allowed under Dutch copyright law. Without very strong evidence the legal committee of FOBID the Netherlands Library Forum (FJC) has suggested that preservation activities in the libraries are hindered by this specific limitation of the preservation exception. Tracing and finding the copyright right owners to ask permission to re-use the digitised works places an administrative and financial burden on the libraries or other cultural or educational organizations which, FJC suggests, causes them to abandon the idea of digitisation. In those cases where libraries try to find a right holder, the results are often unsatisfying. Despite a diligent search, libraries frequently cannot identify or find the right holder. To assist libraries in the search for right holders FJC started to draft guidelines on the subject of a diligent search. FJC has realised that settling the rights on a strictly legal basis is not a useful option for institutions because it is time-consuming and hence expensive, especially when it concerns mass digitisation.

3.3.9 Therefore FJC promotes a different approach: together with the publishers and the collecting societies FJC is working towards a practical solution based on ten so called building blocks. The building blocks set the conditions for mass digitisation of orphan works[154]. The Ministry of Justice of the Netherlands approves of this approach. In its policy letter of December 20th 2007 to the Dutch Parliament the Minister explicitly refers to and praises this initiative.[155]

3.3.10 On 22 April 2008, a letter of intent[156] was signed by FOBID, the National Library Forum[157], and the Dutch Copyright Federation[158] (Stichting Auteursrechtbelangen), representing Dutch organisations for copyright holders, concerning a collaboration to digitise collections in libraries, archives and museums.

3.3.11 Organisations representing creators, working artists, publishers and producers will collaborate in digitising copyright protected works in libraries, when that work has cultural significance and when this digitisation is possible without conflicting with the normal exploitation of this work. The parties aim to make available a broad range of information, in cases where no practical objections exist. In cases where there may be objections, the work will in any event be made available on site (i.e. within the intranet of the institution itself). The parties will work together to examine any problems they come across, and to decide on how those issues can be resolved.

3.3.12 FOBID and the Dutch Copyright Federation share the opinion that a pragmatic approach is required for large scale digitisation of copyright protected works in the collections of libraries, museums and archives. Such an approach prevents real interests of right holders from being damaged and protects libraries from unnecessarily high costs incurred in identifying and locating right holders. Both parties therefore expressed the intention of reaching

[154] FOBID, Netherlands Library Forum, http://www.sitegenerator.bibliotheek.nl/fobid/overig46/overig46.asp?item=165698&.

[155] Directoraat-Generaal Wetgeving, Internationale Aangelegenheden en Vreemdelingenzaken, Auteursrechtbeleidsbrief, http://www.justitie.nl/images/20071220_5520988%20Auteursrechtbeleidsbrief_tcm34-95934.pdf.

[156] Auteursrecht - Archieven en bibliotheken, Letter of intent, http://www.auteursrecht.nl/auteursrecht/pagina.asp?pagkey=100355#Letterofintent.

[157] FOBID, Netherlands Library Forum, http://sitegenerator.bibliotheek.nl/fobid/overig36/overig36.asp.

[158] Auteursrecht, Stichting Auteursrechtbelangen, http://www.auteursrecht.nl/auteursrecht/pagina.asp?pagkey=23939&mode=read.

an agreement regarding the large scale digitisation and making available parts of library, museum and archive collections.

Technological Protection Measures

3.3.13 The law concerning technological protection measures in the Netherlands is discussed above in sections 3.2.38-41. Article 29(a)4 provides a means to undertake digital preservation activities despite the existence of TPMs. In the case that preservation activities cannot be carried out, stakeholders may ask the Ministry of Justice for a government order to provide the user the means to benefit from the preservation exception. The government order might require the right holder to provide a key to unlock the technical measure.

3.4 Overview of Responses to the Issue of Copyright and Digital Preservation in the Netherlands

Copyright Law Reform

3.4.1 At the moment in The Netherlands there are neither proposals nor initiatives for legal reform. However, recently the Ministry of Justice ordered a study to compare the different solutions to the problem of orphan works in different jurisdictions. The Centre of Intellectual Property of Utrecht University is conducting this study. The outcome of the study is expected soon.

3.4.2 Preceding the international symposium, *The Book in the Internet Era: Copyright and the Future for Authors, Publishers and Libraries* in April 2008, the National Library published an article in NRC Handelsblad 17 April 2008 called *Copyright law: an obstacle for the digital library?*. The purpose of the article was to present the perspective of the National Library regarding the impediments in the copyright law to building a digital library. The authors of the article pleaded for a refined combination of the Anglo-Saxon model and the Scandinavian model of extended collective licensing: extended collective licensing combined with the opt-out principle. The authors highlighted the advantages: no diligent search for the right holders needed, users would know in advance the potential costs of using a work, and remuneration to the right holder if he/she comes forward.

3.4.3 The National Library suggests a special internet section in the Copyright Act for non commercial use by cultural and educational institutions.

Activities to Develop Non-Legislative Solutions

Adoption of Alternative Rights Management Frameworks

3.4.4 In the Letter of Intent signed by FOBID (the Netherlands Library Forum) and the Dutch Copyright Federation, both parties express the intention of reaching an agreement regarding the large scale digitisation and making available (parts of) library, museum and archive collections. Per project or collection, via a simple procedure, agreements will be made on:

- the works eligible to digitisation;
- the procedure to make available digitally these works, without financial or commercial benefit to individual members of the public, for education, research or private study;
- the fee owed to the right holders.

3.4.5 The parties will install a committee for a two year period that will assess the requests from cultural institutions regarding digitisation. This committee will promote the conclusion of agreements to this effect with right holders. After two years the committee will report on and evaluate the achieved results.

3.4.6 For developing this alternative framework FOBID and the Dutch Foundation for Copyright Interests have appealed to the government to contribute to the required investments to achieve this goal.

Open Access Repositories and Licensing Mechanisms

3.4.7 In September 2006 a study *Creative Commons Licences for cultural heritage institutions: a Dutch perspective*[159] was issued. This study explores the use of Creative Commons licences as a tool for cultural heritage institutions from the perspective that the influence of copyright in digitisation projects will cause cultural heritage institutions to take up new roles. The study investigates the possibilities for the cultural heritage institutions to provide free access to digital cultural heritage, based on voluntary use of standardized licences. The central question was whether Creative Commons licences constitute a tool allowing cultural heritage institutions to fulfill their mission within their funding and operational framework. The study concludes that cultural heritage institutions can take up new intermediary roles but that Creative

159 See http://www.ivir.nl/creativecommons/CC_for_cultural_heritage_institutions.pdf.

Commons Licences do not offer a solution for orphan works as such.

Collaborative Projects

E-Depot of the National Library

3.4.8 In 1994 the National Library adapted its deposit policy and included electronic publications in its deposit collection. In 1996 the National Library set up small-scale experiments with publishers. At that time discussions were started with Elsevier Science with the aim of acquiring the content of Elsevier electronic journals. In June 1996 the first experimental bilateral archiving agreement was signed. This allowed the National Library to upload electronic journals with a Dutch imprint in the first electronic experimental deposit system. In 2002 the National Library signed a landmark archiving agreement with Elsevier Science. This arrangement turned the National Library into the first official digital archive in the world for journals published by international scientific publishers. Other publishers followed, and at the moment the National Library has agreements with most important international publishers.

3.4.9 In a press release in February 2008 the National Library announced that it has concluded an agreement with the American organization Portico providing that Portico will deposit an off-line copy of its total of more than 6 million articles at the National Library. This arrangement illustrates one way in which organisations internationally recognized for their digital preservation obligations and expertise can cooperate to form a strong, supportive network to safely preserve digital materials.

3.4.10 For depositing electronic publications there are two types of agreements: a general agreement with the Dutch Publishers Association, similar to the agreement the National Library had already for printed publications, and the individual archiving agreements with the international publishers of scholarly journals.

3.4.11 There is a minimum set of conditions to be fulfilled if the National Library enters an agreement: publishers must deposit their publications free of charge, and the National Library has to accept restrictions on access. However in limited cases access is possible. The National Library has required on-site access for any registered user of the Library and has required availability for interlibrary document supply within the Netherlands.

3.4.12 The e-Depot serves as a guarantee to licensees of publishers worldwide. In case of trigger events the National Library safeguards the access licensees have paid for.

3.4.13 The policy of the e-Depot has several cornerstones. It is aimed at future access to the material through long-term preservation and safeguarding long-term accessibility. It is the goal of e-Depot to protect the authenticity and the integrity of the content.

Beelden voor de Toekomst

3.4.14 The project Beelden voor de Toekomst (Images for the Future) has a large copyright component. The consortium estimates that the problem of finding the right holders will be the biggest challenge. Agreements that will make re-use possible will be made with the right holders. Within the project three kinds of agreements are distinguished: collective agreements based on the exception in Dutch copyright law for educational use with a fair compensation for the right holder, voluntary collective agreements for commercial re-use, and agreements with individual right holders.

3.4.15 The collective agreement based on the law is already being used by one of the partners: the Institute for Sound and Images. It is the intention to extend this agreement to the consortium.

3.4.16 For the second type of agreement, the consortium is going to negotiate with collective societies and large content providers. The agreement will include provisions for distribution and sales of the material. The consortium also plans to develop a set of clear guidelines, to make it possible to exchange information between the content providers/holders of collections and private parties.

3.4.17 The consortium would like to negotiate the rights not only for the Netherlands but the whole of Europe.

3.4.18 Other digitisation projects being undertaken with the cooperation of stakeholders are discussed elsewhere in this report.

Practical Measures to Minimize Risk of Infringement

3.4.19 At the moment it is difficult to establish whether there is congruence between the digital preservation by the various sectors and developing best practices. Because of the large impact of copyright law it is clear that most projects or programmes start with digitising material that is out of copyright. For material whose copyright owner cannot be found or located, practical arrangements will be set up and experimented with. It is the intention that these arrangements will be made across sectors. The project Beelden for the Toekomst has chosen to clear all the rights of all the works and make them available to the public. For this agreements were concluded with the right holders.

3.5 Recommendations for Legal Reforms or Practical Solutions in the Netherlands to Facilitate Digital Preservation

3.5.1 The Netherlands implemented an exception to the exclusive right of the author for preservation in its copyright law in 2004. In order for libraries to fulfill one of their core tasks (preserving and making available of information) the Auteurswet should be amended as follows:

- Preservation of analogue and digital copyrighted material which forms part of the collection of a library should always be permitted. Therefore article 16n Auteurswet should be amended to eliminate the following restrictions:

    - Restoration of the specimen of the work; and
    - Retention or a reproduction of the work for the institution if the specimen is threatening to fall into disrepair; and
    - To keep the work in a condition in which it can be consulted if there is no technology available to render it accessible.

- Libraries, educational institutions, museums and archives should be allowed to make available digital material which forms part of their collection on the secure network of the institution that digitised the material.

- A provision concerning orphan works should be inserted. The law should provide that cultural and educational institutions do not infringe copyright when undertaking the preservation and making available of material from orphan works that form part of their collections.

3.6 Bibliography

Beunen, A, T. Schiphof, Archieven en musea online, Taskforce Archieven/Museumvereniging 2006

Beunen, A. Protection for databases. The European Database Directive and its effects in the Netherlands, France and the United Kingdom, Wolf legal Publishers, Nijmegen 2007

Commissie Auteursrecht, Advies over auteursrecht, naburige rechten en de nieuwe media, August 1998

European Commission, Report on Digital Preservation, Orphan Works, and Out of Print Works. Selected Implementation Issues. April 2007

FOBID, Position paper regarding statutory exceptions for libraries to maintain their position in the information society, The Hague, May 2001

Hoorn, E, Creative Commons Licences for Cultural heritage institutions: a Dutch perspective, Amsterdam Instituut voor Informatierecht, September 2006

Hugenholtz, P.B. in Recht en Internet handelingen Nederlandse Juristen Vereniging 128e jaargang/ 1998-I

Intellectuele eigendom, artikelsgewijs commentaar Elsevier juridisch, 's–Gravenhage

Klijn, E, Y. de Lusenet, Tracking the reel world. A survey of audiovisual collections in Europe, Amsterdam European Commission on Preservation and Access, January 2008

Koelman, K B.N. Westerbrink, Auteursrechtelijke aspecten van preservering van elektronische publicaties, Amsterdam Instituut voor Informatierecht February 1998

Koninklijke Bibliotheek, Archiving Agreement, contract voor buitenlandse uitgevers met betrekking tot hun elektronische publicaties in het e-depot

Koninklijke Bibliotheek, Reglement elektronisch depot KB, raamcontract voor Nederlandse uitgevers, goedgekeurd door het Nederlands Uitgevers Verbond op 20 juni 2005

Krikke, J.I., Het bibliotheekprivilege in de digitale omgeving, Kluwer 2000 Deventer

Mossink, W Webarchiveren en auteursrecht in F. den Hollander, G. Voerman Het web gevangen: het archiveren van web sites van de Nederlandse politieke partijen, symposiumbundel Archipol 2002, hoofdstuk 5

Spoor, J.H., D.W.. Verkade, D.J.G. Visser, Auteursrecht. Auteursrecht, naburige rechten en databanken, Kluwer 2005 Deventer

Studiecommissie Informatiemaatschappij van de Vereniging voor Auteursrecht, Reactie op het Wetsvoorstel 28 842 tot uitvoering van de Richtlijn Auteursrechten en naburige rechten in de informatiemaatschappij (2001/29/EG), October 2002

Visser, D.J.G, Enkele opmerkingen bij Wetsvoorstel 28 482. AMI: tijdschrift voor auteurs-, media- en informatierecht 26 (2002) nr 5.

Visser, D.J.G., De beperkingen in de Auteursrechtrichtlijn. Informatierecht/AMI 25 (2001) nr. 1

Part 4: Country Report for the United Kingdom

Adrienne Muir[160]

4.1 Major Digital Preservation Activities in the United Kingdom

4.1.1 There is no national strategy as such for digital preservation in the UK. There is work going on in different sectors and there are some organisations that are trying to bring these sectors together. There has been some strategic activity in science. Her Majesty's Treasury, the (then) Department of Trade and Industry (DTI) and the (then) Department for Education and Skills identified a need for an e-infrastructure for research in 2004. A preservation and curation working group was established by the Office for Science and Innovation to focus on this specific area. This group made several recommendations, including taking into account long-term preservation when reviewing legislation, policy and codes of practice. Another recommendation was that the DTI and Research Councils should fund research by universities and industry to address challenges. Another key recommendation was that there should be a DTI funded "national information infrastructure development programme" (Beagrie 2007).[161]

4.1.2 The Joint Information Systems Committee (JISC), the British Library (BL) and, to a lesser extent, the National Preservation Office (NPO) were instrumental in the development of digital preservation in the libraries and archives communities. The agenda of a JISC and BL sponsored workshop in 1995 was influenced by the draft version of the RLG/CPA Task Force on Digital Archiving Report (1996) report. The JISC and the NPO followed up the recommendations in various ways, including identifying good practice and commissioning a set of studies on digital preservation. The focus of a second workshop in 1999 was

160 Department of Information Science, Loughborough University.

161 See the bibliography in section 4.6.

preservation strategy. Many of the recommendations from this workshop related to the adoption of standards, the need for guidelines and to identify and publicise good practice. Another theme running through the recommendations was the need for coordination and cooperation. The workshop endorsed several recommendations from the JISC/NPO studies, including the need for a national forum and for training. The recommendations for research represented a move from the mainly basic exploratory activities of the JISC/NPO studies.

4.1.3 A national forum has now been established in the form of the Digital Preservation Coalition (DPC). The National Preservation Office had initially taken on a digital preservation role, but it has since relinquished it: the NPO is now an "allied organisation" with the DPC. The DPC has been particularly strong in raising awareness amongst the stakeholders. It has brought together information of best practice in digital preservation management in its handbook, it runs training and other events for members to share knowledge and best practice. The Digital Curation Centre (DCC) is jointly funded by the JISC and the UK's e-Science programme. The DCC undertakes research and disseminates good practice in digital curation and preservation. The JISC continues to support the development in digital preservation through its programmes and funding of projects and initiatives.

4.1.4 The Research Information Network (2007) has developed "a framework of principles and guidelines" for caring for digital research data. This framework includes digital preservation. The Research Data Service (UKRDS) feasibility study is being carried out in 2008. It is funded by the Higher Education Funding Council for England (HEFCE) through its Shared Services programme, with support from JISC. The aim is to assess the feasibility and costs of developing and maintaining a national shared digital research data service for the UK Higher Education sector.

Cultural Heritage Institutions

4.1.5 The British Library and the national libraries of Scotland and Wales are legal deposit libraries. They have developed, or are in the process of developing, digital repositories for their digital collections. There is no legal deposit for digital publications in the UK at the moment, but there has been a voluntary scheme for the deposit of offline digital publications since 2000[162]. The British Library recently ran a pilot project with a small number of

[162] See http://www.bl.uk/aboutus/stratpolprog/legaldep/voluntarydeposit/ for the text of the voluntary code of practice and http://www.bl.uk/aboutus/stratpolprog/legaldep/letterhofta.pdf for an explanatory letter for the re-launched voluntary scheme.

electronic journals publishers to "test the technical infrastructure, mechanisms and procedures relating to the deposit, ingest, storage and preservation"[163].

4.1.6 The British Library is now working with the other legal deposit libraries and publisher partners on developing a voluntary deposit scheme for electronic journals. The libraries are also involved in selective Web archiving through the UK Web Archiving Consortium (UKWAC)[164]. While UKWAC partners share a Web archiving infrastructure, each selects and collects material deemed relevant for its purposes. UKWAC has developed a licence for copying and providing access to archived material[165].

4.1.7 The British Library, along with University College London is involved in the LIFE and LIFE2 projects. The focus is on the lifecycle of digital collections and developing a lifecycle costing methodology. The methodology produced by the first LIFE project includes consideration of rights issues in digital archiving and preservation as part of the acquisitions phase of the lifecycle (Lifecycle Information for E-literature 2006).

4.1.8 The UK National Sound Archive, based at the British Library, benefits from voluntary deposit of recorded sound. The Scottish Screen Archive is part of the National Library of Scotland and the National Library of Wales houses the National Screen and Sound Archive of Wales. While not a national library in the same sense as the British Library or the national libraries of Scotland and Wales, the British Film Institute (BFI) houses the National Film and Television Archive[166]. The BFI's collection includes UK material and material originating in other countries. The Archive is the official UK archive for the output of the UK terrestrial TV channels, video records of UK parliamentary proceedings and films deemed part of the public record in association with The National Archives. Voluntary donation is the primary acquisition method. There are also several public sector regional archives for sound and moving images[167], which may be part of museums, academic institutions and/or local records offices.

---

163 See http://www.bl.uk/aboutus/stratpolprog/legaldep/.

164 See http://www.webarchive.org.uk/.

165 The licence is not publicly available from the UKWAC web site.

166 See http://ahds.ac.uk/depositing/licence.htm.

167 For example, see http://www.brighton.ac.uk/screenarchive/aboutus/aboutus.html for a list of UK public sector film archives.

Government Archives

4.1.9 Public records are deposited in The National Archives, the National Archives of Scotland and the Public Record Office of Northern Ireland. The National Archives (TNA) has had a digital preservation department since 2001 and launched its Digital Archive in 2003[168]. TNA is responsible for the National Digital Archive of Datasets, that is datasets and documents emanating from the UK government. The University of London Computer Centre has cared for these datasets on TNA's behalf for around 15 years. TNA has developed its own digital preservation systems, and Microsoft has provided TNA with copies of its software so that records can still be read in their original formats.

4.1.10 TNA has been working with government departments on the Seamless Flow Project[169] of digital records from departments to TNA. The aim to automate as many of the processes involved as possible and to ensure that the more labour intensive processes take place in the departments and as early as possible. TNA is leading on Digital Continuity on behalf of government departments. The aim here is to ensure that records held in government departments remain readable beyond 5 years through "a shared service solution to the challenges of protecting vital digital files from technological obsolescence"[170]. TNA is also involved in archiving government Web sites through UKWAC. Scotland's national records are archived and preserved by the National Archives of Scotland. These include government, court and legal, Church of Scotland records and the records of some other churches. The Public Record Office of Northern Ireland deals with the province's records. There are also local records offices and archives around the UK[171].

Educational and Research Institutions

4.1.11 Several UK academic libraries took part in the UK LOCKSS pilot[172]. JISC funded the pilot in partnership with the Consortium of Research Libraries (CURL– now known as Research Libraries

168 See http://www.nationalarchives.gov.uk/preservation/digitalarchive/default.htm.

169 See http://www.nationalarchives.gov.uk/electronicrecords/seamless_flow/default.htm.

170 See http://www.nationalarchives.gov.uk/electronicrecords/digitalcontinuity/default.htm.

171 For lists of local records offices and archives in the UK see http://www.nationalarchives.gov.uk/archon/default.htm.

172 See http://www.jisc.ac.uk/whatwedo/programmes/programme_preservation/programme_lockss.aspx.

UK (RLUK)) in the British Isles. Twenty-four libraries trialled the LOCKSS technology and were supported by a central technical support service based at the Digital Curation Centre. There was also a permissions negotiation service to allow LOCKSS-based archiving of electronic journals, provided by JISC's agent for NESLi2 the National e-Journals initiative[173]. The pilot has come to an end and JISC has now invited tenders for an evaluation of the pilot; presumably this will include the rights negotiation aspects.

4.1.12 An increasing number of educational institutions have institutional repositories for research outputs, but the main emphasis is on populating repositories and increasingly visibility of, and access to, these outputs. Major drivers for this trend include research funding council policies. The Research Information Network (2007) issued a report on funding body policies on the management of information outputs from research. Policy on preservation of outputs is less well developed than for deposit.

4.1.13 There are also established digital archives, particularly for research outputs, in the UK. These tend to focus on particular disciplines and serve the academic and sometimes industrial sectors. Some are funded by research councils, others have a variety of revenue streams, including subscriptions, sales or grants. Data centres/archives include the British Atmospheric Data Centre, Earth Observation Data Centre and the Oceanographic Data Centre, which are all supported by the National Environment Research Council. The Science and Technology Facilities Council supports the UK Cluster Data Centre, whereas the Cambridge Crystallographic Data Centre is a not-for profit company.

4.1.14 The Economic and Social Data Service (ESDS)[174] is a distributed service and the UK Data Archive is one of the ESDS constituent centres. The UK Data Archive provides services for other data organisations, and has a deposit licence agreement which includes a clause on preservation copying[175]. The Digital Preservation Coalition[176] produced a list of digital repositories in 2005[177].

---

173 See http://www.nesli2.ac.uk/.

174 See http://www.esds.ac.uk/.

175 See http://www.esds.ac.uk/aandp/create/licenceForm.pdf.

176 See http://www.dpconline.org/.

177 See http://www.dpconline.org/docs/guides/directory.pdf.

4.1.15 Much digital preservation research and development activity in the UK higher and further education sector has been supported by JISC. A major initiative was the CEDARS project, which ran from 1998 until 2001[178]. The JISC's Digital Preservation and Records Management programme was focused on improving the management of JISC's and educational institutions' digital assets, partly through learning from, and building on, what institutions were already doing.[179] Three categories of projects were funded under this programme. One strand focused on the institutional level and corporate assets and involved development of exemplar strategies and practical implementations of these strategies. The digital preservation assessment tools strand aimed to help institutions decide what to preserve. The third strand aimed to integrate functionality and existing standards and tools, such as the Open Archival Information System and the METS metadata standard into institutional repositories[180]. JISC's current Repositories and Preservation programme (2006-9), is focusing on a distributed and shared digital preservation environment and services and the development of new software and tools.

4.1.16 A number of JISC-funded activities have focused on rights issues in digital preservation. For example, a study on archiving electronic journals was funded under this programme. This study included eliciting views on the archiving clauses of the JISC/NESLi model licence for journals[181]. Jones (2003) found that concern about continued archival access was one of the two most cited barriers for libraries to move to electronic only access to journals with any degree of confidence. The NESLi2 licence is discussed below. The LOCKSS pilot discussed above addresses implementing perpetual access.

4.1.17 The Digital Images Archiving Study concluded that "all images within a preservation system must have complete permission clearance, for any current or possible future use, in perpetuity; or, there must be a built in facility or process that enables permissions to be revisited in response to user needs". (Anderson *et al* 2006). Another study (Wilson *et al* 2006) focusing on moving digital images and sound archiving identified the rights to store, preserve and use content as a key issue. Both this study and the Digital Images Archiving Study suggested that rights information should be included in metadata.

---

178 See http://www.leeds.ac.uk/cedars/.

179 See http://www.jisc.ac.uk/whatwedo/programmes/programme_preservation.aspx.

180 For a link to projects see: http://www.jisc.ac.uk/whatwedo/programmes/programme_preservation.aspx.

181 See http://www.nesli2.ac.uk/model.htm for the current NESLi2 licence.

4.1.18 The report of a project on long-term retention and re-use of learning objects suggested that consideration may have to be given to rights for preservation. A recommendation was that a model licence for sharing electronic learning material should not "preclude" standard digital preservation strategies. Another recommendation was that "machine readable digital rights expression language (DREL) may be developed to describe the associated rights for learning resources in such a way that it can be stored with the resource and provide appropriate details for digital rights management" (Barker 2005).

4.1.19 As part of a feasibility study for Web archiving, funded by the JISC and the Wellcome Trust, Charlesworth conducted a study of related legal issues. He commented (2003, p. 8) "… with regard to digital archiving, especially Web archiving, the legislation as currently worded is not terribly helpful. If rights owners control access and use through licence agreements and access is remote, libraries are dependent on them to continue to provide access to the material".

4.1.20 The aim of the Registry of Electronic Licences (RELI) project[182] will be facilitating access to licence terms for access and use of digital resources. While not included in an initial list of possible use cases, presumably any licence terms relating to preservation could be included in this registry for consultation by preservation managers[183]. The project is currently scoping user requirements. The Information Environment Metadata Schema Registry (IEMSR) will be a pilot shared service for "authoritative information about metadata schemas recommended by the JISC IE Standards framework"[184]. While not specifically included within the focus of this project, preservation metadata schemas, including preservation rights metadata, such as the PREMIS schema, could be included in future studies.

4.1.21 The Pilot National Name and Factual Authority Service project[185] aims to facilitate unambiguous linking of digital content to authors and institutions. While the focus of this work is on retrieval, if the service is updated regularly, an additional benefit would be to reduce the number of orphan works in repositories, should repository managers need to seek right holder permissions to

[182] See http://www.lboro.ac.uk/departments/dis/disresearch/RELI/about3.html.

[183] See http://www.jisc.ac.uk/media/documents/programmes/shared_services/reli.doc.

[184] See http://www.ukoln.ac.uk/projects/iemsr/.

[185] See http://www.jisc.ac.uk/whatwedo/programmes/programme_rep_pres/shared_services/project_names.aspx.

preserve deposited content in future. The service may also provide a demonstrator implementation that could be used by the wider digital preservation community to improve provision of right holder information, particularly since the British Library is involved. JISC has recently funded a scoping and feasibility study for a registry of archived electronic journals. In the course of this study, it has become apparent that rights issues have sometimes been managed in an informal way by journal publishers and ejournal archives, and this could have an impact on future preservation of archived journals.

Media Organisations

4.1.22 While there are public sector archives for the output of the media industry, media organisations may also make their own arrangements for their output. The BBC has been working on capturing, archiving and preserving its digital content for some time and is an associate member of the Digital Preservation Coalition. The BBC has a preservation unit and now has a multimedia archive and multimedia archivists. The aim of the Digital Media Initiative is to have end-to-end digital production, with an embedded archive to facilitate re-use and re-distribution.

Third-Party Providers of Preservation-Related Services

4.1.23 There are some service providers providing a range of services from advice and consultancy, to software solutions, to full preservation services. The University of London Computer Centre (ULCC) offers various preservation services, including hosting and preserving data[186]. The National Digital Repository is one of ULCC's services. The ULCC can help clients care for their data or can do this for them. The National Archives is one of the ULCC's clients and ULCC operates the National Digital Archive of Datasets. The ULCC can provide secure off-site storage, it can also undertake data migration and metadata provision. For example, ULCC is cataloguing material captured by UKWAC. Digital rescue is another service offered[187]. The ULCC is a member of the Digital Preservation Coalition and an associate of the Digital Curation Centre. It is involved in research and development and implementing best practice in digital preservation. There are a number of commercial organisations, such as Sungard, that provide "information availability" services, including disaster planning, off-site data warehouses and data and system recovery.

---

[186] See http://www.ulcc.ac.uk/digital-preservation.html.

[187] See http://www.ulcc.ac.uk/digital-preservation/products-services.html for the services offered.

4.1.24 There are also some UK-based third party commercial services which do not store digital material, but offer products or services relevant to archiving and/or preserving digital content. The Digital Archiving Consultancy undertakes studies and provides advice and training to public sector organisations, the pharmaceutical and IT industries[188]. Tessella has been involved in setting up a digital archive service for TNA and is also working with the British Library on its Digital Object Management system[189]. Tessella offers a range of preservation-related services[190] including consultancy and advice, the Safety Deposit Box archival solution or custom software development[191].

Creators and Right Holders

4.1.25 It is hard to know what, if any, arrangements individuals make for the preservation of their own digital output. Individuals create, file and store digital material created in the course of working for their employers. The organisations may have systems and procedures in place for archiving email and/or other documents. JISC has been active in supporting developments in this area in the UK academic sector. However, private citizens are also creating digital content in various formats and are storing it and, increasingly, sharing it with others. Preservation of personal digital collections has been identified as an issue that requires research. The Arts and Humanities Research Council has funded a new research project will explore this topic[192].

4.1.26 When individuals create material and make personal arrangements to keep it accessible, there are unlikely to be any copyright issues. If they are the sole rights owners, they can do as they wish. However, when it comes to sharing material with others, for example by mounting material on sites such as Flickr, MySpace or Facebook, it is not clear to what extent these services will preserve digital content. The publicly available statements and policies of Web 2.0 services do cover copyright issues, but they are geared to mounting, copying and use of other people's material by service users or community members. They do not specifically mention preservation. Ourmedia is one

[188] See http://www.d-archiving.com/clients.htm.

[189] See http://www.bl.uk/aboutus/stratpolprog/digi/dom/index.html.

[190] See http://www.tessella.com/Services/Discipline/digital_preservation.htm.

[191] See http://www.tessella.com/solutions-technologies/solutions/archiving-digital-preservation/#Tessellas_offerings.

[192] See http://www.bl.uk/digital-lives/.

exception which also archives material in the Internet Archive as well as hosting it on the Ourmedia site. The preservation issues associated with Web 2.0 content have been explored in a JISC Technology and Standards Watch report (Anderson 2007). The report makes some points on rights issues. For example, not all services allow users to take back their content whenever they want, the service may encode it in a proprietary format and claim rights in it. The service may also remove or change their service suddenly. If users are not managing their own copies, it may be difficult to ensure preservation (Anderson 2007, p. 42).

4.2 Overview of Copyright, Related Rights, and Legal Deposit Laws of the United Kingdom as Applied to Digital Preservation

Copyright

Exclusive Rights

4.2.1 Under the *Copyright Designs and Patents Act 1988,* the copyright owner has the exclusive right to reproduce a work, issue copies to the public, rent or lend, perform, show or play the work in public, broadcast the work or make an adaptation of the work. The copyright owner also has the right to prevent third parties from carrying out these "restricted" acts without prior permission. Unless permitted under an exception, carrying out a restricted act on all or a substantial part of a copyright work without the permission of the owner, or authorising someone else to do so, is infringing the copyright in that work. Infringement of copyright can carry both civil and criminal penalties, depending on the nature of the infringement (Great Britain 1998, s.16) (Relevant provisions of the Copyright Designs and Patents Act 1988 and other laws are attached as Appendix D.)

4.2.2 There is copyright protection for specific classes of works. The different classes of work that are likely to be found in digital libraries and archives include:

- Original literary works, including novels, poetry and non-fiction and other written works. Their literary merit is not relevant. Computer programs and code are protected as literary works. Letters, memoranda, e-mail messages and Web pages are protected.
- Dramatic works must include some spoken words or actions to perform to distinguish them from literary works.
- Artistic works include graphic works, photographs, sculptures, collages, maps, charts and plans, regardless of artistic merit.

- Musical works and sound recordings recorded on any medium and musical scores including any annotations and directions. Lyrics are protected as literary works.
- Films, including any medium from which a moving image may be reproduced.
- Broadcasts, including any transmission by wireless telegraphy that is capable of lawfully being received by members of the public. This includes satellite transmissions.

Published editions are also protected; there is copyright in the typography and layout of a literary, dramatic or musical work (Great Britain 1988, Ss.3-8).

4.2.3 Copyright exists for a limited period only. *The Copyright Designs and Patents Act 1988* (CDPA) was amended in line with a European Directive (European Parliament and Commission of the European Communities 1993) that harmonised the basic term of copyright in the EU at 70 years from the end of the year the author died (Great Britain 1988, Ss.12-15, Great Britain 1995). However, there are still some differences in terms of copyright protection between the different classes of work.

- Literary, dramatic and musical (other than recorded sound) works are protected for the duration of the author's life until 70 years after his/her death.
- Works of joint authorship are protected for 70 years from the death of the last author.
- Artistic works are protected for the duration of the artist's life plus 70 years after his/her death.
- Published anonymous works are protected for 70 years from first publication.
- Copyright in unpublished literary, dramatic and musical works which have been created by a known author who died before 1 January 1969 expires on 31 December 2039. Copyright in works created by a known author who died on or after January 1969 expires 70 years after the death of the creator.
- Copyright in unpublished anonymous or pseudonymous works created before 1969 expires on 31 December 2039. Copyright in anonymous or pseudonymous works created on or after 1969 expires 70 years after the creation date.
- Films are protected for 70 years from the death of the last to survive of the principal director, the author of the screenplay, the author of the dialogue and the composer of the music specially created for the film.

Copyright protection for some other works is set at 50 years.

- Sound recordings are protected for 50 years from first publication, but 50 years from fixation, if unpublished during that time.
- Broadcasts are protected for 50 years from when the broadcast is first made.
- Computer generated works are protected for 50 years from first creation.

Published editions are protected for 25 years from first publication. Publication or communication to the public of a previously unpublished literary, dramatic or musical or artistic work or film in which copyright has expired will result in 25 years of protection from first publication.

4.2.4 UK copyright law specifies various types of secondary infringement (Great Britain 1988, Ss. 22-26). Infringement occurs if those involved knowingly undertake or facilitate secondary infringement. Acts of secondary infringement are: importing infringing copies; possessing or dealing with infringing copies; providing the means for making infringing copies; permitting the use of premises infringing performances and the provision of "apparatus" for infringing performances. Anyone who knowingly allowed these acts to happen through the supply of apparatus to others or allowing use of premises by other would also be infringing.

Moral Rights

4.2.5 Creators of material have moral rights under UK law (Ss. 79-89) that are distinct and separate from property rights. These include:

- The right of an individual author of a work to be acknowledged as the author or creator. This right must be asserted.
- The right not to have his or her work subjected to "derogatory" treatment.
- The right of any individual to refuse to be associated with something he or she did not create.

Moral rights cannot be transferred, but may be waived. Moral rights do not apply to creators of:

- Computer programs
- The design of a typeface
- Any computer-generated work
- Any work reporting current events

- Works that have appeared in newspapers, magazines or learned journals
- Other collective works, for example encyclopeadia entries
- Most employee-created materials (Great Britain 1988, s.79)

While the copyright in teaching materials created by academics is usually claimed by academic institutions, common practice is that they allow academics to negotiate rights with publishers for academic articles. However, the UK is going against the *Berne Convention* (Article 6bis) in denying moral rights to the authors of learned journal articles, particularly when these rights are so important in the academic world.

Database Rights

4.2.6 A European Directive on databases was issued in 1996 (Directive 96/9/EC of the European Parliament and of the Council of 11 March 1996 on the legal protection of databases, *Official Journal L* 77, 27/03/1996 P. 20 - 28) and a Statutory Instrument was subsequently passed in the UK to implement the Directive (Great Britain 1997). Databases are defined as:

> ... a collection of independent works, data or materials which
> are arranged in a systematic or methodological way, and
> are individually accessible by electronic or other means.
> (Great Britain 1988, s. 3A(1))

4.2.7 Databases, in some circumstances, may enjoy double protection: the database or *sui generis* right, and copyright. A database would be considered a literary work (s. 3(d)) if it is "original". A database is original, "if, and only if, by reason of the selection or arrangement of the contents of the database the database constitutes the author's own intellectual creation." (s. 3A(2)). A decision would need to be taken on what constitutes "original" in individual cases. The database right applies where there has been a substantial investment in obtaining, verifying or presenting the contents of the database. The term of protection in this case is 15 years, but may be renewed if there is a substantial change to the database. The database right prevents the unauthorised extraction and re-utilisation of material from a database, whether it enjoys copyright or not. As a result, both the copyright residing in the structure of the database and the database right restrict the transfer of databases to another medium. For example, if a preservation-related action resulted in some change to the arrangement or an "altered version" of the database, then it might be considered an adaptation (s. 21(3)(ac)).

Performance Rights

4.2.8 Performers' rights in a performance last for fifty years. If their performance is recorded, then they have rights in that recorded performance for fifty years after the performance is released. (Great Britain 1995, s. 10).

Relevant Exceptions and Limitations

4.2.9 Copyright law provides limited exceptions to undertake restricted acts on copyright work for legitimate purposes that do not damage the copyright owners' commercial interests. The *Copyright and related rights regulations 2003* implemented a European directive, which confirmed that all exceptions to copyright are subject to the Berne "three step" test. This is mentioned in the explanatory note to the UK Regulations. This test is used as a standard in framing exceptions to rights and ensures that the exceptions are not in conflict with the normal exploitation of the work and do not unreasonably prejudice the legitimate interests of the right holder. No distinction is usually made between print and non-print material in UK copyright law.

4.2.10 These exceptions are provided in Chapter III of the CDPA 1988: "Acts Permitted in relation to Copyright Works". Sections 37-42 of the Act deal specifically with library privileges. The library privilege of interest to this study is one which permits copying for purposes of preservation or replacement (Great Britain 1988, s.42). Section 42 of UK law permits a librarian or archivist of a *prescribed library*[193] or any *archive* to make a copy from any item in the permanent collection in order to preserve or replace that item, providing that the prescribed conditions are complied with. It also allows for copying in order to replace an item in the permanent collection of another prescribed library or archive. Any library is prescribed for this latter purpose. "A copy" is interpreted to mean a single copy. The exception outlined in S. 42 is only permitted where it is not reasonably practicable to purchase a replacement copy of the item. If a library undertakes copying to replace a copy in another library, the materials must form part of the "permanent collection" of both the donor and the receiver libraries of and must be for reference use only. The term "reference use" is reasonably clear in the print environment in that material may be consulted on the premises only and should not be issued as a loan and taken off the premises. Materials on temporary loan, such as interlibrary loans, are not eligible and so the status of digital material that is subscribed to, but remotely accessed, is not clear. This exception *only* applies to literary,

[193] Prescribed libraries are those that are neither established or conducted for profit nor part of a body established or conducted for profit. (Great Britain 1989, S.3)

dramatic and musical works, not artistic works, sound recordings or films.

4.2.11 Lawful users of computer programs may undertake certain acts that could be relevant to preservation, but under strict conditions (S. 50A). Lawful users may make one backup copy, decompile the software for certain restricted purposes, or copy or adapt it.

Orphan Works

4.2.12 There are provisions in UK copyright law for anonymous or pseudonymous literary, dramatic, musical or artistic work works (Great Britain 1998, S. 57, Great Britain 1995, S. 5, ss. 2). Copyright is not infringed if

- it is not possible by reasonable inquiry to ascertain the identity of the author, and
- it is reasonable to assume—
  - that copyright has expired, or
  - that the author died 70 years or more before the beginning of the calendar year in which the act is done or the arrangements are made.

However, there are currently no provisions permitting copying when the copyright holder is known, but cannot easily be traced.

Legal Deposit

4.2.13 When the Legal Deposit Libraries Act 2003 came into force on January 2004 the long-standing link between legal deposit and copyright law was broken. The *Legal Deposit Libraries Act 2003* (Great Britain 2003) incorporates the *Copyright Act 1911* (Great Britain 1911) legal deposit provisions for the deposit of works "published in print" (Great Britain 2003, S. 1, ss. 3). The 2003 Act requires publishers to send a copy of all printed books to the British Library within a month of publication. In addition, five other libraries have the right to claim copies for their collections within twelve months of publication. These libraries are the National Library of Scotland, the National Library of Wales, the Bodleian Library Oxford, Cambridge University Library and the library of Trinity College Dublin.

4.2.14 At the time of writing, only print material is subject to statutory deposit. The new legal deposit legislation was designed to *enable* the future extension of legal deposit to non-print material. Extension to other categories of material will require further regulation. The enabling section of the new legislation (S. 6) sets out the main elements that subsequent regulations will include: basically the details of what should be deposited by whom, when and in what circumstances. The enabling legislation for legal deposit of non-print material not only indicates the content of future regulations in terms of scope and deposit, it also covers what can be done with deposited material (S. 7) and addresses the copyright and liability issues for legal deposit libraries and depositors (Ss. 8-10). Any future regulations for deposit of particular types of material will specify what can be done in terms of using, copying, lending, transferring or disposing of material and adapting it (S. 7, ss. 1-3). Regulations would specify "the purposes for which relevant material may be used or copied", any embargoes on access, who would be entitled to use material and any limitations on simultaneous access by users (S. 7, ss. 4).

4.2.15 The deposit of UK, English and Welsh public records is governed by the the *Public Records Acts* of 1958 and 1967. Government departments are responsible for managing public records and deciding which records should be archived. Staff of The National Archives provide "guidance, coordination and supervision" of the selection and transfer processes (The National Archives 2007). The legislation specifies that records deemed worthy of preservation should be transferred to The National Archives, or some other place, as designated by the Lord Chancellor, who is charged with overseeing the preservation of public records, "not later than thirty years after their creation" (Great Britain 1958, S. 3, ss. 4). Scotland and Northern Ireland have their own national record offices, the National Archives of Scotland and the Public Record Office of Northern Ireland (PRONI) respectively. The preservation of Scottish records is governed by the *Public Records (Scotland) Act 1937*, the *Public Registers and Records (Scotland) Act 1948*, and some parts of the *Public Records Act 1958*, as amended by the *Public Records Act 1967*. The *Public Records Act (Northern Ireland) 1923* is the relevant legislation for Northern Irish records. Northern Irish government departments must submit records to PRONI for evaluation, where they are archived if deemed worthy of preservation (Public Record Office of Northern Ireland 2002). The *Government of Wales Act 1998* identified the records of certain Welsh organisations as Welsh public records and enabled the National Assembly for Wales to make arrangements for archiving these records. However, for the moment, the records of the National Assembly remain the responsibility of The National Archives in London.

4.2.16 Local government records are the responsibility of local authorities. The *Local Government Act 1972* refers to English and Welsh local records (S. 224). However, it only refers to "principal councils" making "proper arrangements" for "any documents that belong to or are in the custody of the council or any of their officers". The legislation does not explicitly say that records should be deposited and preserved in archives. The *Local*

Government (Scotland) Act 1994 (S. 53) states that local authorities should "make proper arrangements for the preservation and management of any records", they should consult the Keeper of the Records of Scotland about any such arrangements and the Keeper has free access to any local authority records. Local authority records in Northern Ireland are subject to the provisions of the *Public Records Act (Northern Ireland) 1923.*

Technological Protection Measures Provisions

4.2.17 In the UK, technological protection measures are defined as "any technology, device or component" (Great Britain 1998, S. 296ZF) used to (i) control access to, and (ii) use of, digital content. UK law provides legal protection against the circumvention of technological measures. It also provides legal protection against the manufacture of products enabling circumvention. Another provision makes it illegal to produce or distribute tools which enable the circumvention of protection measures (S. 296ZB). TPMs should not prevent users from enjoying permitted exceptions. Preservation copying by libraries and archives is one of the permitted exceptions. The narrowness of the exception and the TPM provisions would mean that it would be difficult to preserve digital material in practice. A user may appeal to the Secretary of State if technological measures prevent them carrying out restricted acts if there is an exception to copyright that permits them to do so (S. 296ZE). This is a cumbersome process and has been rarely used. It would be difficult to prove that any circumvention tools were only intended for use in creating copies under exemptions, and not infringing copies.

4.2.18 UK law also provides legal protection against the removal or alteration of any electronic rights management information with the intention of infringement or concealing infringement. It prevents the distribution, importation for distribution, broadcasting, communication or making available to the public of works or other subject matter from which electronic rights management information has been removed or altered without authority. Rights management information is defined in Section 25 as:

> … any information provided by the copyright owner or the holder of any right under copyright which identifies the work, the author, the copyright owner or the holder of any intellectual property rights, or information about the terms and conditions of use of the work, and any numbers or codes that represent such information.

Copyright Law and Contracts

4.2.19 UK law does not stop licence agreements over-riding copyright exception clauses in most cases. The limited exceptions to this are for certain clauses relating to databases and software. So, it is not an infringement if a person, who has a right (by licence or otherwise) to use a database (databases as literary works), exercises their right to access the database and to use its contents by whatever means necessary. Any term in the contract or licence that prohibits this is irrelevant (Great Britain 1988, s. 296B, s.50 (d1-2)). This exception also applies to legitimate uses in relation to software outlined as in legislation (s. 296A, s. 50A), but only with respect to agreements entered into from 1 January 1993 onward.

4.3 The Impact of Copyright and Related Laws on Digital Preservation Activities in the United Kingdom

Effect of Copyright and Related Laws on Digital Preservation

4.3.1 Current best practice effectively involves multiple and serial copying of digital content. For example, in order to ingest content into a digital archive, content may be copied from its original medium into the archive's storage system. Files may be reformatted at this stage. Storage media will be replaced over time and this will require content to be copied to new storage media. Mitigating the effects of technological obsolescence of file formats will require further reformatting over time. It may also be necessary to alter database structures. In order to retain the look and feel of some digital resources preservation managers may want to use emulation techniques. It may be necessary to keep and reformat electronic support materials over time, for example software, metadata, electronic manuals and specifications. In some cases, preservation institutions may want to make microform copies of digital material as digital preservation is in early stages of development. Librarians and archivists will want to preserve all sorts of digital content, including recorded sound and moving images.

4.3.2 The preservation copying exception in the UK was formulated with offline, non-digital content in mind. The aim is to facilitate the preservation of the intellectual and cultural heritage without affecting the ability of right holders to exploit their intellectual property. The exception hinders the preservation of content which is widely considered to be intellectually and culturally valuable, such as recorded sound, images and artistic works. It also hinders the preservation of digital content. The exception refers to "a" copy, when several need to be made and re-made over time. It refers to material for reference only, when libraries are increasingly making use of network technologies to serve their registered users wherever they happen to be. Copying exceptions introduced through the *Legal Deposit Libraries Act 2003* only apply to legal deposit content, not to content deposited voluntarily.

4.3.3 So the practical effect of current copyright and related laws is that collecting digital content that is in copyright for preservation purposes through Web archiving, copying digital content to storage media and reformatting it will require the permission of right holders. Since there is not yet statutory deposit for digital publications in the UK, copying carried out on voluntary deposited material will also require permission from right holders. The preservation exception does not seem to be adequate for digital material and recorded sound and moving images cannot be digitised for preservation purposes under this exception.

4.3.4 Since digital preservation cannot be carried out effectively under current UK copyright law exceptions, it is necessary to obtain licences from right holders. There is no blanket licensing scheme for digital copying for preservation purposes. There is a model licence for electronic journals for the academic sector that includes archival provisions in the event of subscriptions being terminated (see chapter 4.4)[194].

4.3.5 Some of the organisations submitting evidence to the Gowers review mentioned the difficulties they faced in tracing right holders for permission to carry out restricted acts.

4.3.6 There is no legal deposit for digital publications at the moment, so digital preservation is certainly not facilitated by current law. If further regulations were made for digital publications, then at least there would be a digital legal deposit collection. A point to note is that where “substantially the same” information is made available in more than one medium, it should only be deposited in one medium (S. 2). So, for example, if information is made available in both print and digital forms, it would only be deposited in one medium. The meaning of “substantially the same” and the medium to be deposited would be specified in regulations. At the moment, information that only exists in digital form is not being collected under legal deposit. Another issue is that films and recorded sound are expressly excluded from legal deposit (S.1, ss. 5). However, there are voluntary deposit schemes in place for this material, operated by the British Film Institute and The British Library National Sound Archive respectively. The British Library estimates that it receives around 90% of “commercially-produced

[194] See http://www.nesli2.ac.uk/model.htm.

audio recordings" (British Library 2006, p. 2) through voluntary arrangements with the British Phonographic Industry and the Mechanical Copyright Protection Society.

Potential Risks to Exclusive Rights Held by Creators and Other Right Holders

4.3.7 Copying for preservation purposes does not, in itself, pose a risk to right holders. Providing access to copies potentially poses risks; the nature of the risk would depend mainly on the nature and timing of access. If so-called preservation copying is actually a substitute for purchase or subscription for the preserving or other institutions, then there is a threat. For example, preservation institutions could in theory make several copies and provide access to them instead of purchasing duplicate copies or additional licences. A legal deposit library could provide remote access to deposited material while it is still commercially available. However, the wording of the current preservation exception prohibits this behaviour. As long as preservation institutions have appropriate security and access control measures in place, the interests of right holders should not be threatened.

CASE STUDY 1
UK Web Archiving Consortium members selectively capture Web content. They make individual approaches to site owners for express written permission to capture and make content accessible using a common permissions form. UKWAC also provide a form for reporting possible copyright infringement concerns and UKWAC will take appropriate action, including temporary removal of material. Less than half of all site owners contacted have granted permissions. Positive response rates range between 45% and just over 20% amongst the partners. While some UKWAC members may eventually benefit from extended legal deposit legislation, others will not and would have to continue seeking permissions on an individual basis. There are various reasons for not responding to requests or denying permission. These include not being in a position to grant permission for third party material; lack of awareness or understanding of the legal issues; difficulties in identifying the rights holder(s) and lack of resources to respond. Some sites may even disappear before right holders are located.

CASE STUDY 2
The **BBC** is a public service broadcaster established by Royal Charter. Much of its output is multimedia in format and made available via a variety of platforms. While the BBC may own all rights in content, it has also licensed rights from licensing bodies and rights owners for certain uses of content in its output. As far as preservation is concerned, the BBC's Charter includes an obligation to archive and preserve its output according to common standards. The BBC maintains its own archives and also deposits content in the British Film Archive and the National Sound Archive. Deposits are accompanied with agreements covering storage and access. Copying carried out for preservation purposes should not be prohibited by UK copyright law as it does not prevent acts that are done under statutory authority.

CASE STUDY 3 The National Archives
Records created in government departments are subject to Crown Copyright, so TNA is able to carry out any necessary preservation copying on this material. However, 40% of records deposited at TNA originated elsewhere and are effectively orphan works. As the right holders were private individuals or defunct organisations, there is rarely sufficient information with the records to identify rights owners. The sheer volume of material would make diligent searches practically impossible. TNA also holds records that are not literary, dramatic or musical works. None of the existing licensing bodies have licences for non-published works or for orphan works. There is no publisher that TNA can approach for permission to digitise for preservation purposes or to preserve born digital records.

4.4 Overview of Responses to the Issue of Copyright and Digital Preservation in the United Kingdom

Copyright Law Reform

4.4.1 The *Gowers Review of Intellectual Property* (2006) resulted in various recommendations for legislative and other reforms of the current UK intellectual property system. The Review stated that rights should be flexible and balanced between rights owners and "consumers" (p. 4). Recommendations related to digital preservation include those on orphan works, limited private copying, and archival copying.

4.4.2 For some types of fragile material, for example film and recorded sound, the only feasible means of preservation of the intellectual content is through digitisation. However, if the copyright owner(s) of such works cannot be traced, they cannot be copied as there is neither an existing UK exception nor any relevant provision in EU law. Therefore, Gowers recommended that a proposal for orphan works should be presented to the European Commission (p. 71). Gowers also makes recommendations for the UK Patent Office to clarify what constitutes a "reasonable search" for copyright owners and to make it easier to locate them by establishing a voluntary register of copyright (p. 72).

4.4.3 The recommendations on private copying are aimed at allowing users to "format shift" (p. 63, para. 4.76) the content they acquire legally, so that they can use it in ways most convenient to them. The recommendation is that users should only be allowed to make "one copy per 'format'". This would not allow users to re-format material repeatedly over time in order to keep it accessible or to copy it to new storage devices as existing storage becomes obsolete.

4.4.4 The Gowers Review concluded that UK preservation copying provisions are more stringent than in other countries in terms of the number of copies allowed, the types of work that may be copied and format shifting for preservation purposes (p. 64, para. 4.79). Gowers therefore made recommendations addressing these issues (p. 66).

- Recommendation 10a: Amend s.42 of the CDPA by 2008 to permit libraries to copy the master copy of all classes of work in permanent collections for archival purposes and to allow further copies to be made from the archived copy to mitigate against subsequent wear and tear.
- Recommendation 10b: Enable libraries to format shift archival copies by 2008 to ensure records do not become obsolete.

The wording of these recommendations is vague and will have to be considered carefully. For example the meaning of "permanent collection" will have to defined, as will "archival purposes", which only implies preservation rather than making it explicit. Presumably, "wear and tear" would refer to technological obsolescence as well and media degradation, but it is not clear.

4.4.5 The UK Government accepted the findings and recommendations of the review and the UK Intellectual Property Office (2008) issued a consultation document in January 2008. The term "preservation", rather than just archiving, is used. However, the section on the preservation exception does little more than reiterate Gowers' recommendations and ask what impact these suggestions would have on right holders. The focus is on extending the scope of the exception to include museums and galleries and all classes of work, and whether there should be limits on the numbers of copies made and whether an upper limit could be specified. There are no recommendations as such to be commented on, although there are comments that give the impression that the Government's view is that as long as the purpose of the exception remains the same, and that the provision that copying should only be carried out if it is not reasonable to obtain purchase a replacement copy, expanding the scope should not interfere with the interests of right holders. There is also a comment that "it would not appear sensible to impose a limit on the number of copies of such work if made for preservation purposes" (p. 29). Whilst there are no strong recommendations on expansion of the exception, the document does suggest that if it is expanded, prescribed bodies should be able to complain to the Government if digital rights management prevents preservation copying (p. 30).

4.4.6 Gowers notes that "DRMs may be used to prevent" (p. 73, para. 4.105) copying permitted under the *Copyright Designs and Patents Act 1988*. The current mechanism for addressing this issue is deemed to be unhelpful, so Gowers recommends that this be made easier through "providing an accessible web interface on the Patent Office website by 2008" (p. 73). However, this is hardly a great step forward. It seems that the Government's response to Gowers is that contract should continue to override copyright exceptions in most cases.

Legal Deposit Law

4.4.7 The UK Department for Culture, Media and Sport created the Legal Deposit Advisory Panel (LDAP) in September 2005. The purpose of the Panel is to advise the Secretary of State on regulations for the deposit of particular types of material. The Panel members represent legal deposit libraries and publishers. There are also several independent members with expertise in digital library and legal issues. A representative of the UK Department of Trade and Industry attends its meetings. The Panel has not yet provided any recommendations to the Secretary of State, but has initially been working on three areas: offline publications, electronic journals and Web content. The work of the LDAP is carried out in the context of the UK government's Better Regulation guidelines. This means that alternative means of achieving collection and preservation of the UK's non-print output need to be evaluated to assess which alternative best achieves the aim with least cost and burden on affected parties. Evidence is gathered and presented through Impact Assessments[195]. Possible alternatives to legal deposit include voluntary deposit schemes. The existing offline scheme was re-launched in order to gather the data required to inform the offline recommendation. Work on Web archiving is also at a relatively advanced stage; currently publishers are being consulted on a draft recommendation. Work on ejournals is less advanced. There is an

[195] This also applies to any future changes to copyright law and the UK Government's response to the Gowers Review contains some partially completed Impact Assessments. This document forms part of the consultation process under Better Regulation.

embryonic voluntary deposit scheme, which will be developed over time. Much time has been spent on defining ejournals; the difficulties experienced reflect the complexity of and convergence in the electronic publishing environment.

4.4.8 The *Legal Deposit Libraries Act 2003* specifies changes to the Copyright Designs and Patents Act 1998 and the Copyright and Rights in Databases Regulations 1997 (S.I. 1997/3032). These changes specify that legal deposit libraries will not infringe copyright or database rights if they carry out activities prescribed by any future legal deposit regulations, including copying material from the Internet (S. 8). However, if deposit of digital material is not regulated through legal deposit, but is achieved through voluntary deposit, these provisions would not apply and presumably the legal deposit libraries would have to continue to seek agreements with right holders on preservation-related copying.

4.4.9 Potential liability for infringement of intellectual property rights or breaches of contract arising from the deposit of, and access to, materials are addressed through two 'Exemption from liability' clauses, on 'deposit of publications, etc.' and 'activities in relation to publications' (Ss 9 &10). The first clause includes accompanying material deposited in order to make publications accessible. The clause on activities relating to publications provides exemptions from liability to depositors and libraries for unknowingly depositing and making available defamatory material. The exemptions only apply to defamatory material and there is no mention of other types of illegal material. Again, these exemptions would only apply to material acquired through statutory rather than voluntary means.

Public Records Law

4.4.10 In 2003, The National Archives issued a consultation paper on proposals to amend legislative provisions for records management and archives. The proposals do not apply to Scotland and Northern Ireland. The overall aim was to update the existing legislative provision, including making it more appropriate for digital records, to provide a "firmer legislative basis" (The National Archives 2003, p. 10) for management of public records, to strengthen the provision of and use of guidance and standards and to make the management and preservation of local and authority records subject to the same provisions as public records. As far as digital records are concerned, the consultation paper argued convincingly that, although current legislation is format neutral, its provisions are not entirely appropriate for the effective management and preservation of records in digital form (pp. 25-28, paras. 2.23-2.32). The two recommendations for digital records are to make provision to make sure that they are recognised as records within the Act and that there is provision for standards and guidance to ensure the long-term preservation of digital records (pp. 12-13).

4.4.11 The TNA (2004) subsequently issued a report on responses to its consultative document. The majority of respondents agreed with the proposals. The Act has not been amended in line with the proposals. However, a study on reducing the period before government records are transferred to TNA from 30 years is currently underway. There will have to be new primary legislation in order to achieve this, so the proposals on digital records could be enacted in this legislation.

Activities to Develop Non-Legislative Solutions

Handbooks and Guidelines

4.4.12 The CEDARS project developed some guidance for preservation managers on seeking permissions to carry out preservation copying (CEDARS 2002). In the absence of any licensing solutions from the UK reproduction rights organisations, organisations have been developing standard agreements or negotiating individually with right holders.

4.4.13 The PARADIGM project dealt with archiving, preserving and providing access to personal digital records. A number of legal issues were identified, including copyright. A particular issue for personal records is that the private papers of individuals who are "under contract to public offices" may be subject to Crown Copyright. The papers created by officers and servants of the Crown, including government ministers, in the course of their work would be public records. Some public records are subject to a waiver of Crown Copyright, which would allow various uses, including copying, of the material without requiring licences or payment under certain conditions, including that the papers were unpublished at the point of deposit, the records are open for public inspection and that appropriate attribution is given[196]. A major output of the project is a handbook, which includes guidance on copyright issues[197].

[196] See http://www.opsi.gov.uk/advice/crown-copyright/copyright-guidance/copyright-in-public-records.htm.

[197] See http://www.paradigm.ac.uk/workbook/legal-issues/copyright-archives.html.

Awareness Raising, Sharing Knowledge and Training

4.4.14 JISC funded the development of the Digital Preservation Training Programme for people involved in digital preservation at various levels[198]. One of the modules in this programme addresses legal issues, including copyright and legal deposit. The Digital Curation Centre (DCC) includes legal issues within its remit and the DCC has a legal blog or "blawg"[199]. While copyright and database law is an area of interest, the main focus so far seems to be on use and re-use of digital data by researchers rather than preservation copying. However, the DCC also holds workshops on legal issues in curating data, including copyright and database right and preservation.

Licence Agreements for Deposit and Preservation

4.4.15 When the voluntary deposit scheme for the deposit of non-print material in legal deposit libraries was established in 2000, publishers involved in the scheme completed some standard forms, which included provisions for number of copies to be deposited and access to deposited materials (Working Party on Legal Deposit 1999, S. 13.2). Unless expressly forbidden by the publisher, it was assumed that the deposit library could "copy a publication onto other media for preservation purposes only, subject to the preservation of the individual publication's identity and integrity. The copied version may not be used to provide user access". The scheme was re-launched in February 2007. There is no publicly available documentation on any standard preservation and access agreements for the re-launched scheme.

4.4.16 The UK Web Archiving Consortium Copyright Licence includes questions on the copyright status of content on web sites in order to ascertain whether signatories have rights and/or permissions necessary to allow UKWAC to archive the content. The UKWAC licence states that licensors are granting "a licence to make any reproductions or communications of this web site as are reasonably necessary to preserve it over time and to make it available to the public".

4.4.17 JISC uses the Model NESLi2 Licence[200] in negotiations with publishers. The model licence contains several clauses related to preservation, if preservation is considered to mean keeping content accessible and usable as long as it is needed. These

---

[198] See http://www.ulcc.ac.uk/dptp/.

[199] See http://dccblawg.blogspot.com/.

[200] See http://www.nesli2.ac.uk/model.htm.

include options to allow former subscribers to have access to an archival copy of the material they subscribed to (s. 8.4) and to carry out preservation strategies if the option is that the former subscriber is provided with their own archival copy (s. 8.6). There is also an obligation on the publisher to "inform the Licensee from time to time of the dark archives that the Publisher uses for the deposit of its content". It is not clear from the licence whether the publisher is obliged to ensure such a dark archive has to undertake effective preservation measures over time. Content Complete Ltd is JISC's agent for NESLi2 and negotiated with publishers to grant the rights necessary for libraries to participate in the UK LOCKSS pilot. The LOCKSS system pulls electronic journal content from the publishers. This activity requires both written and machine-readable permissions[201]. In addition libraries need permission to cache and archive their content. Publishers can grant permission once and this can be used by all libraries with authorised access to the content. NESLi publishers were approached first. Apparently a legal appraisal of the archival clauses in NESLi2 model licence was to be carried out by the JISC Services group to ensure that these allow for future LOCKSS-based archiving[202].

4.4.18 There have been developments in licencing to facilitate use of copyright material. For example authors may use Creative Commons licences to let others know what they may and may not do with their material. It is not clear to what extent such licences are being used by authors and creators in the UK. If preservation managers are dealing with material made available with a Creative Commons licence, they will have to check the the licence. For example, depending on the preservation strategies they are using, they may need a licence to make a derivative work. Recently, some academic publishers (for example the Nature Publishing Group) have announced that they will use such licences for their journal content.

4.4.19 The BBC, Channel 4, British Film Institute and the Open University formed the Creative Archive Licence Group in early 2005. The aim was to allow downloading and use of stills and clips of moving images and recorded sound through the Creative Archive Licence (http://creativearchive.bbc.co.uk/licence/-nc_sa_by_ne/uk/prov/). The licence was created for the use of archive material belonging to these institutions and was

201 For the LOCKSS suggested wording for publisher permissions see http://www.lockss.org/lockss/For_Publishers#Permission_to_Librarians.

202 See http://www.jisc.ac.uk/whatwedo/programmes/programme_preservation/programme_lockss.aspx.

apparently "heavily inspired" by the Creative Commons licensing initiative. Other organisations can become members of the group and share their content. It is not clear whether any organisation would wish to download the material made available for preservation purposes, but it is another example of a move towards such licences for non-commercial use of copyright material.

4.4.20 Publishers have been working on developing the Automated Content Access Protocol (ACAP) as an industry standard. The aim of ACAP is to "enable the providers of all types of content published on the World Wide Web to communicate permissions information (relating to access and use of that content) in a form that can be automatically recognized and interpreted, so that business partners can systematically comply with the publishers' policies".[203] This is an international project, with a British project manager and some British reproduction rights organisations, trade organisations and publishers are involved. The first phase of the project, the pilot stage, ended in November 2007. There was a clear intention to carry on. There is potential for ACAP to facilitate Web archiving. Indeed, the British Library was a partner in the pilot project. However, it does not look as if such a use case was fully developed under the pilot project.

4.5 Recommendations for Legal Reforms or Practical Solutions in the United Kingdom to Facilitate Digital Preservation

4.5.1 Before making recommendations for reform of legislative models, it is useful to summarise how current UK law may hinder digital preservation. The preservation exception:

- only applies to libraries and archives and does not extend to other public sector organisations involved in preserving copyright material, such as museums and galleries
- does not apply to commercial organisations that may wish to preserve digital content
- only applies to literary, musical and dramatic works. Other types of digital content that require preservation, such as recorded sound and moving images, are not included
- allows "a" copy to be made, when digital preservation will involve multiple and serial copying and reformatting
- applies to reference material, when the content to be preserved may be accessible to users over networks
- only refers to the making of copies, when some preservation actions may be considered as adaptations

[203] See http://www.the-acap.org/.

- only applies to material in permanent collections when some institutions may wish to gather and preserve material from the Web.

4.5.2 Other aspects of copyright law may hinder digital preservation.

- Copyright and related rights terms differ for different types of material, so seeking permissions to preserve multimedia resources may be complex.
- If the rights owners in categories of material not covered by the preservation exception cannot be traced for permission to copy, the material cannot be copied and may therefore be at risk.
- Provisions to over-ride technological protection measures in order to take advantage of the preservation exception are impractical.
- The preservation exception may be over-ridden by contract terms governing use of materials, except in the case of databases and software.
- Provisions allowing preservation-related copying by legal deposit libraries only come into force when legal deposit for digital publications is enacted.

The Gowers Review and the UK Government's consultation document have already made some relevant recommendations, the Legal Deposit Advisory Panel is examining the case for legal deposit of different categories of digital publication and there is also work at the European level with regard to orphan works. The recommendations in this report re-state some of these recommendations, but also discuss where these recommendations do not go far enough or make further suggestions on issues that are not being addressed.

Revision of the Preservation Copying Exception (CDPA 1988, s. 42)

4.5.3 The Gowers Review recommended that the scope of the preservation exception be amended and the UK Government's consultation document is seeking views on the likely impact on right holders. The aim of the recommendations made here are to facilitate digital preservation without harming the interests of right holders. While the issues of preservation and access are closely linked, in that the aim of preservation is keep material accessible and usable for as long as it is needed, access to preserved material can be managed so that it does not compromise the interests of right holders. At present commercial organisations cannot copy or receive copies for preservation purposes, even if they are no longer able to purchase copies. Extending the preservation exception to such organisations, even if they lose access to material they need and preserving it would not affect the interests of right holders, would set a precedent for other exceptions and undermine the spirit of copyright exceptions.

4.5.4 Museums and galleries have copyright material in their collections. Some museums and galleries have their own libraries and archives of material that is used by users and staff. Curators also collect, store, preserve and display copyright material, such as works of art, recorded sound, moving and still images, maps, designs and music. It is not clear why the preservation exception applies to non-commercial libraries and archives, but not to non-commercial museums and galleries.

4.5.5 The scope of the preservation exception should be expanded to cover the full range of copyright material. There is no obvious reason why literary, dramatic and musical works should be the only categories worth preserving. There is also no obvious reason why preservation copying of other types of work in itself would affect the interests of right holders. Access to preservation copies should be with the agreement of right holders and with appropriate compensation.

4.5.6 While it may have been acceptable to make a single copy when the current law was drafted, this provision is no longer in line with the requirements of long-term preservation or good preservation practice. The Government's consultation document raises the question of whether a maximum number of copies should be specified. It is clear that institutions should not be allowed to make copies of material to avoid purchasing them. The current exception provides for this in that it stipulates that preservation copying can only be carried out when it is no longer reasonably possible to acquire material from the right holder. It seems reasonable to retain this.

4.5.7 Neither Gowers nor the current Government consultation deals with what permanent collections only available for reference purposes means in the digital environment. The inclusion of this stipulation is clearly to prevent libraries and archives from acquiring copies of material from other institutions rather than purchasing their own copies. Presumably, a similar rationale underlies restricting copying to material only available for reference purposes – lending copies should be purchased. However, these restrictions do not take into account changes in libraries and archives, including the way they acquire collections and how they make them available to their users. Physical reference collections are declining in many public sector libraries. Neither does it take into account the changing needs of users, who may be distance learners or who may prefer accessing information from their desktops. Reference works are increasingly made available electronically to registered users outside the library or archive's physical premises and the amount of digital material only available from the premises is decreasing. It does not seem reasonable to prevent preservation of material that will be made available remotely, if the access is controlled in such as way that it does not harm the interests of right holders. The meaning of the term "permanent" needs to be revised in the digital environment. Institutions subscribing to digital sources may not have a physical copy of the material stored on their premises. The material is part of a virtual, rather than a physical collection. Permanent should apply to this material too. The fact that use of such material is governed by contract is a separate issue to be dealt with later. Web archiving is an interesting case. Librarians and archivists may provide links to freely available Web material, making it part of a virtual collection. They may or may not have asked permission to do this. There is no act of physical purchase, neither is there any subscription for access. There is no relationship between right holder and institution. Copying freely available Web material would not harm the commercial interests of right holders in that it would not deny them sales. However, if the right holder does not want their material to be copied in the first place, it is difficult to see how this could ever be considered legitimate under a preservation exception.

4.5.8 Amending the copyright exception along the lines suggested above would also address the following issues.

- The issue of different lengths of terms for different types of content making rights seeking a complex exercise is resolved for material that falls under the exception.
- The issue of being unable to copy orphan works for preservation purposes is resolved for material that falls under the exception.

Technological Protection Measures and Licence Agreements

4.5.9 However, some issues would not be resolved by amending the preservation exception in the ways suggested. There would still be a need for a more practical mechanism for overcoming the problem of TPMs preventing implementation of the preservation exception. Even if a more practical way of dealing with TPMs is found, the problem that the preservation exception can be over-ridden by contract law for all material except databases and software remains. The obvious suggestion is that the the law should be amended so that the preservation exception cannot be over-ridden by contract terms at all. Right holders may well object strongly to this suggestion as they are likely to perceive it as a potential loss of control of their intellectual property. They would need to be thoroughly reassured that this would not be the case.

Legal Deposit and Web Archiving

4.5.10 If the Legal Deposit Advisory Panel finds that statutory deposit is the best alternative for ensuring the preservation of the recorded heritage, legal deposit should be extended to cover all types of digital publication, without exception. The exclusion of recorded sound and film from legal deposit provisions should be reviewed. If regulations are made to enact digital legal deposit, the legal deposit libraries will be able to copy for preservation purposes and to archive Web material. There is a clear case for the collection and preservation of Web material by legal deposit libraries and archives with a long-term preservation remit, such as the national archives of the constituent parts of the UK, as they perform a similar function to the legal deposit libraries for government and other types of official records. Indeed TNA does need to seek permission for most of the government sites it harvests as this is part of its remit.

Other Non-Legislative Reforms

4.5.11 Bodies funding activities that result in the creation of digital content may wish that this content is preserved. The Research Information Network report on research funders' policies (2007) indicated that although there is increasing recognition of a need to manage and disseminate research outputs, there has been more focus on published outputs rather than other outputs such as datasets. There has also been more emphasis on deposit and access rather than preservation. The conclusion is that policies are needed and these need to be co-ordinated across various stakeholders. Mandating archiving and preservation in contractual relationships with funded research institutions and researchers would avoid the need for preserving agencies to find, collect and ask for permission to preserve such digital content.

4.5.12 For organisations wishing to carry out Web archiving and preservation copying that is not covered by the preservation copying exception, the situation is messy and complex. Commercial organisations will require permission to copy for preservation purposes. While there are currently no licensing schemes available for these organisations, if there was an identified need existing reproduction rights organisations may be able to develop such schemes. Previous research on copyright and digital preservation (Ayre & Muir 2004) indicated that right holders had little enthusiasm for blanket licensing schemes. Without carrying out further research, it is not clear whether this is still the case.

4.5.13 Moves towards open access may ease the rights clearance burden on preserving organisations that are not able to rely on existing legislative provision or collective licensing such as the NESLi2 licence. If more digital content is made available with accompanying terms of use, such as a Creative Commons licence, it reduces the need to identify and seek clearance from individual right holders. It is beyond the scope of this study to survey the current situation with regard to use of such licences and analyse to what extent they would allow for digital preservation. It would, however, be useful to carry out a multi-sector study of attitudes towards the use of such licences and the underlying perceptions that inform attitudes.

4.6 Bibliography

Anderson, P., 2007. *What is Web 2.0? Ideas, technologies and implications for Education*, http://www.jisc.ac.uk/media/documents/techwatch/tsw0701b.pdf, [accessed 8.8.07].

Anderson, S. *et al.*, 2006. *Digital images archiving study.* http://www.jisc.ac.uk/uploaded_documents/FinaldraftImagesArchivingStudy.pdf, [accessed 6.8.07].

Ayre, C. & A. Muir, 2004. *The right to preserve: copyright and licensing for digital preservation: a report for the Arts and Humanities Research Board.* http://hdl.handle.net/2134/343, [accessed 13.2.08].

Barker, E. *et al.*, 2004. *Long-Term Retention and Reuse of E-Learning Objects and Materials.* http://www.jisc.ac.uk/uploaded_documents/LTR_study_v1-4.doc, [accessed 6.8.07].

Beagrie, N., 2007. *E-infrastructure strategy for research: final report from the OSI Preservation and Curation Working Group.* http://www.nesc.ac.uk/documents/OSI/preservation.pdf, [accessed 20.3.08].

Beagrie, N. & M. Jones, 2002. *Preservation management of digital materials: a handbook.* Online version available at http://www.dpconline.org/graphics/handbook/, [accessed 6.8.07].

British Library, 2006. *Gowers review of intellectual property: response submitted by the British Library.* http://www.hm-treasury.gov.uk/media/5/6/british_library_375_132kb.pdf, [accessed 22.8.07].

CEDARS Project, 2002. *Cedars guide to intellectual property rights.* http://www.leeds.ac.uk/cedars/guideto/ipr/guidetoipr.pdf, [accessed 1.10.07].

Feeney, M., 1999. *Digital culture: maximising the nation's investment.* London: National Preservation Office.

Gowers review of intellectual property, 2006. Norwich: HMSO.

Great Britain, Public and General Acts, 1911. *Copyright Act 1911,* 1 & 2 Geo. V, ch. 46, s.15.

Great Britain, Public and General Acts, 1923. *Public Records Act (Northern Ireland) 1923,* ch. 20.

Great Britain, Public and General Acts, 1937. *Public Records (Scotland) Act 1937.* Geo. VI, ch. 43.

Great Britain, Public and General Acts, 1948. *Public Registers and Records (Scotland) Act 1948.* 11 & 12 Geo. VI, ch. 57

Great Britain, Public and General Acts, 1958. *Public Records Act 1958.* Eliz. II, ch. 51.

Great Britain, Public and General Acts, 1967. *Public Records Act 1967.* Eliz. II, ch. 44.

Great Britain, Public and General Acts, 1972. *Local Government Act 1972.* ch. 70.

Great Britain, Public and General Acts, 1994. *Local Government (Scotland) Act 1994.* ch. 39.

Great Britain, Public and General Acts, 1997. *Copyright rights in databases: the copyright and rights in databases regulations 1997,* http://www.opsi.gov.uk/si/si1997/19975110.htm, [accessed 2.07.08].

Great Britain, Public and General Acts, 2000. *Freedom of Information Act 2000.* Eliz. II, ch. 36.

Great Britain, Public and General Acts, 2003. *Legal Deposit Libraries Act 2003,* Eliz. II, ch. 28.

Great Britain, Statutory Instruments, 1989. Copyright (Librarians and Archivists) (Copying of Copyright Material) Regulations 1989, S.I. 1212.

Great Britain, Statutory Instruments, 2003. *The Copyright and Related Rights Regulations 2003*, S.I. 2498.

Lifecycle Information for E-literature, 2006. *A summary from the LIFE project Report Produced for the LIFE conference 20 April 2006.* http://eprints.ucl.ac.uk/archive/00001855/01/LifeProjSummary.pdf, [accessed 6.8.07].

The National Archives, 2003. Proposed national records and archives legislation: proposals to change the current legislative provision for records management and archives: consultation paper. http://www.nationalarchives.gov.uk/documents/policy-consultation.pdf, [accessed 2.7.07].

The National Archives, 2004. *Report on responses to The National Archives' consultation paper CP03/01*, http://www.nationalarchives.gov.uk/documents/report.pdf, [accessed 2.7.07].

The National Archives, 2007. *The history of the Public Records Act*. http://www.nationalarchives.gov.uk/policy/act/history.htm, [accessed 25.6.07].

Public Record Office of Northern Ireland, 2002. *List of Government department records*. http://www.proni.gov.uk/index/research_and_records_held/records_held_in_proni/public_records_departmental.htm, [accessed 2.07.08].

Research Information Network, 2007. *Research funders' policies for the management of information outputs: a report commissioned by the Research Information Network*. http://www.rin.ac.uk/files/Funders'%20Policy%20&%20Practice%20-%20Final%20Report.pdf, [accessed 6.2.08].

Research Information Network, 2007. *Stewardship of digital research data: a framework of principles and guidelines: responsibilities of research institutions and funders, data managers, learned societies and publishers*. http://www.rin.ac.uk/files/Research%20Data%20Principles%20and%20Guidelines%20full%20version%20-%20final.pdf, [accessed 20.3.08].

UK Intellectual Property Office, 2008. *Taking forward the Gowers Review of Intellectual Property: proposed changes to copyright exceptions*. http://www.ipo.gov.uk/consult-copyrightexceptions.htm, [accessed 9.1.08].

Wilson, A. *et al.*, 2006. *Moving Images and Sound Archiving Study.* http://www.jisc.ac.uk/media/documents/programmes/preservation/moving_images_and_sound_archiving_study1.pdf, [accessed 2.07.08]

Working Party on Legal Deposit, 1999. *Code of practice for the voluntary deposit of non-print publications.* Revised version, September 1999. http://www.bl.uk/aboutus/stratpolprog/legaldep/voluntarydeposit/, [accessed 2.07.08]

Part 5: Country Report for the United States

June M. Besek,[204] William G. LeFurgy[205]
and Christopher D. Weston[206]

5.1 Major Digital Preservation Activities in the United States

5.1.1 A wide range of digital preservation-related activities takes place in the United States. These activities include assembling and maintaining digital archives, developing technical tools for digital preservation, and identifying best practices for ensuring long term availability of digital content. Much of this work is decentralized, and is occurring both in the public and in the private sectors. Entities undertaking such efforts have taken different approaches to the technical, legal and administrative issues raised by digital preservation. Standards and practices are still developing, and this is likely to continue for some time to come.

5.1.2 Initial efforts to bring digital information under institutional stewardship have focused largely on research materials, including scholarly literature. Digital preservation activities are now addressing a wider range of content, however, as evidenced by some of the project descriptions below. Current digital preservation projects encompass both "born digital" material and digitized analog material. Preservation activities extend to public domain materials as well as to those protected by copyright. In the latter case, preservation projects generally rely on copyright exceptions or on agreements with right holders.

---

[204] Executive Director, Kernochan Center for Law, Media and the Arts, Columbia Law School.

[205] Project Manager, Digital Initiatives, Office of Strategic Initiatives, U.S. Library of Congress.

[206] Attorney-Advisor, U.S. Copyright Office, Library of Congress.

Cultural Heritage Institutions

5.1.3 The Library of Congress has worked collaboratively with government, academic, commercial, and professional communities across the nation on many digital preservation activities, primarily through the National Digital Information Infrastructure and Preservation Program (NDIIPP),[207] but also through its other programs, discussed below. NDIIPP is the national digital preservation effort led by the Library of Congress. Its mission is to "develop a national strategy to collect, archive and preserve the burgeoning amounts of digital content, especially materials that are created only in digital formats, for current and future generations."[208] Launched in 2001, NDIIPP is principally concerned with the three areas outlined below.

- Capturing, preserving, and making available significant digital content. From the start, a priority for NDIIPP has been to safeguard important bodies of at risk digital content. Content now under stewardship by NDIIPP partners is varied, but focuses on geospatial information; web sites; audio visual productions; images and text; and materials related to critical public policy issues (e.g., public health and medical preparedness, state and local digital publications and agency policy documents).

- Building and strengthening a national network of partners. The NDIIPP approach is based on findings from its early planning process that no single entity could realistically undertake sole responsibility to comprehensively preserve digital content, and that partnerships are necessary to ensure that information vital to scholars and researchers now and in the future will be saved. The NDIIPP national network currently has about 130 partners drawn from federal agencies, state and local governments, academia, professional and nonprofit organizations, and commercial entities.

- Developing a technical infrastructure of tools and services. NDIIPP partners work collaboratively to develop a technical infrastructure by building the information systems, tools, and services that support digital preservation. These include utilities that automate stewardship tasks and processing; operational services for digital content curation; and digital content delivery mechanisms among partners and between the Library of Congress preservation and access technical environments.

---

207 *See* Digital Preservation, http://www.digitalpreservation.gov/.

208 *See* What the Library is Doing, http://www.digitalpreservation.gov/library/about.html.

5.1.4 The following examples illustrate some of the projects under the NDIIPP umbrella:

- University of California, California Digital Library, *Web at Risk – A Distributed Approach to Preserving Our Nation's Political Cultural Heritage* focuses on collecting and preserving political and cultural web content from state and local governments, the federal government and certain nonprofit sources.[209]
- University of Maryland, Robert H. Smith School of Business, *Birth of the Dot Com Era* preserves at risk digital materials from the American business culture during the early years of the commercialization of the Internet, and is authorized to create a special "closed archive for restricted material."[210]
- Educational Broadcasting Corporation, *Preserving Digital Public Television* works to design an archive for the long-term preservation of public television programs now being recorded directly onto a digital medium instead of film.[211]
- Washington State Archives, Multi-state Preservation Consortium builds on Washington's advanced digital archives framework to implement a centralized repository for eight other states.[212]

5.1.5 Besides its management of NDIIPP, the Library of Congress engages in a number of other digital preservation programs, examples of which are:

- Web Capture. The Library's Web Capture team is charged with building a Library-wide understanding and technical infrastructure for capturing Web content. The team, in collaboration with a variety of Library staff, and national and international partners, is identifying policy issues, establishing best practices, and building tools to collect and preserve Web content. It is also a founding member of the International Internet Preservation Consortium.[213]
- The National Audio-Visual Conservation Center (NAVCC) is the first centralized facility in America specifically planned and designed for the acquisition, cataloging, storage and

---

209 *See* The Web at Risk: Preserving our Nation's Cultural Heritage, http://www.cdlib.org/inside/projects/preservation/webatrisk/.

210 *See* Dot Com Archive, http://www.dotcomarchive.org/.

211 *See* Preserving Digital Television, http://www.ptvdigitalarchive.org/.

212 *See* Multi-State Preservation Partnership, http://www.digitalarchives.wa.gov/content.aspx?txt=LoCProjectSite.

213 *See* Net Preserve, http://netpreserve.org/about/index.php.

preservation of the nation's collection of moving images and recorded sounds. This collaborative initiative is the result of a partnership between the Packard Humanities Institute, the United States Congress, the Library of Congress and the Architect of the Capitol. The NAVCC will use state-of-the-art technologies to significantly increase preservation capacities and capabilities, and new large-scale digital acquisition and archiving systems that will serve as a prototype for the global audiovisual community.

5.1.6 The National Agricultural Library (NAL) houses and provides access to a large agricultural information collection in analog and digital forms and serves as the nexus for a national network of state land-grant and U.S. Department of Agriculture field libraries. A key institutional responsibility involves preserving agricultural works of national and international importance indefinitely into the future. In addition, NAL has a leadership role to assist in the preservation of important agricultural literature held by other U. S. institutions. NAL has worked on preservation of journals and other materials in electronic form for many years, and has a long history of providing enhanced access to its digital information.

5.1.7 The National Library of Medicine (NLM) is taking a leadership role in ensuring permanent access to important digital materials in health and biomedicine, including electronic journals, databases, documents published on the web, and new kinds of scholarly communication. Collection development and acquisitions staff have seen an increasing availability of born digital materials that NLM needs to add to its collection. The NLM preservation program has embraced digitization as a preservation format to replace microfilming. By identifying high-level functional requirements and policy considerations, the NLM's Digital Repository Working Group has outlined an infrastructure and a standards-based approach to the management, preservation and access of NLM's existing and future digital resources.

5.1.8 The Government Printing Office (GPO)[214] is the U.S. government's primary centralized resource for gathering, cataloging, producing, providing, authenticating, and preserving published information in all forms. As a large volume of this

[214] It is NARA, discussed below, that has the legal responsibility for determining which U.S. government records should become part of the official Archives of the United States, and for maintaining custody of those records. In a 2003 agreement, NARA delegated physical custody of permanent records contained within "GPO Access" (GPO's public web site) to GPO, but NARA retains legal custody and ultimate responsibility for preservation of and access to those records. GPO and other U.S. government agencies also maintain other types of information of long term value that are not part of the official Archives of the United States. For these reasons, GPO, as well as NLM and NAL, are categorized as cultural heritage institutions rather than as government archives.

information is issued in digital form, GPO is developing the Federal Digital System (FDsys) to allow federal content creators to publish content that can then be preserved, authenticated, managed and delivered upon request.[215] This digital system will form the core of GPO's future operations. All known Federal Government documents within the scope of GPO's Federal Depository Library Program, whether printed or born digital, will be included in the FDsys. Content will be available for Web searching and Internet viewing, downloading and printing, and as document masters for conventional and on-demand printing, or other dissemination methods.

Government Archives

5.1.9 The National Archives and Records Administration (NARA) is responsible for federal records disposition. Disposition is a comprehensive term that includes both destruction and transfer of federal records to the National Archives of the United States. NARA has preserved electronic records since the 1970s, but is faced with bringing in a vastly greater volume of digital material. The agency has been working on a system since 1998 to address this challenge. The Electronic Records Archives (ERA) will enable NARA to improve its services to other federal agencies, researchers and teachers. In 2005, the agency entered into a multi-million dollar contract with a vendor to build the ERA system.[216]

5.1.10 Most U.S. state governments have made limited progress with preserving electronic records and other official information in digital form. The Library of Congress Preserving State Government Information initiative is meant to serve as a catalyst for preservation of digital data valuable to state governments. The initiative supports four demonstration projects working with 23 states that are collecting and preserving digital content of interest to Congress, including geospatial information, state legislative records and state executive agency documentation. Each project will also share tools, services and best practices to help every state make progress in managing its digital heritage. Overall, the initiative aims to promote development of standards, best practices and technical infrastructure necessary to provide for permanent access to a national collection of state and local government information.[217]

---

[215] *See* U.S. Government Printing Office, http://www.gpo.gov/projects/fdsys.htm.

[216] *See* Electronic Records Archive, http://www.archives.gov/era/.

[217] *See* Digital Preservation: Partners, http://www.digitalpreservation.gov/partners/states.html.

Educational and Research Institutions

5.1.11 The National Science Foundation (NSF) is an independent U.S. government agency that provides grants and other funding for approximately 20 percent of all federally supported basic research conducted by America's colleges and universities. The agency has supported many significant programs in connection with digital preservation. An example is the Digital Archiving and Long-Term Preservation program, a 2004 partnership with the Library of Congress that supported ten novel research projects designed to produce practical tools, services, and practices for digital preservation. NSF sponsored a research committee that issued *Long-Lived Digital Data Collections Enabling Research and Education in the 21st Century*, a report that outlines the need for effective preservation practices for data sets generated through scientific research.[218] A major current program known as Sustainable Digital Data Preservation and Access Network (DataNet) provides for multi-million dollar funding for projects that have promise for developing new methods, management structures and technologies to manage the diversity, size, and complexity of current and future data sets.

5.1.12 The Association of Research Libraries (ARL) is a nonprofit membership organization comprising the libraries of North American research institutions and influences public policies that affect research libraries and the communities they serve. In 2004, ARL published a report endorsing digitization as an accepted preservation reformatting option. This report has been influential in promoting digital preservation as not only critical for the short term, but viable for the long term.

5.1.13 The Coalition for Networked Information (CNI) promotes digital preservation by contributing to standards efforts and encouraging communication across allied communities. Sponsored by ARL and EDUCAUSE, CNI hosts conferences in which major digital preservation issues are discussed. CNI also participates in a number of conferences and initiatives that support digital preservation activities, including the Library of Congress's NDIIPP preservation initiatives.

5.1.14 The Center for Research Libraries (CRL) is a consortium of North American universities, colleges and independent research libraries. It acquires and preserves various traditional and digital resources for research and teaching (including, for example, newspapers, journals and other documents), which it then makes

[218] *See* National Science Foundation Office of Cyberinfrastructure, http://www.nsf.gov/dir/index.jsp?org=OCI.

available to its members.[219] CRL is engaged in a variety of preservation activities, analog and digital. The political communications Web archive project, a joint project with CRL and several universities, is designed to develop effective methodologies for the systematic, sustainable preservation of Web-based political communications by individuals and organizations from Latin America, Sub-Saharan Africa, Southeast Asia, and Western Europe. CRL is also engaged in a project to study successful or long-lived collections of data by federal agencies and nonprofit and for-profit institutions to identify practices and strategies that have enabled those collections to persist, and to create tools and metrics for developing and assessing new repositories. CRL, together with OCLC/RLG and NARA developed *The Trustworthy Repositories Audit & Certification: Criteria and Checklist (TRAC),* published in 2007,[220] discussed below in section 5.4.23.

5.1.15 The Andrew W. Mellon Foundation is a nonprofit foundation that has played a critical role in addressing digital preservation needs by providing funding for specific preservation-related projects and encouraging the development of organizations to undertake digital preservation. Among the many projects it has funded are Portico, JSTOR and ArtSTOR. The Mellon Foundation has also funded the development of the Global Digital Format Registry (GDFR), which aims to provide authoritative information about digital formats. The GDFR intends to become a key international infrastructure component for the digital preservation programs of libraries, archives and other institutions with the responsibility for keeping digital resources viable over time.

5.1.16 The Institute of Museum and Library Services is the primary source of federal support for the nation's 122,000 libraries and 17,500 museums.[221] Recent grants in digital preservation have provided support for establishing a repository for preserving digital images at Cornell University, establishing a LOCKSS (Lots Of Copies Keep Stuff Safe) system in Alabama, creating preservation strategies for Computer-Aided Design architectural documents at MIT, and developing a digital preservation training

---

219 *See* Center for Research Libraries, http://www.crl.edu.

220 *See* Trustworthy Repositories Audit & Certification: Criteria and Checklist (Feb. 2007), available at http://www.crl.edu/PDF/trac.pdf. This project built on an earlier report Trusted Digital Repositories: Attributes and Responsibilities (May 2002), www.oclc.org/programs/ourwork/past/trustedrep/repositories.pdf, that resulted from a collaboration between OCLC and Research Libraries Group, as well as on CRL's Auditing and Certification of Digital Archives project, work from the Nestor project (Germany), and from the Digital Curation Center in the UK.

221 *See* Institute of Museum and Library Services, http://www.imls.gov/.

program for staff in libraries, archives, museums, and other cultural heritage organizations.

Third Party Providers of Preservation-Related Services

5.1.17 The Internet Archive is a nonprofit organization that regularly browses, copies and archives sites on the Internet.[222] It collaborates with a variety of institutions, including national libraries around the world, to create a broad record of web content for use by scholars and researchers. The Internet Archive's activities are discussed in more detail in sections 5.4.45-46, below.

5.1.18 The Online Computer Library Center (OCLC) is a nonprofit library service and research organization dedicated to the public purposes of furthering access to the world's information and reducing the rate of rise of library costs. A major OCLC initiative is the Digital Archive, which provides a centralized, secure storage environment. It provides fee-based digital preservation services, and is presently working with libraries and other organizations in a number of states.

Creators and Right Holders

5.1.19 Creators and right holders are working with NDIIPP on projects involving the preservation of comic art, video games and electronic literature through the Preserving Creative America initiative. Some right holders have undertaken digital preservation of their own materials to ensure their continuing ability to commercially exploit them. However, detailed information about such efforts is not generally publicly available.[223]

5.1.20 The NDIIPP Preserving Creative America initiative is working with creators and right holders in the motion picture, photography and recorded sound industries on digital preservation tools and educational outreach. Other collaborative preservation projects involving right holders (e.g., Portico and CLOCKSS) are described in sections 5.4.35-41, below.

---

[222] *See* Internet Archive, http://www.archive.org/about/about.php; Michele Kimpton, Written Response to Section 4, Section 108 (Apr. 7, 2006), available at http://www.section108.gov/docs/Kimpton_Internet-Archive.pdf.

[223] Also, there is no certainty as to whether all of those works will continue to be made available to the public in the future, and on what terms.

5.2 Overview of Copyright, Related Rights and Legal Deposit Laws of the United States as Applied to Digital Preservation

Copyright

5.2.1 United States copyright law (contained in Title 17 of the U.S. Code) protects any original work of authorship that is fixed in a tangible medium.[224] "Original" is not a high threshold; it simply means that the work has not been copied, and that it has at least a modicum of creativity. The Copyright Act lists the following categories of works eligible for copyright protection, but the list is non-exclusive: literary works; musical works, including any accompanying words; dramatic works, including any accompanying music; pantomimes and choreographic works; pictorial, graphic, and sculptural works; motion pictures and other audiovisual works; sound recordings; and architectural works. Copyright lasts for the life of the author and seventy years thereafter.[225] (Relevant provisions of the U.S. Copyright Act are attached as Appendix E.)

Exclusive Rights

5.2.2 U.S. copyright law provides a copyright owner with the following rights:

- the right to reproduce the work (the right to make copies).[226]
- the right to create adaptations (also known as derivative works).
- the right to distribute copies of the work to the public. The distribution right is limited by the "first sale doctrine" (an exhaustion principle), which provides that the owner of a particular copy of a copyrighted work may sell or transfer that copy.[227]

---

[224] 17 U.S.C. § 102(a) (2006).

[225] Certain works, such as works made for hire and works first published prior to January 1, 1978, have different terms of protection. 17 U.S.C. § 302(c), 304 (2006). See Lolly Gasaway, When Works Pass Into the Public Domain, http://www.unc.edu/%7Eunclng/public-d.htm.

[226] "Copy" is defined broadly under U.S. law to include any form in which the work is fixed, or embodied, and from which it can be perceived, reproduced or communicated, either directly or with the aid of a machine. 17 U.S.C. § 101 (2006). Technically, a copy of a sound recording is known as a "phonorecord," but for convenience all reproductions of copyrighted works will be referred to herein as "copies."

[227] 17 U.S.C. §109(a) (2006). There is no digital first sale doctrine, because a digital transmission involves making a copy, not merely transferring a copy.

- the right to perform the work publicly; [228] and
- the right to display the work publicly.

5.2.3 "Publicly" is a broad concept in copyright. To perform or display a work publicly means to perform or display it anywhere that is open to the public or anywhere that a "substantial number of persons outside of a normal circle of a family and its social acquaintances is gathered." [229] Transmitting the performance or display to such a place also makes it public. It does not matter if members of the public receive the performance at the same time or different times, at the same place or different places.

5.2.4 The United States does not have a "making available" right denominated as such, but making a work available generally implicates at least one, and sometimes more, of the existing rights under copyright.[230]

The Significance of Publication under U.S. Copyright Law

5.2.5 Before the 1976 Copyright Act went into effect, works were not eligible for federal copyright protection until they were published, with notice of copyright. Unpublished works were protected under state law. Consequently, a work's publication status was of critical importance. The 1976 Act embraced both published and unpublished works, largely preempting state laws. However, the law still treats published and unpublished works differently in ways that may be significant with respect to digital preservation. Specifically, the exceptions that a library or archives has under section 108 to copy works for preservation and replacement depend on whether the work is published or unpublished. The scope of fair use is generally narrower with respect to works that are unpublished, particularly with respect to works that have not

---

[228] Sound recordings have only a limited public performance right that protects them when the performance is by means of a digital audio transmission. 17 U.S.C. § 106(6), 114 (2006).

[229] 17 U.S.C. §101 (2006).

[230] The copyright owner's exclusive distribution right, discussed above, is not limited to distribution of tangible copies. Making a work available to be received or viewed by the public over an electronic network has been held to be a public performance or display of the work. *E.g.*, Playboy Enters., Inc. v. Frena, 839 F. Supp. 1552 (M.D. Fla. 1993); *see* Metro-Goldwyn-Mayer Studios Inc. v. Grokster, Ltd., 545 U.S. 913, 929-30, 937-38 (2005); New York Times Co. v. Tasini, 533 U.S. 483, 497, 499-501 (2001). *But see* Atlantic Recording Corp. v. Howell, 2008 U.S. Dist. Lexis 35284 (D. Ariz. 2008) (making sound recordings available for downloading on the internet without authorization is not an infringement without evidence of actual distribution). "Streaming" a work over the internet is a public performance, and implicates the reproduction right as well; downloads of copyrighted works implicate both the distribution right (as discussed above) and the reproduction right.

been publicly disseminated in any form. And only published works are required to be deposited for the Library of Congress under the copyright law. These legal provisions will be discussed further below.

5.2.6 The law defines "publication" as the distribution of copies or phonorecords of a work to the public by sale or other transfer of ownership, or by rental, lease, or lending. The offering to distribute copies or phonorecords to a group of persons for purposes of further distribution, public performance, or public display, constitutes publication. A public performance or display of a work does not of itself constitute publication.[231]

5.2.7 The latter point deserves emphasis. The fact that a public performance or display does not alone amount to publication means that a work that is widely disseminated to the public through performance on the radio or television but not distributed in copies is technically still considered unpublished under the statute. Under the same reasoning, Internet sites that permit streaming but not downloading are technically unpublished, although this has not yet been conclusively resolved. Whether or not a work is published has implications for preservation, as will be discussed further below.

Infringement

5.2.8 Infringement occurs when someone exercises one or more of the exclusive rights without permission of the right holder or legal authorization in the form of an applicable exception or limitation. Infringement is said to be direct when the infringer is the individual that actually commits the wrongful act of copying, public distribution, etc.

5.2.9 Under U.S. copyright law, one can be liable for infringement even if one is not a direct infringer. There are two types of secondary liability. Vicarious liability applies where the defendant has the right and ability to supervise the infringing activity, and derives a direct financial benefit from it. Contributory liability applies where the defendant has knowledge of the infringing conduct, and induces or materially contributes to it. In *Sony Corp. of America v. Universal City Studios, Inc.*, the U.S. Supreme Court held that the mere sale of copying equipment does not result in secondary liability if the product has a substantial noninfringing use.[232] In

[231] 17 U.S.C. § 101 (2006).

[232] 464 U.S. 417, 441 (1984). The Supreme Court held that Sony was not liable for distributing videotape recorders because they were widely used for legal purposes: private, in-home taping of free television programs for later viewing was fair use; moreover, some rights holders consented to having their programs copied.

Metro-Goldwyn-Mayer Studios, Inc. v. Grokster,[233] however, the Court held that the distributor of a device capable of noninfringing use (in that case, peer to peer file-sharing software), can still be liable for infringement by third parties where the device is distributed with the object of promoting its use to infringe copyright, as demonstrated by statements or other affirmative steps taken to foster infringement.[234]

Moral Rights

5.2.10 When the United States joined the Berne Convention, it had no moral rights provisions in its copyright law. It took the position that the moral rights required by article 6bis of Berne were provided by a patchwork of laws including the federal Trademark Act ("the Lanham Act"),[235] state trademark and unfair competition laws, state moral rights laws and defamation law. The Visual Artists Rights Act (VARA), passed after the U.S. adhered to Berne and codified in section 106A of the U.S. Copyright Act, provides the moral rights of attribution and integrity to authors of certain types of visual works. However, VARA applies only to a narrowly defined category of works, and is more concerned with the integrity of the "original copies" than with reproductions.[236] The

---

233 125 S. Ct. 2764 (2005).

234 *Id.* at 2770. The court found evidence of defendants' intent to induce infringement in (1) their targeting advertisements promoting infringing use to former Napster users; (2) their failure to try to develop filtering tools or other means to reduce infringement; and (3) their business model, which relied on sales of advertising space for revenue, and was enhanced by the high volume infringing use.

235 *But see* Dastar Corp. v. Twentieth Century Fox Film Corp., 539 U.S. 23 (2003) (holding that the Lanham Act, in protecting against confusion concerning the "origin of goods," refers to the producer of tangible goods offered for sale – in that case, videotapes of a motion picture substantially based on an earlier work without attribution – and not to the author of any work embodied in those goods).

236 VARA applies to works of visual art, defined in 17 U.S.C. § 101 as

> (1) a painting, drawing, print or sculpture, existing in a single copy, in a limited edition of 200 copies or fewer that are signed and consecutively numbered by the author, or, in the case of a sculpture, in multiple cast, carved, or fabricated sculptures of 200 or fewer that are consecutively numbered by the author and bear the signature or other identifying mark of the author; or
> (2) a still photographic image produced for exhibition purposes only, existing in a single copy that is signed by the author, or in a limited edition of 200 copies or fewer that are signed and consecutively numbered by the author.
>
> A work of visual art does not include —
>
> (A) (i) any poster, map, globe, chart, technical drawing, diagram, model, applied art, motion picture or other audiovisual work, book, magazine, newspaper, periodical, data base, electronic information service, electronic publication, or similar publication;

exclusions from VARA make it unlikely that it will present issues for digital preservation.[237]

Database Rights

5.2.11 A database may be protected by copyright as a compilation if there is originality in the selection, coordination or arrangement of the contents, but that protection does not extend to underlying facts or data.[238] The United States has no *sui generis* protection for databases to supplement copyright protection. The U.S. Supreme Court in *Feist Publications, Inc. v. Rural Telephone Service*[239] rejected the notion that mere industry or "sweat of the brow" invested in the collection of data is sufficient to qualify a compilation for copyright. In rejecting copyright protection for a garden-variety "white pages" telephone directory, the Court held that some creativity in the selection, coordination or arrangement of the contents is required. Copyright in compilations and databases is said to be "thin," and does not extend to facts and data contained in them, which may be freely taken as long as the protectable selection, coordination or arrangement is not copied.

Performance Rights

5.2.12 The owners of copyrighted works (e.g., sound recordings (phonograms) and audiovisual works) have a right of public performance, as described above. The performer(s) may not be the right holders in such works, however, either because they are not deemed to be the author in the first instance or because they have transferred their rights to another. Copyright protects only works already fixed in a tangible medium of expression. Until 1994 there was no protection under federal law for the unauthorized fixation of performances. In connection with United States' adherence to the TRIPs agreement, U.S. law was amended to provide protection for performers against (1) fixation

---

(ii) any merchandising item or advertising, promotional, descriptive, covering, or packaging material or container;
(iii) any portion or part of any item described in clause (i) or (ii);
(B) any work made for hire; or
(C) any work not subject to copyright protection under this title

[237] VARA does not apply to reproductions of works of visual arts in books, periodicals, data bases, electronic information services, electronic publications and other categories excluded from the definition of "work of visual art." 17 U.S.C. 106A(c) (3) (2006). In addition, the modification of a work of art as the result of conservation or public presentation is not actionable unless it is the result of gross negligence. 17 U.S.C. 106A(c) (2) (2006).

[238] Feist Publications, Inc. v. Rural Telephone Service Co., 499 U.S. 340 (1991).

[239] 499 U.S. 340 (1991).

of a musical performance without their consent, (2) the unauthorized transmission of a live musical performance without their consent, or (3) the unauthorized distribution of a copy of any fixation made without the performers' consent.[240] The law applies only to musical performances, however.

5.2.13 Unfixed performances (whether or not musical) may have protection under state law. For example, in *Zacchini v. Scripps-Howard Broadcasting Co.*,[241] the U.S. Supreme Court upheld a state law right of publicity claim by a performer against a local TV news station that videotaped and broadcast his entire "human cannonball act" in the course of its coverage of entertainment at a state fair. The nature and scope of protection for unfixed performances can vary from state to state, however, and the law in this area is not well-developed.

Relevant Exceptions and Limitations

5.2.14 The rights under U.S. copyright law are subject to many exceptions and limitations. Those most relevant to digital preservation are fair use and the exceptions for libraries and archives in section 108 of the Copyright Act.[242]

5.2.15 "Fair use" excuses otherwise infringing activity. Whether a use is fair depends on the facts of a particular case. Certain uses are favored in the statute: criticism, comment, news reporting, teaching (including multiple copies for classroom use), scholarship and research. However, these uses are not automatically considered fair (nor are other uses automatically considered unfair). There are four factors that must be evaluated in every case: (1) the purpose and character of the use, (2) the nature of the copyrighted work, (3) the amount and substantiality of the portion used, and (4) the effect of the use on the potential market for or value of the copyrighted work.[243]

---

240 17 U.S.C. § 1101 (2006).

241 Zacchini v. Scripps-Howard Broadcasting Co., 433 U.S. 562 (1977).

242 All works created by U.S. government employees in the course of their employment are in the public domain in the United States. 17 U.S.C. § 105 (2006). It is important to bear this in mind in reviewing the descriptions of various federal government preservation initiatives that provide access to government materials.

243 17 U.S.C. §107 (2006). The legislative history of the 1976 Copyright Act indicates that preservation activities may qualify as fair use. H.R. Rep. 94-1476, 94th Cong. 2d Sess. 73 (1976) (citing the urgency of preserving pre-1942 motion pictures and stating that making duplicate copies of such works for archival preservation "certainly falls within the scope of 'fair use'").

5.2.16 Section 108 contains several exceptions specific to libraries and archives. To qualify for any of the section 108 exceptions, the library or archives must be open to the public, or at least to researchers in a specialized field; the reproduction and distribution may not be for commercial advantage; and the library or archives must include a copyright notice or legend on copies.[244]

5.2.17 Section 108(b) allows libraries and archives to make up to three copies of an *unpublished* copyrighted work in their collections "solely for purposes of preservation and security or for deposit for research use in another library or archives." The work must be currently in the collections of the library or archives, and any copy made in digital format may not be made available to the public in that format outside the library premises.

5.2.18 Section 108(c) allows libraries and archives to make up to three copies of a *published* work to replace a work in their collections that is damaged, deteriorating, lost or stolen or whose format has become obsolete, if the library determines after reasonable effort that an unused replacement cannot be obtained at a fair price.[245] "Obsolete" means the machine or device needed to "render perceptible a work stored in that format" is "no longer manufactured or is no longer reasonably available in the commercial marketplace."[246] As with copies of unpublished works, copies in digital format may not be made available to the public outside the library premises.[247]

---

[244] This report focuses on the provisions of section 108 that relate to preservation, but section 108 also allows libraries and archives to make single copies for users under certain conditions. They may reproduce articles and short excerpts at the request of users, and they may reproduce a complete work or a substantial portion thereof at a user's request if the work cannot be obtained at a fair price. 17 U.S.C. § 108(d) (e) (2006). However, they may not engage in systematic reproduction and distribution of copies. Libraries may enter into interlibrary arrangements provided the copies they receive under the arrangement do not substitute for a purchase or subscription. 17 U.S.C. § 108(g) (2006).

[245] Until the Digital Millennium Copyright Act (DMCA), Pub. L. No. 105-304, 112 Stat. 2860, 2889, was passed in 1998, the copying privileges in sections 108(b) and (c) were limited to "a copy" of a work "in facsimile form." The DMCA changed these sections to permit up to three copies and to allow those copies to be made in digital form. Although Congress was attempting to accommodate the changing needs of libraries and archives in the digital world, the three copy limit reflected the preservation standard for microfilm rather than any digital preservation standard. The legislative history of the DMCA also indicates that the section 108 exceptions were not intended to apply to digital archives available exclusively via the Internet. S. Rep. No. 105-190, 105th Cong., 2d Sess. 61-62 (1998).

[246] 17 U.S.C. § 108(c)(2) (2006).

[247] The Copyright Office has stated that this provision does not permit "preemptive archival activity to preserve works before they become obsolete." *Recommendation of the Register of Copyrights in RM 2002-4; Rulemaking on Exemptions from the Prohibition*

5.2.19 Section 108(f)(3) allows libraries and archives to reproduce and distribute "a limited number of copies and excerpts . . . of an audiovisual news program." This exception was intended to allow libraries to make off-the-air recordings of daily newscasts of the national television networks "for limited distribution to scholars and researchers for use in research purposes."[248] Section 108(h) allows a library, archives, or nonprofit educational institution to reproduce, distribute, perform or display in facsimile or digital form a copy of a published work during the last 20 years of its copyright term, for purposes of preservation, scholarship or research. The exception applies only if the work is not subject to normal exploitation and cannot be obtained at a reasonable price.[249]

5.2.20 Section 108(f)(4) makes clear that nothing in section 108 affects the ability of libraries and archives to rely on fair use. In other words, section 108 does not represent the outer limits of permissible activities by libraries and archives.

Legal Deposit

5.2.21 The copyright owner of a work published in the United States is required to deposit two copies of the "best edition"[250] in the Copyright Office "for the use or disposition of the Library of Congress."[251] Mandatory deposit is one of the principal means by which the Library of Congress builds its collections. The law provides the Library with an opportunity to acquire the deposit copies, but it does not require the Library to acquire them, or to preserve them.[252] The Library may exempt certain categories, or require the deposit of only one copy.

---

on Circumvention of Copyright Protection Systems for Access Control Technologies (Oct. 27, 2003) at 63.

248 H.R. Rep. No. 94-1476, 94th Cong., 2d Sess. 77 (1976).

249 17 U.S.C. § 108(h) (2006). To take advantage of this privilege, an institution must first make a reasonable investigation to determine that the work meets these criteria and that the copyright owner has not filed a notice to the contrary in the Copyright Office.

250 17 U.S.C. § 407(a) (2006). Failure to comply with deposit requirements can result in fines.

251 17 U.S.C. § 407(b) (2006).

252 17 U.S.C. § 704 (2006). Rights holders are required to deposit works for the Library regardless of whether they register the copyright, but if they do register, the copies submitted with registration application can serve as the deposit copies. *Id.* § 408(b). Deposits made in connection with registration that are not selected by the Library are retained by the Copyright Office "for the longest period considered practical and desirable by the Register of Copyrights and the Librarian of Congress." After that period they may, in their joint discretion, order the disposal or other disposition of copies of published works. *Id.* § 704 (d). While the Library collects widely, what it "particularly preserves

5.2.22 The Copyright Act allows the Library of Congress to retain deposited published works for its collections, or to use them for exchange or transfer to any other library.[253] The Copyright Office is entitled to make "a facsimile reproduction" for its records of works deposited in connection with applications for registration before transferring the copies to the Library of Congress.[254]

5.2.23 As discussed above, under the definition of publication in the Copyright Act, a work is deemed published only if it is distributed in copies. Works distributed over the Internet in a manner that allows downloading (with the right holder's authorization) are generally considered published.[255] On the other hand, works that are publicly disseminated solely through performance (for example, on the radio or television, or streamed over the Internet) but not distributed in copies are generally considered unpublished and therefore not subject to the general mandatory deposit requirement.

5.2.24 To allow the Library to acquire non-syndicated radio and television programming for its collections without imposing undue hardship on copyright owners, the law permits the Library to tape "transmission programs" and make a copy for archival purposes. It also allows the Register of Copyrights to make a demand for deposit of a specific transmission program (which the broadcaster can satisfy by gift, a loan to allow the Library to copy it, or by sale at cost), but does not permit blanket demands.[256] A transmission program is "a body of material that, as an aggregate, has been produced for the sole purpose of transmission to the public in sequence and as a unit."[257]

Technological Protection Measures Provisions

5.2.25 Technological protection measures encompass software, devices or other technologies used to block or limit access to a work, or

---

tends to be its special collections – those unique maps, manuscripts, photographs, films, radio broadcasts, and materials in other formats held only by the Library of Congress." Deanna Marcum and Amy Friedlander, Keepers of the Crumbling Culture, D-Lib Magazine May 2003, available at http://www.dlib.org/dlib/may03/friedlander/-05friedlander.html.

[253] 17 U.S.C. § 704 (b) (2006).

[254] 17 U.S.C. § 704 (c) (2006).

[255] *But see* discussion in section 5.2.7, *supra.*

[256] 17 U.S.C. § 407(e) (2006).

[257] 17 U.S.C. § 101 (2006).

certain actions with respect to the work (e.g., copying). TPMs include such things as encryption, passwords, and access controls.

5.2.26 Section 1201 of Title 17, enacted as part of the 1998 the Digital Millennium Copyright Act, prohibits anyone from circumventing a "technological measure that effectively controls access to a work . . . ."[258] There is no ban on circumventing a technological measure that protects a right of a copyright owner (such as a copy control).[259] Section 1201 also prohibits manufacturing, providing, or trafficking in devices or services primarily intended to circumvent access controls *or* rights controls.[260]

5.2.27 There are a number of exceptions to these anti-circumvention provisions set out in section 1201, but none of them apply to library and archives copying for preservation.[261] In addition to the specific exemptions set out in the statute, section 1201 provides for a rulemaking proceeding conducted by the Copyright Office every three years. The purpose of the proceeding is to determine whether users of any particular class of copyrighted works are, or are likely to be, adversely affected in their ability to make non-infringing uses by the prohibition against circumventing technological access controls. If so, the Librarian of Congress, upon the recommendation of the Copyright Office, will promulgate additional exemptions. Those exemptions remain in effect only until the next rulemaking proceeding, however, so a new application must be filed every three years if an exemption is to remain in effect.

5.2.28 In the most recent rulemaking proceeding the Office allowed an exception for

> Computer programs and video games distributed in formats that have become obsolete and which require the original media or hardware as a condition of

---

[258] 17 U.S.C. § 1201(a)(1)(A) (2006).

[259] If the circumventor goes on to make an infringing use of the protected work, he will be liable under copyright law. With current technologies, however, there is not always a clear line between access controls and rights controls. *See, e.g.*, Register's Recommendation of Oct. 27, 2003, *supra* note 247 at 44-45.

[260] 17 U.S.C. 1201(a)(2) and (b) (2006).

[261] 17 U.S.C. 1201(d) (2006) provides an exemption for nonprofit libraries, archives and educational institutions for purposes of determining whether to purchase a work, but it is not applicable to preservation copying. There are also exemptions for law enforcement and other government activities, reverse engineering, encryption research, preventing access by minors to material on the internet, protection of personally identifying information, and security testing. 17 U.S.C. 1201(e)-(j) (2006).

> access, when the circumvention is accomplished for the purpose of preservation or archival reproduction of published digital works by a library or archive.[262]

The Internet Archive, which sought the exemption, demonstrated that the ability to circumvent access controls on those works was critical to its preservation efforts.

5.2.29 Even though the Librarian is empowered to create additional exemptions, he cannot affect the ban on trafficking in circumvention devices and services, so the means to take advantage of the exception may not be available.

Copyright Law and Contracts

5.2.30 In general, the copyright law provides "default rules" that may be overridden by valid contracts. Subsection 108(f)(4) makes clear that the provisions of section 108 do not supersede any contractual obligations a library may have (e.g., under a subscription or donor agreement) with respect to a work that it wishes to copy.

5.3 The Impact of Copyright and Related Laws on Digital Preservation Activities in the United States

Effect of Copyright and Related Laws on Digital Preservation

5.3.1 U.S. copyright law presents significant challenges to digital preservation of copyrighted works. Section 108 was intended to enable certain preservation activities, but because it was created in an earlier era it is not broad enough to encompass many digital preservation activities, as explained below. For that reason, libraries and archives must rely on both section 108 and the fair use doctrine.

5.3.2 *Preservation of published works.* There is no specific authorization for libraries and archives to make preservation copies of *published* works in their collections. Section 108(c) deals with copying for replacement and does not specifically address preservation. It is sometimes viewed as a preservation provision because it enables libraries to maintain in their collections copies of works that would otherwise be lost. But to be eligible for copying under this section, the work must be lost, stolen, damaged, deteriorating or in an obsolete format, and then may be copied only if, after reasonable effort, the library or

---

[262] *Exemption to Prohibition on Circumvention of Copyright Protection Systems for Access Control Technologies*, 71 Fed. Reg. 68472, 68474 (Nov. 27, 2006).

archives determines that an unused replacement cannot be obtained at a fair price. It does not allow preservation before one of these triggering events occurs, and thus is ineffective as a means to preserve works that can easily be damaged or lost before preservation copies can be made, such as born digital works, and fragile or rare works. Moreover, "obsolete" is narrowly defined, as explained above. Under the statutory definition, even vinyl LP record albums are not considered obsolete, because record players are still readily available in the marketplace.

5.3.3 *Three-copy limit.* As discussed above, preservation requires making numerous copies to create and maintain preservation copies. "Copies," however, are defined broadly under U.S. law, and include even temporary reproductions in the short-term memory of a computer when a user views a work.[263] As described above, digital preservation necessitates the making of numerous copies, including the multiple, distributed permanent copies called for under best practices, as well as the innumerable temporary copies created whenever a digital work is accessed or transmitted in the course of collecting, curating, maintaining and providing access to the work. Section 108 (b) of the Copyright Act – which authorizes copying of unpublished works for preservation or for deposit in another library or archives – limits a library or archives to making only three copies. Similarly, section 108 (c) limits a library or archives to making only three copies of published works for replacement purposes. The three-copy limit is impracticable in the context of digital preservation.

5.3.4 *No copying for acquisition*. With few exceptions,[264] the library and archives exceptions in U.S. copyright law allow libraries to make copies only of works already in their collections; they do not permit libraries to copy for purposes of acquisition. However, many works are now made available to the public without making copies available for purchase or sale (e.g., much Internet content, many television and radio programs, etc.). As a result, these

[263] *E.g.,* MAI Systems Corp. v. Peak Computer, 991 F.2d 511 (9th Cir. 1993), cert. dismissed, 114 S. Ct. 671 (1994); see U.S. Copyright Office, DMCA Section 104 Report 118 (August 2001). Thus, there is no exemption for temporary acts of reproduction to facilitate a lawful use as is provided for in Art. 5(1) of Directive 2001/29/EC of the European Parliament and of the Council of 22 May 2001 on the harmonisation of certain aspects of copyright and related rights in the information society, Official Journal L 167, 22/06/2001 P. 0010 – 0019. In some cases, however, temporary, incidental copies made to facilitate a lawful use might be considered a fair use.

[264] 17 U.S.C. § 108 (b) (2006) does permit copying for deposit in another library, thus potentially adding to the depository library's collections. In addition, libraries may copy audiovisual news programs under section 108(f)(3), and they may copy works in the last 20 years of copyright pursuant to section 108(h) if the requirements of that section are met. *See* discussion in section 5.2.19, *supra*. In some cases copying for acquisition may be permissible under the doctrine of fair use, discussed in section 5.2.15, *supra*.

works do not become part of the libraries' collections through purchase or sale, and there is no specific exception that allows libraries to copy general programming from television, radio or the Internet. Works not distributed in copies may be at risk, because (with the exception of television news programming) they are not being acquired by libraries and archives and are therefore not being systematically preserved. See, however, the discussion of the Internet Archive in sections 5.4.45 and 5.4.46, below.

Limitations of mandatory deposit

5.3.5 Although the mandatory deposit provisions require that two copies of the best edition of works published in the United States be deposited with the Copyright Office for the benefit of the Library of Congress, the law presents a number of obstacles to comprehensive digital preservation for these works. First, as discussed above, not all copyrighted works are embraced within the mandatory deposit provisions. They apply only to published works, that is, those that are distributed in copies with the authorization of the copyright owner. Assuming that works that can be downloaded from the Internet with the authorization of the right holder are published, deposit of such works could be required under section 407, although the regulations currently do not require deposit of such works. There are many works that are available on the Internet, however, that are available only for streaming and not for downloading, and assuming those works are not considered published under the law, they are generally not subject to mandatory deposit.

5.3.6 Second, the statute specifically requires the deposit of copies of the published edition(s) of each work, but many electronic works published over the Internet are not published in preservation-quality copies. For example, an e-journal made available on the Internet is deemed published if copies can be downloaded, but those copies generally are in formats that are not of preservation quality. Even for works distributed in tangible copies, such as CD or DVD format, there may be characteristics of the work as published – for example, technological protection measures – that make it unsuitable to serve as a preservation copy.

5.3.7 Third, there are limits to what the Library can do with the deposits it receives through mandatory deposit. The law allows the Library to keep the work deposited or to give it to another library. It provides the Library with no specific authorization to exercise any of the copyright owner's rights. Thus the Library may not make and distribute copies, or publicly perform a motion picture that it received through mandatory deposit. Moreover, the Library does not currently have the clear right even to make incidental, temporary copies in managing, preserving, or providing access to such works acquired without a license, and thus, unless statutory authority to do so were granted, the Library would have to rely on arguments of fair use or implied license.

5.3.8 The legal limitations of mandatory deposit are not the only obstacle to preservation of digital materials, however. The Library does not have the capacity to retain and preserve all digital works published in the United States. While the Library is working on updating its regulations, those regulations currently do not require deposit of materials published only electronically (e.g., on websites), because of the large number of still unresolved issues raised by the mandatory deposit of such materials, including those related to best edition. This issue is discussed further below.

Fair use

5.3.9 Other than section 108 and mandatory deposit, fair use is the legal doctrine that provides the greatest support for preservation activities with respect to copyrighted works. As noted above, section 108 limits libraries to making three copies to preserve unpublished works in their collections or to replace lost, stolen, damaged, deteriorating or obsolete copies of published works that they cannot obtain on the market at a fair price. But a three-copy limit is simply unworkable in the context of digital preservation, so libraries rely on fair use in making the necessary additional copies. Similarly, they sometimes rely on fair use to make replacement copies of works that technically do not meet the criteria – for example, of very rare or fragile copies that are not yet damaged but easily could be with regular user access, or of works whose playback device is no longer common in the marketplace, though still available and therefore the work is not technically obsolete. Libraries and archives also rely on fair use when they authorize independent contractors to act on their behalf in taking advantage of the section 108 exceptions, since by its terms section 108 applies only to library and archives employees.

5.3.10 Web archiving activities also use fair use for their legal justification. Under section 108, libraries and archives are generally not permitted to copy in order to acquire new materials for their collections.[265] The Internet Archive relies on fair use to justify its copying and archiving of web material, as does the Library of Congress in specific cases. Relying on fair use rather than section 108 or another exception does affect the scope of

[265] There are a few exceptions to this general principle: libraries and archives are allowed to copy and circulate copies of audiovisual news programs; a library or archives may make and provide to another library a copy of an unpublished work in its collections, thus adding to the collection of the second library or archives; and the Library of Congress may copy "transmission programs" under certain circumstances.

libraries' and archives' activities, however. The Internet Archive, presumably to bolster its claim of fair use and to avoid the risk of suit, will respect right holders' requests not to crawl and copy their sites, and will take down any sites it has already archived on request of the owner. As a result, it does not acquire a comprehensive web archive.

5.3.11 Libraries and archives that copy online content in reliance on fair use must be careful about diverting users from websites, because the effect on the right holder's actual or potential market is an important fair use consideration. For this reason, the Library of Congress's general practice is to seek permissions in connection with any media sites that it crawls, and it will make publicly available only those sites whose owners grant permission. Another way that libraries and archives attempt to minimize harm to the website is to delay providing access to collected web material for some period of time.

5.3.12 It is important to recognize that legal restrictions are not the only obstacle to digital preservation, and perhaps not even the most significant obstacle. Uncertainty as to preservation practices and standards, lack of technical expertise, lack of resources, and a general lack of understanding of these complex issues all compound the problem.

Potential Risks to Exclusive Rights Held by Creators and Other Right Holders

5.3.13 Right holders may perceive digital preservation activities as a threat to their economic interests. It is not digital preservation per se that is problematic, but rather access to digital preservation copies. Libraries and other preservation institutions commonly regard access as a necessary component of preservation activities. For example, they may be unable to justify the investment in preservation if the works are not accessible to users until the copyrights expire (which could take many decades).[266] They may also believe that user access to the digital archive is essential to evaluating and maintaining the integrity of the data.

5.3.14 Right holders of "born digital" works often rely on a subscription model in which they provide access to those works rather than selling copies outright, and they fear that libraries and archives, by providing access to preservation copies, will compete directly with

266 *See, e.g., YEA: The Yale Electronic Archive, Report on the Digital Preservation Planning Project* 22-23, 33 (February 2002), *available at* http://www.library.yale.edu/~okerson/yea/frontmatter.pdf. This project was a collaboration between the Yale University Library and Elsevier Science, funded by the Andrew W. Mellon Foundation.

them. Even where their business models rely on sales, right holders may be concerned that if libraries and archives can provide free access to their works, sales will diminish. These concerns are most acute for right holders of works with small profit margins whose sales are predominately to libraries and educational institutions – but they are not limited to those right holders. Right holders are also concerned about the proliferation of digital copies and resulting security risks.

5.3.15 For works whose principal economic return occurs within a short time of their release, the concerns about library and archives competition diminish significantly over time.[267] But markets are changing, and some types of works once thought to exhaust their economic potential within a short time after their release could provide revenue long into the future.[268]

5.3.16 The digitization of analog works for preservation raises additional concerns for right holders. They fear that allowing public access to those digital preservation copies will restrict their ability to enter new markets. Right holders may delay market entry in order to negotiate the necessary rights for digital distribution, which can sometimes be a time-consuming process. Moreover, in some cases it was a conscious decision on the part of the right holder not to make the work available in digital form. In right holders' view, libraries and archives that digitize these works and make them accessible to users compete with an unfair advantage since they can bypass rights clearance issues. Such activities, in their view, could effectively preempt the introduction of a digital version of an existing analog work, and deprive authors and other right holders of any financial return from the exploitation of their works in digital markets.

5.4 Overview of Responses to the Issue of Copyright and Digital Preservation in the United States

Copyright Law Reform

5.4.1 There are a number of proposals for amendment of the copyright law currently under discussion. Those most relevant to digital preservation are discussed below.

[267] See the discussion of JSTOR in sections 5.4.33-34, below.

[268] Internet distribution channels such as Amazon.com make it possible to provide consumers with a wider range of products than ever before, effectively allowing older works to stay in "inventory" and continue to generate revenues for their copyright owners for many years, instead of being removed to make way for newly-introduced works. *See generally* Chris Anderson, *The Long Tail* (2007).

Section 108

5.4.2 The Section 108 Study Group was convened as an independent group by the National Digital Information Infrastructure and Preservation Program of the Library of Congress and by the U.S. Copyright Office. It was formed to consider whether and how section 108 of the Copyright Act should be amended to address the issues and concerns of libraries and archives, as well as those of creators and other right holders, and to provide recommendations on how to revise the copyright law to insure an appropriate balance that serves the national interest. The Study Group, composed of experts from the library and archives community, the right holder communities, and others, issued its final report in March 2008.[269]

5.4.3 The Study Group made several recommendations relevant to digital preservation. Proposals in the report were characterized as recommendations when the group unanimously agreed that a legislative change is appropriate and on the general nature of that change. In many cases, however, the recommendations are subject to the resolution of related outstanding issues, discussed in detail in the Report.[270]

Section 108 Group Recommendations Concerning Eligibility for Library and Archives Exceptions

5.4.4 The Study Group had a cluster of recommendations concerning eligibility for the libraries and archives exceptions.

- *Museums.* First, it recommended that museums should be eligible under section 108. It is unclear why museums were not included when the law was originally drafted, but the group agreed that museums' legitimate need to reproduce copyright protected materials is greater than in the past, and that there are strong public policy grounds for adding museums to the

---

[269] *See* The Section 108 Study Group Report (Mar. 2008), *available at* http://www.section108.gov/docs/Sec108StudyGroupReport.pdf [hereafter, "Section 108 Group Report"].

[270] For more detail on the recommendations themselves and the underlying issues still to be resolved in formulating legislation, see the Section 108 Group Report, *supra* note 269. The report also describes the Group's conclusions in areas in which the Group had substantive discussions and agreed that a legislative solution might be appropriate, but had no specific recommendations on major issues, as well as other outcomes concerning additional issues that the Group discussed.

cultural institutions granted copyright exceptions in section 108.[271]

- *Functional requirements.* Second, the group recommended that institutions seeking to avail themselves of the section 108 exceptions should have to meet certain threshold eligibility requirements. Currently the law does not define "library" or "archive" and provides only minimal eligibility requirements.[272] When the law was drafted there was a common understanding of what was meant by a library or an archive, but now many collections of materials – analog and digital – use those terms. The Study Group found it difficult to create definitions, but decided that including functional requirements would appropriately distinguish between those institutions that should be permitted to use the section 108 exceptions and those that should not. The new eligibility requirements recommended by the Study Group would supplement those already in the statute. They include possessing a public service mission, providing professional services normally associated with libraries and archives, employing a trained library or archives staff, and possessing a collection comprising lawfully acquired and/or licensed materials.

- *Outside contractors.* Third, the Study Group recommended that libraries and archives should be allowed to use outside contractors to assist them in their activities pursuant to the section 108 exceptions, under certain conditions. The Study Group recognized that because many libraries and archives do not have the specialized expertise required for digital preservation and other permitted library activities, it may be more efficient and practical for them to outsource certain activities. Specifically, the recommendation is that libraries and archives may use outside contractors, provided:

    a. The contractor is acting solely as the provider of a service for which compensation is made by the library or archives, and not for any other direct or indirect commercial benefit.

    b. The contractor is contractually prohibited from retaining copies other than as necessary to perform the contracted-for service.

    c. The agreement between the library or archives and the

---

271 Thus, while the recommendations generally refer to "libraries and archives," the report makes clear that the recommendations are applicable to museums as well.

272 The current requirements are that the institution must be open to the public, or at least to researchers in a specialized field; the reproduction may not be for any purpose of direct or indirect commercial advantage; and any copy made must include a copyright notice or legend. 17 U.S.C. § 108(a) (2006).

> contractor preserves a meaningful ability on the part of the right holder to obtain redress from the contractor for infringement by the contractor.[273]

These conditions are designed to ensure that the contractors will not exploit the right holders' works for their own purposes, and that there is some means of enforcing the law against contractors in the event they misuse the copyrighted works provided to them in the course of their work for a library or archives. Otherwise, there may be significant obstacles to effective enforcement of the law against a contractor, particularly if the contractor is not subject to U.S. jurisdiction or has no significant assets in the United States.

Section 108 Study Group Recommendation Concerning Preservation of Publicly Disseminated Works

5.4.5 Many published works are at risk of loss if copies are not made before harm occurs. This is particularly true with respect to works in digital form, which can deteriorate very quickly to the point at which they cannot be used or restored. Preservation must begin early in the work's life. As explained above, digital preservation requires making multiple copies over a work's life – for example, to monitor the integrity of the work, to migrate it to new formats as technology progresses, and to provide backup copies in case of catastrophic failure. Section 108 as currently drafted, however, does not provide for the making of preservation copies of published works – only of unpublished works.

5.4.6 Accordingly, the Study Group proposed a new exception to allow libraries and archives qualified for digital preservation to undertake preemptive preservation of "at risk" publicly disseminated works in their collections, which could extend as well to those works in their collections that have been publicly disseminated but nevertheless are technically considered unpublished under the law.[274] Specifically, the group recommended:

> An exception should be added to section 108 to permit a library or archives qualified under the proposed exception to make a limited number of copies as reasonably necessary to create and maintain a preservation copy of any at risk published or other

273 Section 108 Group Report, *supra* note 269, at 39.

274 As discussed above, under U.S. law a work can be widely disseminated via a broadcast, stream or other performance but is technically unpublished as long as it has not been distributed in copies. Such works occasionally make their way into library collections. *See, e.g.,* 17 U.S.C. § 108 (f)(3) (2006) (permitting libraries and archives to copy and lend audiovisual news programs).

publicly disseminated work in its collections, provided that:

a. The number of copies made is limited to those that are reasonably necessary to create and maintain a copy of the work for preservation purposes, in accordance with recognized best practices;

b. The library or archives restricts access to the preservation copies to that which is necessary to effectively maintain and preserve the work;

c. The preservation copies may be used to make copies pursuant to subsections 108(c) or (h); and

d. The preservation copies are labeled as such.[275]

5.4.7 Among the most difficult issues the group faced was how "recognized best practices" should be identified, and who should determine whether a particular library or archive is qualified to make digital preservation copies. The group acknowledged that best practices are still developing and could not be described in detail in the statute. The Section 108 Study Group Report suggested that best practices might be defined with reference to trusted sources of best practices, or through regulations that could be updated from time to time. The recommendation includes general criteria relevant to determining if a library or archives is qualified:

> Criteria to determine if a particular library or archives is "qualified" to avail itself of this exception should include whether the library or archives:
>
> a. Maintains preservation copies in a secure, managed, and monitored environment utilizing recognized best practices. The following general principles for "best practices" should be observed for digital preservation (and for analog preservation to the extent applicable):
>
> i) A robust storage system with backup and recovery services;
>
> ii) A standard means of verifying the integrity of incoming and outgoing files, and for continuing integrity checks;
>
> iii) The ability to assess and record the format, provenance, intellectual property rights, and other significant properties of the information to be preserved;
>
> iv) Unique and persistent naming of information

[275] Section 108 Group Report, *supra* note 269, at 69.

objects so that they can be easily identified and located;

v) A standard security apparatus to control authorized access to the preservation copies; and

vi) The ability to store digital files in formats that can be easily transferred and used should the library or archives of record need to change.

b. Provides an open, transparent means of auditing archival practices;

c. Possesses the ability to fund the cost of long-term preservation;

d. Possesses a demonstrable commitment to the preservation mission; and

e. Provides a succession plan for preservation copies in the event the qualified library or archives ceases to exist or can no longer adequately manage its collections.[276]

The Study Group did not reach agreement on a procedural mechanism for determining whether a library or archives qualifies for this new exception, e.g., whether a library or archives could determine for itself whether it qualifies or whether it must be certified by a third party, whether compliance audits would be required, etc. The group did, however, agree that it was important not to exclude smaller institutions such as local archives that hold valuable material. Accordingly, part of the recommendation is that the qualifying criteria "should make allowances for institutions with limited resources that cannot create their own sophisticated preservation systems."

Section 108 Study Group Recommendation Concerning Publicly Available Online Content

5.4.8 Copyright protected material that is publicly disseminated online, including for example websites, blogs and various forms of "user generated content," presents new and unique preservation issues. Much of this material is not available for purchase by libraries and archives that wish to preserve it, and U.S. law generally does not allow libraries and archives to copy material for the purpose of adding it to their collections. Asking permission can be a time-consuming and often fruitless endeavor, and may simply not be possible where the material is ephemeral (for example, Web content concerning fast-breaking political events or natural disasters).

[276] *Id.* at 69-70.

5.4.9 Accordingly, the Study Group recommended:

> A new exception should be added to section 108 to permit libraries and archives to capture and reproduce publicly available online content for preservation purposes, and to make those copies accessible to users for purposes of private study, scholarship, or research.
>
> a. "Publicly available" for purposes of this exception is defined as publicly disseminated online content (such as websites) that is not restricted by access controls or any type of registration, password, or other gateway requiring an affirmative act by the user to access the content.
>
> b. Once a library or archives has captured publicly available online content, it should be allowed to provide access to its preservation copies of this content to researchers on the library's or archives' premises.
>
> c. Libraries and archives should be permitted to make the captured content available remotely to their users, but only after a specified period of time has elapsed.[277]

5.4.10 Under the recommendation, right holders would be able to opt out of allowing libraries and archives to capture their publicly available online content, provided that the Library of Congress is entitled to copy and preserve all publicly available online content, regardless of the right holder's desire to opt out. Government and political websites would not be entitled to opt out, however. Right holders that permit capture and preservation of their publicly available online content may separately opt out of allowing libraries and archives to make their content available remotely to users.

5.4.11 There are two additional conditions to this recommendation. Libraries and archives would be prohibited from engaging in activities that are likely to materially harm the value or operations of the Internet site hosting the online content that is sought to be captured and made available. Libraries and archives would also have to label copies of captured online content that are made accessible to users with the date of capture and a legend indicating that it is an archived copy for use only for private study, scholarship, and research.

---

277 *Id.* at 80.

Other Recommendations by the Section 108 Study Group Relevant to Digital Preservation

5.4.12 In addition to the recommendations discussed above, the Study Group made several other recommendations relevant to digital preservation. With respect to replacement copies of unpublished works in section 108 (c), it recommended:

- The 3-copy limit for replacement copies should be changed to allow libraries and archives to make "a limited number of copies as reasonably necessary." The Study Group agreed that the 3-copy limit is not feasible in the context of digital preservation, which requires multiple copies over time. Because there is no precise number of copies that would allow a library or archives to digitally replace and preserve analog works, the group recommended a flexible standard, while limiting the number of copies available to users to the number actually replaced.

- A new "trigger" should be added to section 108 (c) to permit replacement copying of "fragile" originals. A "fragile" copy is one "embodied in a physical medium that is at risk of becoming unusable because it is delicate or easily destroyed or broken and cannot be handled without risk of harm."[278] This change would allow libraries and archives to make replacement copies of works likely to deteriorate so the fragile copy can be kept in storage and the replacement provided to users.

- A library or archives would be required to search for a usable copy – rather than an unused copy – at a fair price before it could make a replacement copy. The Study Group recognized that it is much easier to search for pre-owned copies now with Internet search tools, and that many pre-owned copies are new or virtually new. The copy must be in good condition and suitable for library or archives purposes, however.

5.4.13 With respect to preservation and security copies of unpublished works in section 108 (b), the group recommended:

- The exception in section 108 (b) should be limited to unpublished works that have not been publicly disseminated.[279] In the Study Group's view, section 108 (b)

[278] *Id.* at 54-55.

[279] For purposes of the Section 108 Report, "publicly disseminated" refers to works that have been intentionally made available to the public by any means whatsoever, including broadcast or electronic transmission via the Internet or other online media, whether or not distributed or offered for distribution in material copies.

was intended primarily to cover works neither publicly disseminated nor intended for public dissemination. Those unpublished works that have been publicly disseminated through streaming or broadcast are better addressed through the recommended exceptions for "preservation-only" copying of publicly disseminated works in libraries' and archives' collections, and for preservation of online content.

- The 3-copy limit for preservation and security copies of unpublished works should be changed to allow libraries and archives to make "a limited number of copies as reasonably necessary." The Group's rationale was the same as that for providing a similar formulation for replacement copies of published works.

- The number of deposit copies of unpublished works that can be made should be amended to a reasonable limit on the number of institutions to which libraries and archives can deposit a copy of an unpublished work. A library or archive that receives a deposit copy of an unpublished work from another library or archives should not be permitted to make further copies for preservation or for deposit in other libraries or archives. The Study Group's position was that this recommendation would increase scholarly access to unpublished works and guard against catastrophic loss, while use of these works on the premises of these institutions would not have a significant adverse impact on the authors' right of first publication.

Areas Where the Study Group Did Not Agree on Recommendations

5.4.14 There were certain issues potentially relevant to digital preservation that the Study Group discussed, but did not agree on.

- *Licenses and Other Contracts.* Currently section 108(f)(4) states that nothing in section 108 in any way affects contractual obligations. The Study Group explored whether there were circumstances in which any of the section 108 exceptions should apply despite contrary terms of a license or other contract. The Study Group agreed that the terms of any negotiated, enforceable contract should continue to apply notwithstanding the section 108 exceptions. The group disagreed, however, as to whether the exceptions in section 108, particularly those dealing with preservation and replacement, should trump contrary terms in non-negotiable agreements.

- *Circumvention of Technological Protection Measures.* Currently libraries and archives are not permitted to circumvent TPMs that effectively control access to a work ("technological access controls") for the purposes of exercising the section 108 exceptions. The Study Group explored whether circumvention of technological access controls should ever be permitted, particularly for replacement and preservation copying. The Group did not agree on whether a recommendation in this area was needed, and, if so, what kind of recommendation would be appropriate.

5.4.15 The Study Group made some additional recommendations and conclusions that address other aspects of section 108, such as the copies for users provisions, which are not discussed here.

5.4.16 The Study Group's report was issued in March 2008. The report was presented to the U.S. Copyright Office, which will review it and solicit further input before making its recommendations to Congress.

Orphan Works Legislation

5.4.17 In 2005 the Copyright Office undertook an inquiry into the problem of copyrighted works whose owners cannot be identified or located by potential users, referred to as "orphan works." The Office was concerned that the inability to locate copyright owners was discouraging beneficial uses of copyrighted works. Potential users were reluctant to make orphan works available to the public, or use them as the basis for new creative endeavors, because they were concerned that if the copyright owner later came forward they could incur substantial damages, or be forced to settle for an amount disproportionate to the value of the use in order to avoid an injunction.

5.4.18 The Office issued its report in January 2006, and recommended that the Copyright Act be amended to limit the remedies available against users of orphan works who (1) demonstrate that they performed a reasonably diligent search to find the copyright owner without success and (2) provide reasonable attribution to the author and copyright owner. The limitation on remedies the Office proposed was twofold. First, it would limit monetary relief to reasonable compensation for the use – completely eliminating monetary relief where the use is noncommercial and the user ceases the use upon notice. Second, it would limit the ability of the copyright owner to obtain injunctive relief, so that a user who relied on the work's orphan status could continue to exploit a derivative work based on that orphan work, with appropriate compensation to the right holder. Orphan works legislation, based in part on the Copyright Office report, was introduced but not passed in 2006. It was recently reintroduced in both houses of Congress.[280]

5.4.19 The new bills follow the same general framework of the Copyright Office proposal. If a user does a "qualifying search" and is unable to locate the copyright owner, then he or she may use the work with limited liability. Both bills provide additional conditions to the exception, however. For example, the user must include a symbol indicating that the work used is an orphan work, and must retain and be prepared to come forward promptly with evidence of the search that was made. Both bills give the Copyright Office responsibility for maintaining information about best practices in connection with searching for right holders. The House bill requires users to file a Notice of Use in the Copyright Office prior to commencing use of the orphan work.

5.4.20 If orphan works legislation is enacted, it will provide some relief to libraries and archives, which then will be able to copy and disseminate orphan works with a greatly diminished fear of liability for copyright damages. It would not respond to all of their concerns, however, because not all of the works that libraries and archives want to copy for preservation and to make available to remote users are orphan works.

Legal Deposit Law

5.4.21 In many respects the current mandatory deposit law is ill suited to the requirements of digital preservation. As discussed above, the law requires the deposit of the best edition of works published in the United States. But in many cases – particularly with digital materials – the published version may not be the best version for purposes of long-term preservation. For example, an e-book may contain technological protection measures that will hamper preservation activities. Material published online may be in html code rather than in a format more suited to the Library's long-term preservation needs. The Library may not have the resources or the legal right to migrate such copies to more preservable formats.

5.4.22 The Library of Congress has thus far refrained from demanding deposit of Web content and certain other kinds of digital materials, until it can develop procedures to make the ingest and preservation of a large volume of electronic content efficient and workable. It is in the process of developing such procedures, which will likely require revisions to the regulations governing

280 H.R. 4279, 110th Cong., 2d Sess. (introduced April 24, 2008); S. 2913, 110th Cong., 2d Sess. (introduced April 24, 2008).

demand deposit, and possibly also entail changes to the Copyright Act to, among other things, allow the Library to require deposit of the version best suited to its needs and authorize it to make the copies necessary for digital preservation and to provide onsite user access. No proposals for changes to copyright law or regulations to address these issues have yet been introduced.

Activities to Develop Non-Legislative Solutions

Development of Best Practices

5.4.23 CRL, working with OCLC/RLG, has been working to develop "best practices" in the area of digital preservation. Specifically, these organizations have developed an audit and certification methodology to evaluate the trustworthiness of digital repositories. The audit criteria, which were tested with several major digital repositories, were published in a 2007 report, *Trustworthy Repositories Audit & Certification: Criteria and Checklist (TRAC).*[281] The TRAC document is designed to delineate a process for the certification of digital repositories using checklists, and to serve as a resource when planning the development of digital archives.[282]

5.4.24 The Automated Content Access Protocol, or ACAP, was developed by publishers from different sectors of the publishing industry, together with representatives of major search engines, technical partners and others.[283] ACAP was designed to serve as an industry standard to enable providers of all types of content published on the web to automate communications of rights and permissions information by providing a framework that search engines' crawlers can be programmed to understand.

Voluntary Guidelines and Model Contract Terms

5.4.25 Consortia of libraries and university library systems have developed (and continue to refine) model contract terms to ensure long-term access to electronic scholarly materials to which they subscribe. Such terms generally allow the licensee to archive a copy of subscription materials that it creates or receives from the licensor, or requires the licensor to deposit the materials in a digital preservation repository. However, these are model license

281 *See Trustwothy Repositories Audit & Certification: Criteria and Checklist* (Feb. 2007), *available at* http://www.crl.edu/PDF/trac.pdf.

282 The report built as well as on CRL's Auditing and Certification of Digital Archives project, work from the Nestor project (Germany), and the Digital Curation Center in the UK).

283 *See* Automated Content Access Protocol, http://www.the-acap.or.

provisions, so it is unclear the extent to which these terms have found their way into negotiated agreements.

Open Access Repositories and Licensing Mechanisms

5.4.26 The development of open access digital repositories such as PubMed Central (PMC) has ensured long-term preservation of and access to many scholarly works. PMC is a free digital archive of biomedical and life sciences research journal literature. It is managed by the National Library of Medicine in the National Institutes of Health (NIH). PMC is committed to preserving the journal literature "in a form that ensures unrestricted access to it over the longer term."[284] Participation by publishers is voluntary, though the terms of research grants may require that certain articles be placed in the PMC database (see 5.4.28). Only journals that qualify based on the scientific quality of the journal and the technical quality of their digital files can be included. It includes only peer-reviewed research.

5.4.27 PMC, opened in 2000, was developed in response to the trend toward publishing exclusively online, with the goal of permanently preserving the e-journal literature, and improving access to biomedical information. Some publishers deposit their content in PMC immediately. Others, however, wait for a time in order to avoid adversely affecting their own market. PMC strongly encourages deposit of full articles within one year of publication and other editorial content within three years.[285]

5.4.28 Increasingly, government agencies and private foundations that fund research are requiring grantees to make the articles based on their research publicly accessible through PMC within a specified period after publication. For example, PMC has been designated as the repository for research funded by NIH Public Access,[286] the Howard Hughes Medical Institute,[287] and the Wellcome Trust.[288]

---

[284] *See* PMC Overview, http://www.pubmedcentral.nih.gov/about/intro.html.

[285] *See PubMed Central, Policies and Guidelines for Depositing and Providing Access to Full Text,* http://www.pubmedcentral.nih.gov/about/guidelines.html.

[286] *See* NIH Public Access Policy, http://publicaccess.nih.gov/ , implementing Division G, Title II, Section 218 of P.L. 110-161 (Consolidated Appropriations Act, 2008).

[287] *See* Research Policies, http://www.hhmi.org/about/research/sc320.pdf.

[288] *See* Wellcome Trust, Authors Guide and FAQ, http://www.wellcome.ac.uk/About-us/Policy/Spotlight-issues/Open-access/Guides-and-FAQ/WTD018855.htm.

5.4.29 Another significant development for digital archives of scholarly materials are the efforts of universities to ensure that faculty research and writings are made freely available. For example, the Faculty of Arts and Sciences at Harvard University recently voted to allow the university to make their scholarly works freely available online. [289] Of course, "open access" databases do not necessarily equate with long term preservation, but it is likely that such databases will be preserved in accordance with best practices for digital preservation as universities develop preservation archives.[290]

5.4.30 Creative Commons provides a license/permissions system by which right holders may affix a designation to their works indicating how they may be used (e.g., they may be copied, copied with attribution, allowing derivative works, etc.).[291] The rights required for digital preservation would appear to fall within many of the various permutations of Creative Commons licenses, and therefore such licenses potentially provide an easy means to determine whether digital preservation is permitted for works whose right holders use them. It is unclear as yet what effect Creative Commons licenses are having in practice with respect to digital preservation.

Collaborative Projects

5.4.31 One strategy that has been used to overcome restrictions that copyright laws may place on digital preservation activities is to design preservation projects that involve collaboration between right holders and archives, so that right holders agree to the activities necessary for preservation. This approach has been used in particular in the preservation of scholarly materials.

Preservation of digitized scholarly journals

5.4.32 Libraries and archives now often license access to journals in electronic form rather than subscribing to hard copies that they

---

[289] *See* Patricia Cohen, "At Harvard, a Proposal to Publish Free on the Web," N.Y. Times Feb. 12, 2008; Robert Mitchell, "Harvard to collect, disseminate scholarly articles for faculty," Harvard Gazette Online, Feb. 13, 2008, available at http://www.news.harvard.edu/gazette/2008/02.14/99-fasvote.html. While faculty are permitted to "opt out," the move will likely bring more pressure to bear on the publishers of scholarly journals, which may be are reluctant to allow the articles they publish to be made freely available (or may permit open access only after a specified period of time after publication).

[290] *See, e.g.*, Overview: Digital Repository Service (DRS), http://hul.harvard.edu/ois/systems/drs/.

[291] *See* Creative Commons: License Your Work, http://creativecommons.org/about/license/.

can retain for archival purposes. In some cases, subscribing to hard copy journals is no longer possible, as certain journals publish only in electronic form. Libraries and archives have become increasingly concerned about ensuring long-term preservation of and access to scholarly journals. For this reason, scholarly journals have been the focus of many of the preservation initiatives to date.

5.4.33 JSTOR is dedicated to preserving, archiving, and making available past issues of important scholarly journals.[292] JSTOR delivers its contents as scanned images in order to preserve the journals exactly as they were produced on paper. Publishers give JSTOR a nonexclusive license to create and use the image files, but retain all copyrights. They also give JSTOR a perpetual license to the material that goes into JSTOR's archives, so that JSTOR can continue to provide libraries with access to journals to which they have already subscribed, even if the publisher ends its agreement and ceases to make new materials available.[293] This way, libraries can remove hard-copy back issues of journals with confidence that they will have access to these issues in the future. JSTOR pays no licensing fees to participating publishers, though it offers a small amount of revenue sharing. Publishers benefit from having their materials digitized and preserved by JSTOR.

5.4.34 JSTOR attempts to balance the broad societal interest in preservation, libraries' interests in access to content, and right holders' interests in maintaining revenue streams. It does this by using a "moving wall" approach to making content available. In other words, journals are not made immediately available through JSTOR, to avoid a significant adverse effect on publishers' ability to get a return on their investment. The "moving wall" is generally a period of three to five years, after which JSTOR has the rights to digitize and make available the back issues of a particular journal. Each year, another year of older journals is made available.[294] Libraries pay a one-time "Archive Capital Fee" and a yearly "Annual Access Fee" for user access to JSTOR archives, based on their size and the nature of the research collections they wish to access.

---

292 *See* JSTOR Archiving Practices, http://www.jstor.org/page/info/about/archives/index.jsp.

293 Roger C. Schonfeld, *JSTOR: a History* 142 (2003).

294 *See* Moving Wall, http://www.jstor.org/page/info/about/archives/journals/movingWall.jsp.

Preservation of e-journals

5.4.35 Portico and CLOCKSS illustrate two different approaches to preservation of e-journals. Portico is an e-journal archive launched in 2005 with support from JSTOR (discussed above), Ithaka,[295] the Library of Congress and the Andrew W. Mellon Foundation.[296] Its mission is to preserve scholarly electronic journals to ensure their continued availability to scholars and researchers. Its primary funding comes from annual contributions from publishers and from libraries, with additional support from government agencies and charitable foundations. Many journal publishers and libraries are participating in Portico.[297]

5.4.36 Portico receives source files (containing graphics, text, etc.) of electronic journals directly from publishers, and systematically "normalizes" them by converting them from the publishers' proprietary formats to a standard archival format.[298] It retains both the original and the source files in the archive, and commits to long-term preservation of the materials, including future content migrations as technology changes. Portico's focus is preservation rather than on current access. Portico can deliver archival versions of journals to participating institutions when a "trigger event" occurs. Trigger events occur when (1) a publisher stops operations; or (2) a publisher ceases to publish a title; or (3) a publisher no longer offers back issues; or (4) upon catastrophic and sustained failure of a publisher's delivery platform.[299]

5.4.37 Publishers make an annual contribution based on their total journal revenues. Publishers benefit from participating in Portico because they can rely on Portico to convert their journals to an archival format, to preserve them for the long term and to migrate them forward as technology changes. Although Portico's focus is on long-term preservation, publishers can get access to their own content through a Portico web portal. Moreover, Portico provides a means for publishers to respond to library concerns that e-journal content be maintained and preserved by a trusted third-party archive.[300] Portico also provides publishers a means of

[295] *See* Ithaka, http://www.ithaka.org/.

[296] *See* The Andrew W. Mellon Foundation, http://www.mellon.org/.

[297] Portico's current list of libraries and publishers is on its website, http://www.portico.org.

[298] Eileen Fenton, *Preserving Electronic Scholarly Journals: Portico*, Ariadne Issue 47, at 3 (Apr. 2006), http://www.ariadne.ac.uk/issue47/fenton/.

[299] *See* Service for Libraries, http://www.portico.org/libraries/.

[300] *See* Service for Publishers http://www.portico.org/publishers/.

fulfilling commitments to ensure "perpetual access" to materials to which the user subscribed even after the subscription has lapsed, although using Portico as a perpetual access mechanism is optional.

5.4.38 Libraries make an annual payment based on their annual Library Materials Expenditure. Libraries benefit from participating in Portico because it allows them to rely more heavily on e-journals – with attendant cost savings – while ensuring that they will not lose access to valuable content because of publisher failure. Portico gives them the opportunity to use their collective resources more efficiently to ensure long-term preservation. They can be confident that, upon one of the triggering events, they will have access to the necessary materials. Portico also provides an efficient means to secure perpetual access, provided that a participating publisher agrees to allow Portico to provide post-cancellation access.

5.4.39 CLOCKSS, which provides a different approach to digital preservation of e-journals, is built upon LOCKSS (Lots of Copies Keep Stuff Safe), an international nonprofit initiative that originated at Stanford University. LOCKSS provides tools and services to partner libraries to enable the preservation of web-published content.[301] LOCKSS was designed to give libraries a simple and sustainable means to archive their electronic journals locally. Participating libraries configure a local computer with the LOCKSS software. They can then archive any journal title to which they subscribe and for which (a) the publisher has granted permission, (b) the publishing platform is supported by LOCKSS, and (c) a "critical mass of libraries" agree to archive the title. The archiving is done through a regular web crawl of the publisher's site. LOCKSS software continuously checks the integrity of the archived content against that in LOCKSS archives (or "boxes") maintained by other libraries and automatically restores damaged content in a participant's box.

5.4.40 CLOCKSS (Controlled LOCKSS) is an international nonprofit partnership of libraries and publishers that uses the LOCKSS technology to create an e-journal digital repository.[302] Each participating library houses two "CLOCKSS boxes." These CLOCKSS boxes store and preserve scholarly work from the participating publishers in digital form, including works to which the particular library subscribes as well as works to which it does

---

[301] *See* LOCKSS, http://www.lockss.org/lockss/Home. Currently, over 200 publishers allow their content to be stored by LOCKSS at over 150 libraries around the world. *Id.*

[302] *See* CLOCKSS, http://www.clockss.org/clockss/Home.

not subscribe. CLOCKSS boxes use the LOCKSS software to continuously monitor and, where necessary, to correct the stored content.

5.4.41 The archived copies in the CLOCKSS boxes remain "dark" (i.e., unavailable for use) until a trigger event occurs. A trigger event is an event that renders the digital content unavailable from the publisher, such as occurs if a publisher goes out of business or discontinues a particular publication. Once a trigger event occurs, the CLOCKSS Board votes to "light up" the content. If the vote passes, the content is moved to a hosting platform and becomes available world-wide for free. Presently, CLOCKSS is implementing a pilot program, which includes seven libraries (six in the U.S. and one in the U.K.) and 11 publishers. Once the CLOCKSS pilot program concludes in 2008, additional publishers and libraries will be invited to participate.[303]

Practical Measures Used to Minimize the Risk of Infringement in Undertaking Digital Preservation.

5.4.42 The Internet Archive's and the Library of Congress's web capture activities illustrate two different approaches to minimizing the risk of infringement in the preservation of publicly available web content.

Library of Congress Web Capture Project

5.4.43 In 2000, the Library of Congress established a pilot project to collect and preserve primary source web materials.[304] A multidisciplinary team of Library staff studied methods to evaluate, select, collect, catalog, provide access to, and preserve these materials for future generations of researchers. The Library has developed thematic Web archives on such topics such as the United States National Elections of 2000, 2002, and 2004, the Iraq War, and the events of September 11, 2001.

5.4.44 Prior to collection of any website, the Library typically sends an email notification, which gives the website owner notice of the collection activity and of the Library's intention to include the website in its archive. For media sites, the Library usually seeks separate permission to crawl and collect the website and to provide remote access to researchers. For other sites, where the claim of fair use is stronger, the Library provides notification that it will crawl the site and collect it unless it receives notice of a desire to opt-out. It will not provide remote access to users without

303 A list of the current participants is available at http://www.clockss.org/clockss/Home.

304 *See* Web Capture, http://www.loc.gov/webcapture/.

express permission. The types of notices and permission requests that are sent are determined in consultation with legal counsel for the Library and depend on factors such as the type of website and content on the site, the urgency of capture, and the source of the site (U.S. or foreign).

The Internet Archive

5.4.45 The Internet Archive is a nonprofit organization designed to build an Internet library and make it available to the public.[305] Unlike the Library of Congress's web collection efforts, which focus on particular topics, the Internet Archive seeks to create a comprehensive record of web content for use by scholars and researchers. It has been archiving web pages for almost twelve years, and archives approximately two billion web pages per month. It makes this material available over its website, http://www.archive.org, after a delay ranging from one week to six months after collection.

5.4.46 The Internet Archive relies on a protocol known as the "Oakland Archive Policy" in collecting and providing access to web content.[306] Website owners can opt out of having their content copied, or "harvested." This can be done mechanically by putting a robots.txt file on the site. The Internet Archives web crawling utility will respond to the file and bypass the site. Upon notification, Internet Archive will also block access to previously collected website material.[307] The ability to opt out protects website owners that derive financial and other benefits from making available older material, and minimizes the risks of a copyright infringement lawsuit against Internet Archive.

5.5 Recommendations for Legal Reforms or Practical Solutions in the United States to Facilitate Digital Preservation

5.5.1 The Section 108 Study Group has made detailed recommendations for changes to U.S. law to accommodate digital preservation.[308] Most of the recommendations below are based

[305] *See* Internet Archive, http://www.archive.org/about/about.php; Michele Kimpton, *Written Response to Section 4, Section 108* (Apr. 7, 2006), available at http://www.section108.gov/docs/Kimpton_Internet-Archive.pdf.

[306] *See* Comments submitted by the Internet Archive to the 108 Study Group 4-6 (Apr. 7, 2006), available at http://www.section108.gov/docs/Kimpton_Internet-Archive.pdf.

[307] The Internet Archive has also developed a web application to allow "noncommercial 'memory' institutions" around the world that lack technical resources to archive content they regard as important. Statement of Michele Kimpton, *supra* note 305.

[308] *See generally* Section 108 Group Report, *supra* note 269.

on those of the Study Group. (The only exception is the final recommendation, as the Section 108 Group did not consider issues with respect to the Library of Congress and mandatory deposit.)

5.5.2 Although these recommendations are at a more general level than the Section 108 Study Group recommendations, they are intended to be consistent with the Section 108 Study Group recommendations. Accordingly, the Section 108 Study Group Report should be consulted for important qualifications and further discussion concerning the issues raised by the recommendations below (e.g., what does it mean to be for a library or archive (or museum) to be "qualified to undertake digital preservation," how are best practices determined, when is a work "at risk," when is it permissible to access preservation copies, what is meant by "publicly available online content," and so on.)

5.5.3 The United States Congress should amend the law to:

1. Eliminate the three-copy limit for replacement and preservation copies, since it is not feasible in the digital environment, and replace it with a standard such as "a limited number as reasonably necessary" for the required purpose (i.e., for making and maintaining *a* replacement copy or for preservation copying).

2. Allow libraries and archives qualified to undertake digital preservation in accordance with best practices to proactively preserve works in their collections that are at risk, provided that they restrict access to the preservation copies.[309]

3. Allow libraries and archives to copy publicly available online content for their collections and make that content available to users on the premises of the library or archives, and, after a reasonable delay to protect the economic interests of right holders, to remote users. Right holders should be allowed to opt out except where collection of the content is a matter of fundamental public policy (such as government and political websites), and right holders should be protected from excessive crawling of their sites that impairs the functioning of those sites.

4. Allow libraries and archives to make replacement copies of works that are fragile (i.e., "embodied in a physical medium

[309] More detail concerning appropriate conditions for libraries and archives that wish to make "preservation-only" copies can be found in the Section 108 Group Report, *supra* note 269 at 69-70.

that is at risk of becoming unusable because it is delicate or easily destroyed or broken and cannot be handled without risk of harm"), even if those works are not yet damaged or deteriorating.

5. Allow libraries and archives to use outside contractors to assist them in the preservation and replacement activities authorized under section 108, provided that (a) the contractor is acting solely as the provider of a service for which compensation is made by the library or archives, and not for any other direct or indirect commercial benefit; (b) the contractor is contractually prohibited from retaining copies other than as necessary to perform the contracted-for service; and (c) the agreement between the library or archives and the contractor preserves a meaningful ability on the part of the right holder to obtain redress from the contractor for infringement by the contractor.

6. Allow museums to use the section 108 exceptions.

7. Amend the mandatory deposit provisions of section 407 to allow the Library of Congress (a) in the case of works published in digital form, to require deposit of the version most suitable for its needs, and (b) to make a limited number of copies of works deposited under section 407 as reasonably necessary to preserve those works and to make the deposit copies available to users on the premises of the Library, with appropriate protection for right holders. The Library should also be permitted to copy *any* publicly available online content, regardless of whether the right holder has opted out of web harvesting by other libraries and organizations, provided that content of right holders that have "opted out" may be made available only on Library premises.

Part 6: Summary of Findings and Joint Recommendations

6.1 Summary of Findings

6.1.1 Digital preservation is vital to ensure that works created and distributed in digital form will continue to be available over time to researchers, scholars and other users. Digital works are ephemeral, and unless preservation efforts are begun soon after such works are created, they will be lost to future generations. Although copyright and related laws are not the only obstacle to digital preservation activities, there is no question that those laws present significant challenges.

6.1.2 The four countries surveyed in this report all have exceptions in their copyright and related laws that allow reproduction (and sometimes other activities) in connection with the preservation of protected works. However, many of the exceptions were enacted in an analog era and do not adequately accommodate all of the activities necessary for *digital* preservation. Some countries have begun the process of changing their laws to create exceptions to allow digital preservation by libraries, archives and other preservation institutions, but applying the preservation exceptions that currently exist to digital preservation is often an uncertain and frustrating exercise.

6.1.3 The existing exceptions for preservation apply inconsistently across the jurisdictions with regard to which institutions may make use of them, the materials they apply to, the degree of copying they allow, and whether and how preservation copies may be accessed by the public.

6.1.4 Further complicating matters are the evolving commercial markets for digital works, and the apprehension among creators and right holders concerning the impact that further exceptions might have on the market for their works.

6.1.5 Most of the countries represented here have laws in some form that require the deposit of copyrighted materials for the benefit of one or more preservation institutions. None of them, however, has a uniform national system for collection of digital materials, either through a compulsory or a voluntary scheme.

6.1.6 Libraries, archives and other preservation institutions have responded in different ways to the challenges that copyright laws currently present for digital preservation. For example, entities in all of the surveyed jurisdictions have embarked upon projects that rely on collaborative agreements between preservation institutions and right holders. These agreements are important both for the materials they save and for the best practices they engender. Such arrangements are much more prevalent for some types of digital works than for others, however. Legal reform is needed to ensure comprehensive preservation of the vast range of copyrighted materials now being made available in digital form.

6.1.7 The individual country recommendations in sections 2.5, 3.5, 4.5 and 5.5, and the joint recommendations below, focus on amendments to copyright and legal deposit laws that will help to bring these laws into the digital age. Implementation of these recommendations must, of course, be consistent with the legitimate interests of right holders.

6.1.8 Along this line, the joint recommendations include two recommendations for further research into areas that are particularly important to digital preservation and particularly sensitive to right holders: access to preservation copies, and the relationship of contracts to copyright exceptions (and in particular, to exceptions that facilitate digital preservation).

6.2 Joint Recommendations

These recommendations are intended to provide guidelines for national copyright and related rights laws and policies that concern the digital preservation of copyrighted works.

Countries should establish laws and policies to encourage and enable the digital preservation of at risk copyrighted materials. These laws and policies should, at a minimum:

1. Apply to all non-profit libraries, archives, museums and other institutions as may be authorized by national law (hereafter, "preservation institutions") that are open to the public, provided they do not undertake these activities for any purpose of commercial advantage.

2. Apply equally to all categories of copyrighted materials, including literary, artistic, musical and dramatic works, as well as to motion pictures and sound recordings.

3. Apply equally to copyrighted materials in all media and formats, whether hard copy or electronic, born digital or digitized for preservation.

4. Allow preservation institutions to pro-actively preserve at risk copyrighted materials before they deteriorate, are damaged or are lost, and before any software or hardware required to access and use the material becomes obsolete, subject to measures appropriate to protect the legitimate interests of right holders.

5. Allow preservation institutions to undertake preservation activities as necessary and in accordance with international best practices for digital preservation, including

   (a) Reproduction and retention of such copies as may be necessary for effective digital preservation;
   (b) The serial transfer of copyrighted works into different formats for preservation in response to technological developments and changing standards, and
   (c) The communication of works within the preservation institution for administrative activities related to preservation, or between the preservation institution and legally authorized third party preservation repositories as necessary for the purpose of maintaining redundant preservation copies to protect against catastrophic loss.

   All of the foregoing should be subject to measures appropriate to protect the legitimate interests of right holders.

6. Enable relevant preservation institutions comprehensively to preserve copyrighted materials that have been made available to the public in digital form, by means of

   (a) A legal deposit system,
   (b) The legal ability to harvest publicly available online content for preservation purposes,
   (c) Incentives for contractual arrangements for preservation activities, and/or
   (d) Some combination of the foregoing.

It is also recommended that

7. Preservation institutions should work with right holders to develop workable approaches to the digital preservation of copyrighted materials protected by technological measures such as encryption or copy protection.

8. Preservation institutions should develop best practices for digital preservation.

9. Further research should be undertaken on the national level with regard to whether and under what circumstances access to digital preservation copies can be provided without harm to right holders.

10. Further research should be undertaken on the national level to reexamine the interaction between copyright and private agreements as it relates to digital preservation.

The research suggested in recommendations 9-10 will help in determining whether common approaches to these issues can be developed.

Appendix A

Selected Provisions of International Treaties and Laws Relevant to Digital Preservation

The Berne Convention

Article 9(2) of the Berne Convention for the Protection of Literary and Artistic Works[1] provides:

> It shall be a matter for legislation in the countries of the Union to permit the reproduction of [protected literary and artistic] works in certain special cases, provided that such reproduction does not conflict with a normal exploitation of the work and does not unreasonably prejudice the legitimate interests of the author.

The WIPO Copyright Treaty

Article 10 of the WIPO Copyright Treaty[2] provides:

> (1) Contracting Parties may, in their national legislation, provide for limitations of or exceptions to the rights granted to authors of literary and artistic works under this Treaty in certain special cases that do not conflict with a normal exploitation of the work and do not unreasonably prejudice the legitimate interests of the author.
>
> (2) Contracting Parties shall, when applying the Berne Convention, confine any limitations of or exceptions to rights provided for therein to certain special cases that do not conflict with a normal exploitation of the work and do not unreasonably prejudice the legitimate interests of the author.[3]

The WIPO Performances and Phonograms Treaty[4] has an analogous provision in Article 16.

---

[1] Berne Convention for the Protection of Literary and Artistic Works, opened for signature September 9, 1886, 1 B.D.I.E.L. 715, http://www.wipo.int/treaties/en/ip/berne/trtdocs_wo001.html.

[2] The WIPO Copyright Treaty, adopted Dec. 20, 1996, 36 I.L.M. 65, http://www.wipo.int/treaties/en/ip/wct/trtdocs_wo033.html.

[3] *Id.* art. 10 (footnotes omitted).

[4] The WIPO Performances and Phonograms Treaty, adopted Dec. 20, 1996, 36 I.L.M. 76, http://www.wipo.int/treaties/en/ip/wppt/trtdocs_wo034.html.

European Community Information Society Directive

Directive 2001/29/EC of the European Parliament and of the Council of 22 May 2001 on the harmonisation of certain aspects of copyright and related rights in the information society[5] provides:

> Article 5
>
> Exceptions and limitations
>
> ...
>
> 2. Member States may provide for exceptions or limitations to the reproduction right provided for in Article 2 in the following cases:
>
> ...
>
> (c) in respect of specific acts of reproduction made by publicly accessible libraries, educational establishments or museums, or by archives, which are not for direct or indirect economic or commercial advantage;
>
> ...
>
> 3. Member States may provide for exceptions or limitations to the rights provided for in Articles 2 and 3 in the following cases:
>
> (n) use by communication or making available, for the purpose of research or private study, to individual members of the public by dedicated terminals on the premises of establishments referred to in paragraph 2(c) of works and other subject-matter not subject to purchase or licensing terms which are contained in their collections;
>
> 4. Where the Member States may provide for an exception or limitation to the right of reproduction pursuant to paragraphs 2 and 3, they may provide similarly for an exception or limitation to the right of distribution as referred to in Article 4 to the extent justified by the purpose of the authorised act of reproduction.
>
> 5. The exceptions and limitations provided for in paragraphs 1, 2, 3 and 4 shall only be applied in certain special cases which do not conflict with a normal exploitation of the work or other subject-matter and do not unreasonably prejudice the legitimate interests of the rightholder.
>
> Article 6
>
> Obligations as to technological measures

[5] Official Journal L 167, 22/06/2001 P. 0010 – 0019.

1. Member States shall provide adequate legal protection against the circumvention of any effective technological measures, which the person concerned carries out in the knowledge, or with reasonable grounds to know, that he or she is pursuing that objective.

2. Member States shall provide adequate legal protection against the manufacture, import, distribution, sale, rental, advertisement for sale or rental, or possession for commercial purposes of devices, products or components or the provision of services which:
(a) are promoted, advertised or marketed for the purpose of circumvention of, or
(b) have only a limited commercially significant purpose or use other than to circumvent, or
(c) are primarily designed, produced, adapted or performed for the purpose of enabling or facilitating the circumvention of,
any effective technological measures.

3. For the purposes of this Directive, the expression "technological measures" means any technology, device or component that, in the normal course of its operation, is designed to prevent or restrict acts, in respect of works or other subject-matter, which are not authorised by the rightholder of any copyright or any right related to copyright as provided for by law or the sui generis right provided for in Chapter III of Directive 96/9/EC. Technological measures shall be deemed "effective" where the use of a protected work or other subject-matter is controlled by the rightholders through application of an access control or protection process, such as encryption, scrambling or other transformation of the work or other subject-matter or a copy control mechanism, which achieves the protection objective.

4. Notwithstanding the legal protection provided for in paragraph 1, in the absence of voluntary measures taken by rightholders, including agreements between rightholders and other parties concerned, Member States shall take appropriate measures to ensure that rightholders make available to the beneficiary of an exception or limitation provided for in national law in accordance with Article 5(2)(a), (2)(c), (2)(d), (2)(e), (3)(a), (3)(b) or (3)(e) the means of benefiting from that exception or limitation, to the extent necessary to benefit from that exception or limitation and where that beneficiary has legal access to the protected work or subject-matter concerned.

A Member State may also take such measures in respect of a beneficiary of an exception or limitation provided for in accordance with Article 5(2)(b), unless reproduction for private use has already been made possible by rightholders to the

extent necessary to benefit from the exception or limitation concerned and in accordance with the provisions of Article 5(2)(b) and (5), without preventing rightholders from adopting adequate measures regarding the number of reproductions in accordance with these provisions.
The technological measures applied voluntarily by rightholders, including those applied in implementation of voluntary agreements, and technological measures applied in implementation of the measures taken by Member States, shall enjoy the legal protection provided for in paragraph 1.
The provisions of the first and second subparagraphs shall not apply to works or other subject-matter made available to the public on agreed contractual terms in such a way that members of the public may access them from a place and at a time individually chosen by them.

When this Article is applied in the context of Directives 92/100/EEC and 96/9/EC, this paragraph shall apply mutatis mutandis.

Appendix B

Selected Provisions of Australian law

Copyright Act of 1968

10 Definitions

archives means:

(a) archival material in the custody of:

(i) the Australian Archives;

(ii) the Archives Office of New South Wales established by the *Archives Act* 1960 of the State of New South Wales;

(iii) the Public Record Office established by the *Public Records Act* 1973 of the State of Victoria; or

(iv) the Archives Office of Tasmania established by the *Archives Act* 1965 of the State of Tasmania; or

(b) a collection of documents or other material to which this paragraph applies by virtue of subsection (4)

...

(4) Where:

(a) a collection of documents or other material of historical significance or public interest that is in the custody of a body, whether incorporated or unincorporated, is being maintained by the body for the purpose of conserving and preserving those documents or other material; and

(b) the body does not maintain and operate the collection for the purpose of deriving a profit; paragraph (b) of the definition of *archives* in subsection (1) applies to that collection.

Example: Museums and galleries are examples of bodies that could have collections covered by paragraph (b) of the definition of *archives*.

48 Interpretation

In this Division, a reference to an article contained in a periodical publication shall be read as a reference to anything (other than an artistic work) appearing in such a publication.

48A Copying by Parliamentary libraries for members of Parliament

The copyright in a work is not infringed by anything done, for the sole purpose of assisting a person who is a member of a Parliament in the performance of the person's duties as such a member, by an authorized officer of a library, being a library the principal purpose of which is to provide library services for members of that Parliament.

49 Reproducing and communicating works by libraries and archives for users

(1) A person may furnish to the officer in charge of a library or archives:

(a) a request in writing to be supplied with a reproduction of an article, or a part of an article, contained in a periodical publication or of the whole or a part of a published work other than an article contained in a periodical publication, being a periodical publication or a published work held in the collection of a library or archives; and

(b) a declaration signed by him or her stating:

(i) that he or she requires the reproduction for the purpose of research or study and will not use it for any other purpose; and

(ii) that he or she has not previously been supplied with a reproduction of the same article or other work, or the same part of the article or other work, as the case may be, by an authorized officer of the library or archives.

(2) Subject to this section, where a request and declaration referred to in subsection (1) are furnished to the officer in charge of a library or archives, an authorized officer of the library or archives may, unless the declaration contains a statement that to his or her knowledge is untrue in a material particular, make, or cause to be made, the reproduction to which the request relates and supply the reproduction to the person who made the request.

Note: The reproduction could be made from another reproduction of the article or published work in the collection of the library or archives that was made without infringing copyright because of subsection 51A(1), to replace the article or published work because it was damaged, had deteriorated or had been lost or stolen.

(2A) A person may make to an authorized officer of a library or archives:

(a) a request to be supplied with a reproduction of an article, or part of an article, contained in a periodical publication, or of the whole or a part of a published work other than an article contained in a periodical publication, being a periodical publication or a published work held in the collection of a library or archives; and

(b) a declaration to the effect that:

(i) the person requires the reproduction for the purpose of research or study and will not use it for any other purpose;

(ii) the person has not previously been supplied with a reproduction of the same article or other work, or the same part of the article or other work, as the case may be, by an authorized officer of the library or archives; and

(iii) by reason of the remoteness of the person's location, the person cannot conveniently furnish to the officer in charge of the library or archives a request and declaration referred to in subsection (1) in relation to the reproduction soon enough to enable the reproduction to be supplied to the person before the time by which the person requires it.

(2B) A request or declaration referred to in subsection (2A) is not required to be made in writing.

(2C) Subject to this section, where:

(a) a request and declaration referred to in subsection (2A) are made by a person to an authorized officer of a library or archives; and

(b) the authorized officer makes a declaration setting out particulars of the request and declaration made by the person and stating that:

(i) the declaration made by the person, so far as it relates to the matters specified in subparagraphs (2A)(b)(i) and (ii), does not contain a statement that, to the knowledge of the authorized officer, is untrue in a material particular; and

(ii) the authorized officer is satisfied that the declaration made by the person is true so far as it relates to the matter specified in subparagraph (2A)(b)(iii);

an authorized officer of the library or archives may make, or cause to be made, the reproduction to which the request relates and supply the reproduction to the person.

Note: The reproduction could be made from another reproduction of the article or published work in the collection of the library or archives that was made without infringing copyright because of subsection 51A(1), to replace the article or published work because it was damaged, had deteriorated or had been lost or stolen.

(3) Where a charge is made for making and supplying a reproduction to which a request under subsection (1) or (2A) relates, subsection (2) or (2C), as the case may be, does not apply in relation to the request if the amount of the charge exceeds the cost of making and supplying the reproduction.

(4) Subsection (2) or (2C) does not apply in relation to a request for a reproduction of, or parts of, 2 or more articles contained in the same periodical publication unless the articles are requested for the same research or course of study.

(5) Subsection (2) or (2C) does not apply to a request for a reproduction of the whole of a work (other than an article contained in a periodical publication), or to a reproduction of a part of such a work that contains more than a reasonable portion of the work unless:

(a) the work forms part of the library or archives collection; and

(b) before the reproduction is made, an authorized officer has, after reasonable investigation, made a declaration stating that he or she is satisfied that a reproduction (not being a second-hand reproduction) of the work cannot be obtained within a reasonable time at an ordinary commercial price.

(5AA) For the purposes of subsection (5), if the characteristics of the work are such that subsection 10(2) or (2A) is relevant to the question whether the reproduction contains only a reasonable portion of the work, then that question is to be determined solely by reference to subsection 10(2) or (2A) and not by reference to the ordinary meaning of *reasonable portion*.

(5AB) For the purposes of paragraph (5)(b), in determining whether a reproduction (not being a second-hand reproduction) of the work cannot be obtained within a reasonable time at an ordinary commercial price, the authorized officer must take into account:

(a) the time by which the person requesting the reproduction requires it; and

(b) the time within which a reproduction (not being a second-hand reproduction) of the work at an ordinary commercial price could be delivered to the person; and

(c) whether an electronic reproduction of the work can be obtained within a reasonable time at an ordinary commercial price.

(5A) If an article contained in a periodical publication, or a published work (other than an article contained in a periodical publication) is acquired, in electronic form, as part of a library or archives collection, the officer in charge of the library or archives may make it available online within the premises of the library or archives in such a manner that users cannot, by using any equipment supplied by the library or archives:

(a) make an electronic reproduction of the article or work; or

(b) communicate the article or work.

(6) The copyright in an article contained in a periodical publication is not infringed by the making, in relation to a request under subsection (1) or (2A), of a reproduction of the article, or of a part of the article, in accordance with subsection (2) or (2C), as the case may be, unless the reproduction is supplied to a person other than the person who made the request.

(7) The copyright in a published work other than an article contained in a periodical publication is not infringed by the making, in relation to a request under subsection (1) or (2A), of a reproduction of the work, or of a part of the work, in accordance with subsection (2) or (2C), as the case may be, unless the reproduction is supplied to a person other than the person who made the request.

(7A) Subsections (6) and (7) do not apply to the making under subsection (2) or (2C) of an electronic reproduction of:

(a) an article, or a part of an article, contained in a periodical publication; or

(b) the whole or part of a published work, other than such an article;

in relation to a request under this section for communication to the person who made the request unless:

(c) before or when the reproduction is communicated to the person, the person is notified in accordance with the regulations:

(i) that the reproduction has been made under this section and that the article or work might be subject to copyright protection under this Act; and

(ii) about such other matters (if any) as are prescribed; and

(d) as soon as practicable after the reproduction is communicated to the person, the reproduction made under subsection (2) or (2C) and held by the library or archives is destroyed.

(7B) It is not an infringement of copyright in an article contained in a periodical publication, or of copyright in a published work, to communicate it in accordance with subsection (2), (2C) or (5A).

(8) The regulations may exclude the application of subsection (6) or (7) in such cases as are specified in the regulations.

(9) In this section:

archives means an archives all or part of whose collection is accessible to members of the public.

library means a library all or part of whose collection is accessible to members of the public directly or through interlibrary loans.

supply includes supply by way of a communication.

Note: Under section 203F, it is an offence to make a false or misleading declaration for the purposes of this section. Sections 203A, 203D and 203G create offences relating to the keeping of declarations made for the purposes of this section.

50 Reproducing and communicating works by libraries or archives for other libraries or archives

(1) The officer in charge of a library may request, or cause another person to request, the officer in charge of another library to supply the officer in charge of the first-mentioned library with a reproduction of an article, or a part of an article, contained in a periodical publication, or of the whole or a part of a published work other than an article contained in a periodical publication, being a periodical publication or a published work held in the collection of a library:

(a) for the purpose of including the reproduction in the collection of the first-mentioned library;

(aa) in a case where the principal purpose of the first-mentioned library is to provide library services for members of a Parliament—for the purpose of assisting a person who is a member of that Parliament in the performance of the person's duties as such a member; or

(b) for the purpose of supplying the reproduction to a person who has made a request for the reproduction under section 49.

(2) Subject to this section, where a request is made by or on behalf of the officer in charge of a library to the officer in charge of another library under subsection (1), an authorized officer of the last-mentioned library may make, or cause to be made, the reproduction to which the request relates and supply the reproduction to the officer in charge of the first-mentioned library.

Note: The reproduction could be made from another reproduction of the article or published work in the collection of the other library that was made without infringing copyright because of subsection 51A(1), to replace the article or published work because it was damaged, had deteriorated or had been lost or stolen.

(3) Where, under subsection (2), an authorized officer of a library makes, or causes to be made, a reproduction of the whole or part of a work (including an article contained in a periodical publication) and

supplies it to the officer in charge of another library in accordance with a request made under subsection (1):

(a) the reproduction shall, for all purposes of this Act, be deemed to have been made on behalf of an authorized officer of the other library for the purpose for which the reproduction was requested; and

(b) an action shall not be brought against the body administering that first-mentioned library, or against any officer or employee of that library, for infringement of copyright by reason of the making or supplying of that reproduction.

(4) Subject to this section, if a reproduction of the whole or a part of an article contained in a periodical publication, or of any other published work, is, by virtue of subsection (3), taken to have been made on behalf of an authorised officer of a library, the copyright in the article or other work is not infringed:

(a) by the making of the reproduction; or

(b) if the work is supplied under subsection (2) by way of a communication—by the making of the communication.

(5) The regulations may exclude the application of subsection (4) in such cases as are specified in the regulations.

(6) Where a charge is made for making and supplying a reproduction to which a request under subsection (1) relates, subsection (3) does not apply in relation to the request if the amount of the charge exceeds the cost of making and supplying the reproduction.

(7) Where:

(a) a reproduction (in this subsection referred to as the *relevant reproduction*) of, or of a part of, an article, or of the whole or a part of another work, is supplied under subsection (2) to the officer in charge of a library; and

(b) a reproduction of the same article or other work, or of the same part of the article or other work, as the case may be, has previously been supplied under subsection (2) for the purpose of inclusion in the collection of the library;

subsection (4) does not apply to or in relation to the relevant reproduction unless, as soon as practicable after the request under subsection (1) relating to the relevant reproduction is made, an authorized officer of the library makes a declaration:

(c) setting out particulars of the request (including the purpose for which the relevant reproduction was requested); and

(d) stating that the reproduction referred to in paragraph (b) has been lost, destroyed or damaged, as the case requires.

(7A) If:

(a) a reproduction is made of the whole of a work (other than an article contained in a periodical publication) or of a part of such a work, being a part that contains more than a reasonable portion of the work; and

(b) the work from which the reproduction is made is in hardcopy form; and

(c) the reproduction is supplied under subsection (2) to the officer in charge of a library;

subsection (4) does not apply in relation to the reproduction unless:

(d) in a case where the principal purpose of the library is to provide library services for members of a Parliament—the reproduction is so supplied for the purpose of assisting a person who is a member of that Parliament in the performance of the person's duties as such a member; or

(e) as soon as practicable after the request under subsection (1) relating to the reproduction is made, an authorized officer of the library makes a declaration:

(i) setting out particulars of the request (including the purpose for which the reproduction was requested); and

(ii) stating that, after reasonable investigation, the authorized officer is satisfied that a copy (not being a second-hand copy) of the work cannot be obtained within a reasonable time at an ordinary commercial price.

(7B) If:

(a) a reproduction is made of the whole of a work (including an article contained in a periodical publication) or of a part of such a work, whether or not the part contains more than a reasonable portion of the work; and

(b) the work from which the reproduction is made is in electronic form; and

(c) the reproduction is supplied under subsection (2) to the officer in charge of a library;

subsection (4) does not apply in relation to the reproduction unless:

(d) in a case where the principal purpose of the library is to provide library services for members of a Parliament—the reproduction is so supplied for the purpose of assisting a person who is a member of that Parliament in the performance of the person's duties as such a member; or

(e) as soon as practicable after the request under subsection (1) relating to the reproduction is made, an authorized officer of the library makes a declaration:

(i) setting out particulars of the request (including the purpose for which the reproduction was requested); and

(ii) if the reproduction is of the whole, or of more than a reasonable portion, of a work other than an article—stating that, after reasonable investigation, the authorised officer is satisfied that the work cannot be obtained in electronic form within a reasonable time at an ordinary commercial price; and

(iii) if the reproduction is of a reasonable portion, or less than a reasonable portion, of a work other than an article—stating that, after reasonable investigation, the authorised officer is satisfied that the portion cannot be obtained in electronic form, either separately or together with a reasonable amount of other material, within a reasonable time at an ordinary commercial price; and

(iv) if the reproduction is of the whole or of a part of an article—stating that, after reasonable investigation, the authorised officer is satisfied that the article cannot be obtained on its own in electronic form within a reasonable time at an ordinary commercial price.

(7BA) For the purposes of subsections (7A) and (7B), if the characteristics of the work are such that subsection 10(2) or (2A) is relevant to the question whether the reproduction contains only a reasonable portion of the work, then that question is to be determined solely by reference to subsection 10(2) or (2A) and not by reference to the ordinary meaning of *reasonable portion*.

(7BB) For the purposes of subparagraphs (7A)(e)(ii) and (7B)(e)(ii), (iii) and (iv), in determining whether a copy of the work, the work, the portion of the work or the article (as appropriate) cannot be obtained within a reasonable time at an ordinary commercial price, the authorized officer must take into account:

(a) the time by which the person requesting the reproduction under section 49 requires the reproduction; and

(b) the time within which a reproduction (not being a second-hand reproduction) of the work at an ordinary commercial price could be delivered to the person; and

(c) whether the copy, work, portion or article can be obtained in electronic form within a reasonable time at an ordinary commercial price.

(7C) If:

(a) a reproduction is made in electronic form by or on behalf of an authorised officer of a library of the whole of a work (including an article contained in a periodical publication) or of a part of such a work; and

(b) the reproduction is supplied under subsection (2) to the officer in charge of another library;

subsection (3) does not apply in relation to the reproduction unless, as soon as practicable after the reproduction is supplied to the other library the reproduction made for the purpose of the supply and held by the first-mentioned library is destroyed.

(8) Subsection (4) does not apply to a reproduction or communication of all or part of 2 or more articles that are contained in the same periodical publication and that have been requested for the same purpose unless:

(a) the purpose is the one described in paragraph (1)(aa) (assisting a member of a Parliament perform his or her duties); or

(b) the purpose is the one described in paragraph (1)(b) (supplying a reproduction to a person requesting it under section 49 for research or study) and the reproduction of the articles was requested under section 49 for the same research or course of study.

(10) In this section:

library means:

(a) a library all or part of whose collection is accessible to members of the public directly or through interlibrary loans; or

(b) a library whose principal purpose is to provide library services for members of a Parliament; or

(c) an archives all or part of whose collection is accessible to members of the public.

supply includes supply by way of a communication.

Note: Under section 203F, it is an offence to make a false or misleading declaration for the purposes of this section. Sections 203A, 203D and 203G create offences relating to the keeping of declarations made for the purposes of this section.

51 Reproducing and communicating unpublished works in libraries or archives

(1) Where, at a time more than 50 years after the end of the calendar year in which the author of a literary, dramatic, musical or artistic work died, copyright subsists in the work but:

(a) the work has not been published; and

(b) a reproduction of the work, or, in the case of a literary, dramatic or musical work, the manuscript of the work, is kept in the collection of a library or archives where it is, subject to any regulations governing that collection, open to public inspection;

the copyright in the work is not infringed:

(c) by the making or communication of a reproduction of the work by a person for the purposes of research or study or with a view to publication; or

(d) by the making or communication of a reproduction of the work by, or on behalf of, the officer in charge of the library or archives if the reproduction is supplied (whether by way of communication or otherwise) to a person who satisfies the officer in charge of the library or archives that the person requires the reproduction for the purposes of research or study, or with a view to publication, and that the person will not use it for any other purpose.

(2) If the manuscript, or a reproduction, of an unpublished thesis or other similar literary work is kept in a library of a university or other similar institution, or in an archives, the copyright in the thesis or other work is not infringed by the making or communication of a reproduction of the thesis or other work by or on behalf of the officer in charge of the library or archives if the reproduction is supplied (whether by communication or otherwise) to a person who satisfies an authorized officer of the library or archives that he or she requires the reproduction for the purposes of research or study.

51AA Reproducing and communicating works in Australian Archives

(1) The copyright in a work that is kept in the collection of the Australian Archives, where it is open to public inspection, is not infringed by the making or communication by, or on behalf of, the officer in charge of the Archives:

(a) of a single working copy of the work;

(b) of a single reference copy of the work for supply to the central office of the Archives;

(c) on the written request for a reference copy of the work by an officer of the Archives in a regional office of the Archives, where the officer in charge is satisfied that a reference copy of the work has not been previously supplied to that regional office—of a single reference copy of the work for supply to that regional office;

(d) where the officer in charge is satisfied that a reference copy of the work supplied to a regional office of the Archives is lost, damaged or destroyed and an officer of the Archives in that regional office makes a written request for a replacement copy of the work—of a single replacement copy of the work for supply to that regional office; or

(e) where the officer in charge is satisfied that a reference copy of the work supplied to the central office of the Archives is lost, damaged or destroyed—of a single replacement copy of the work for supply to that central office.

(2) In this section:

reference copy, in relation to a work, means a reproduction of the work made from a working copy for supply to the central office, or to a regional office, of the Australian Archives for use by that office in providing access to the work to members of the public.

replacement copy, in relation to a work, means a reproduction of the work made from a working copy for the purpose of replacing a reference copy of the work that is lost, damaged or destroyed.

working copy, in relation to a work, means a reproduction of the work made for the purpose of enabling the Australian Archives to retain the copy and use it for making reference copies and replacement copies of the work.

51A Reproducing and communicating works for preservation and other purposes

(1) Subject to subsection (4), the copyright in a work that forms, or formed, part of the collection of a library or archives is not infringed by the making or communicating, by or on behalf of the officer in charge of the library or archives, of a reproduction of the work:

(a) if the work is held in manuscript form or is an original artistic work—for the purpose of preserving the manuscript or original artistic work, as the case may be, against loss or deterioration or for the purpose of research that is being, or is to be, carried out at the library or archives in which the work is held or at another library or other archives;

(b) if the work is held in the collection in a published form but has been damaged or has deteriorated—for the purpose of replacing the work; or

(c) if the work has been held in the collection in a published form but has been lost or stolen—for the purpose of replacing the work.

(2) The copyright in a work that is held in the collection of a library or archives is not infringed by the making, by or on behalf of the officer in charge of the library or archives, of a reproduction of the work for administrative purposes.

(3) The copyright in a work that is held in the collection of a library or archives is not infringed by the communication, by or on behalf of the officer in charge of the library or archives, of a reproduction of the work made under subsection (2) to officers of the library or archives by making it available online to be accessed through the use of a computer terminal installed within the premises of the library or archives with the approval of the body administering the library or archives.

(3A) The copyright in an original artistic work that is held in the collection of a library or archives is not infringed in the circumstances described in subsection (3B) by the communication, by or on behalf of the officer in charge of the library or archives, of a preservation reproduction of the work by making it available online to be accessed through the use of a computer terminal:

(a) that is installed within the premises of the library or archives; and

(b) that cannot be used by a person accessing the work to make an electronic copy or a hardcopy of the reproduction, or to communicate the reproduction.

(3B) The circumstances in which the copyright in the original artistic work is not infringed because of subsection (3A) are that either:

(a) the work has been lost, or has deteriorated, since the preservation reproduction of the work was made; or

(b) the work has become so unstable that it cannot be displayed without risk of significant deterioration.

(4) Subsection (1) does not apply in relation to a work held in published form in the collection of a library or archives unless an authorized officer of the library or archives has, after reasonable investigation, made a declaration:

(a) stating that he or she is satisfied that a copy (not being a second-hand copy) of the work, or of the edition in which the work is held in the collection, cannot be obtained within a reasonable time at an ordinary commercial price; and

(b) if he or she is satisfied that a copy (not being a second-hand copy) of another edition of the work can be obtained within a reasonable time at an ordinary commercial price—stating why the reproduction should be made from the copy of the work held in the collection.

Note: Under section 203F, it is an offence to make a false or misleading declaration for the purposes of this section. Sections 203A, 203D and 203G create offences relating to the keeping of declarations made for the purposes of this section.

(5) Where a reproduction of an unpublished work is made under subsection (1) by or on behalf of the officer in charge of a library or archives for the purpose of research that is being, or is to be, carried out at another library or archives, the supply or communication of the reproduction by or on behalf of the officer to the other library or archives does not, for any purpose of this Act, constitute the publication of the work.

(6) In this section:

administrative purposes means purposes directly related to the care or control of the collection.

officers of the library or archives includes volunteers assisting with the care or control of the collection.

preservation reproduction, in relation to an artistic work, means a reproduction of the work made under subsection (1) for the purpose of preserving the work against loss or deterioration.

51B Making preservation copies of significant works in key cultural institutions' collections

(1) This section applies in relation to a work held in the collection of a library or archives if:

(a) the body administering the library or archives:

(i) has, under a law of the Commonwealth or a State or Territory, the function of developing and maintaining the collection; or

(ii) is prescribed by the regulations for the purposes of this subparagraph; and

(b) an authorized officer of the library or archives is satisfied that the work is of historical or cultural significance to Australia.

Manuscript

(2) If the work is held in the form of a manuscript, the copyright in the work is not infringed by an authorized officer of the library or archives making up to 3 reproductions of the work from the manuscript for the purpose of preserving it against loss or deterioration.

Original artistic work

(3) If the work is held in the form of an original artistic work, the copyright in the work is not infringed by an authorized officer of the library or archives making up to 3 comprehensive photographic reproductions of the work from the original artistic work for the purpose of preserving it against loss or deterioration if the officer is satisfied that a photographic reproduction (not being a second-hand reproduction) of the work cannot be obtained within a reasonable time at an ordinary commercial price.

Published work

(4) If the work is held in published form, the copyright in the work is not infringed by an authorized officer of the library or archives making up to 3 reproductions of the work from the copy held in the collection, for the purpose of preserving the work against loss or deterioration, if the officer is satisfied that:

(a) a copy (not being a second-hand copy) of the work, or of the edition in which the work is held in the collection, cannot be obtained within a reasonable time at an ordinary commercial price; and

(b) if the officer is satisfied that a copy (not being a second-hand copy) of another edition of the work can be obtained within a reasonable time at an ordinary commercial price—it is appropriate that the reproduction should be made from the copy of the work held in the collection.

Electronic copies and commercial availability

(5) In determining for the purposes of subsection (3) or (4) whether a reproduction or copy (not being a second-hand reproduction or copy) of the work, or of a particular edition of the work, cannot be obtained within a reasonable time at an ordinary commercial price, the authorized officer must take into account whether an electronic copy of the work or edition can be obtained within a reasonable time at an ordinary commercial price.

Relationship with the rest of this Division

(6) This section does not limit the rest of this Division. The rest of this Division does not limit this section.

52 Publication of unpublished works kept in libraries or archives

(1) Where:

(a) a published literary, dramatic or musical work (in this section referred to as *the new work*) incorporates the whole or a part of a work (in this section referred to as *the old work*) to which subsection 51(1) applied immediately before the new work was published;

(b) before the new work was published, the prescribed notice of the intended publication of the work had been given; and

(c) immediately before the new work was published, the identity of the owner of the copyright in the old work was not known to the publishers of the new work;

then, for the purposes of this Act, the first publication of the new work, and any subsequent publication of the new work whether in the same or in an altered form, shall, in so far as it constitutes a publication of the old work, be deemed not to be an infringement of the copyright in the old work or an unauthorized publication of the old work.

(2) The last preceding subsection does not apply to a subsequent publication of the new work incorporating a part of the old work that was not included in the first publication of the new work unless:

(a) subsection 51(1) would, but for this section, have applied to that part of the old work immediately before that subsequent publication;

(b) before that subsequent publication, the prescribed notice of the intended publication had been given; and

(c) immediately before that subsequent publication, the identity of the owner of the copyright in the old work was not known to the publisher of that subsequent publication.

(3) If a work, or part of a work, has been published and, because of this section, the publication is taken not to be an infringement of the copyright in the work, the copyright in the work is not infringed by a person who, after the publication took place:

(a) broadcasts the work, or that part of the work; or

(b) electronically transmits the work, or that part of the work (other than in a broadcast) for a fee payable to the person who made the transmission; or

(c) performs the work, or that part of the work, in public; or

(d) makes a record of the work, or that part of the work.

53 Application of Division to illustrations accompanying articles and other works

Where an article, thesis or literary, dramatic or musical work is accompanied by artistic works provided for the purpose of explaining or illustrating the article, thesis or other work (in this section referred to as *the illustrations*), the preceding sections of this Division apply as if:

(a) where any of those sections provides that the copyright in the article, thesis or work is not infringed—the reference to that copyright included a reference to any copyright in the illustrations;

(b) a reference in section 49, section 50, section 51 or 51A to a reproduction of the article, thesis or work included a reference to a reproduction of the article, thesis or work together with a reproduction of the illustrations;

(c) a reference in section 49 or section 50 to a reproduction of a part of the article or work included a reference to a reproduction of that part of the article or work together with a reproduction of the illustrations that were provided for the purpose of explaining or illustrating that part; and

(d) a reference in section 51A or section 52 to the doing of any act in relation to the work included a reference to the doing of that act in relation to the work together with the illustrations.

140A Acts done by Parliamentary libraries for members of Parliament

A copyright subsisting by virtue of this Part is not infringed by anything done, for the sole purpose of assisting a person who is a member of a Parliament in the performance of the person's duties as such a member, by an authorized officer of a library, being a library the principal purpose of which is to provide library services for members of that Parliament.

110A Copying and communicating unpublished sound recordings and cinematograph films in libraries or archives

Where, at a time more than 50 years after the time at which, or the expiration of the period during which, a sound recording or cinematograph film was made, copyright subsists in the sound recording or cinematograph film but:

(a) the sound recording or cinematograph film has not been published; and

(b) a record embodying the sound recording, or a copy of the cinematograph film, is kept in the collection of a library or archives where it is, subject to any regulations governing that collection, accessible to the public;

the copyright in the sound recording or cinematograph film and in any work or other subject matter included in the sound recording or cinematograph film is not infringed:

(c) by the making of a copy or the communication of the sound recording or cinematograph film by a person for the purpose of research or study or with a view to publication; or

(d) by the making of a copy or the communication of the sound recording or cinematograph film by, or on behalf of, the officer in charge of the library or archives if the copy is supplied or communicated to a person who satisfies the officer that he or she requires the copy for the purpose of research or study, or with a view to publication and that he or she will not use it for any other purpose.

112AA Making preservation copies of significant published editions in key cultural institutions' collections

(1) This section applies in relation to a published edition of one or more works held in the collection of a library or archives if:

(a) the body administering the library or archives:

(i) has, under a law of the Commonwealth or a State or Territory, the function of developing and maintaining the collection; or

(ii) is prescribed by the regulations for the purposes of this subparagraph; and

(b) an authorized officer of the library or archives is satisfied that the edition is of historical or cultural significance to Australia.

Published editions

(2) The copyright in the published edition is not infringed by an authorized officer of the library or archives making up to 3 facsimile copies of the edition from the copy held in the collection, for the purpose of preserving the edition against loss or deterioration, if the officer is satisfied that a copy or facsimile copy of the edition (not being a second□hand copy) cannot be obtained within a reasonable time at an ordinary commercial price.

(3) In determining whether a copy (not being a second□hand copy) cannot be obtained within a reasonable time at an ordinary commercial price, the authorized officer must take into account whether an electronic copy of the edition can be obtained within a reasonable time at an ordinary commercial price.

Works in published editions

(4) If, under this section, copyright in the published edition is not infringed by the making of a facsimile copy of the edition, the making of that copy does not infringe copyright in any of the works in the published edition.

Relationship with the rest of this Division

(5) This section does not limit any of the other provisions of this Division that provide that an act (however described) does not infringe copyright. Those other provisions do not limit this section.

200AB Use of works and other subject-matter for certain purposes

(1) The copyright in a work or other subject matter is not infringed by a use of the work or other subject matter if all the following conditions exist:

(a) the circumstances of the use (including those described in paragraphs (b), (c) and (d)) amount to a special case;

(b) the use is covered by subsection (2), (3) or (4);

(c) the use does not conflict with a normal exploitation of the work or other subject matter;

(d) the use does not unreasonably prejudice the legitimate interests of the owner of the copyright.

Use by body administering library or archives

(2) This subsection covers a use that:

(a) is made by or on behalf of the body administering a library or archives; and

(b) is made for the purpose of maintaining or operating the library or archives (including operating the library or archives to provide services of a kind usually provided by a library or archives); and

(c) is not made partly for the purpose of the body obtaining a commercial advantage or profit.

Use by body administering educational institution

(3) This subsection covers a use that:

(a) is made by or on behalf of a body administering an educational institution; and

(b) is made for the purpose of giving educational instruction; and

(c) is not made partly for the purpose of the body obtaining a commercial advantage or profit.

Use by or for person with a disability

(4) This subsection covers a use that meets all the following conditions:

(a) the use is made by:

(i) a person with a disability that causes difficulty in reading, viewing or hearing the work or other subject matter in a particular form; or

(ii) someone else;

(b) the use is made for the purpose of the person obtaining a reproduction or copy of the work or other subject matter in another form, or with a feature, that reduces the difficulty;

(c) the use is not made partly for the purpose of obtaining a commercial advantage or profit.

This section does not apply if under another provision the use does not, or might not, infringe copyright

(6) Subsection (1) does not apply if, because of another provision of this Act:

(a) the use is not an infringement of copyright; or

(b) the use would not be an infringement of copyright assuming the conditions or requirements of that other provision were met.

Example 1: Paragraph (a)--Without using an appliance adapted for producing multiple copies or an appliance that can produce copies by reprographic reproduction, a school teacher reproduces a literary work in the course of educational instruction. Under subsection 200(1), the reproduction is not an infringement of copyright in the work, so this section does not apply.

Example 2: Paragraph (b)--A body administering an institution assisting persons with a print disability makes a Braille version of a published literary work. Under subsection 135ZP(2), making such a version does not infringe copyright in the work if certain conditions (relating to remuneration etc.) are met, so this section does not apply.

Cost recovery not commercial advantage or profit

(6A) The use does not fail to meet the condition in paragraph (2)(c), (3)(c) or (4)(c) merely because of the charging of a fee that:

(a) is connected with the use; and

(b) does not exceed the costs of the use to the charger of the fee.

Definitions

(7) In this section:

"conflict with a normal exploitation" has the same meaning as in Article 13 of the TRIPS Agreement.

"special case" has the same meaning as in Article 13 of the TRIPS Agreement.

"unreasonably prejudice the legitimate interests" has the same meaning as in Article 13 of the TRIPS Agreement.

"use" includes any act that would infringe copyright apart from this section.

201 Delivery of library material to the National Library

(1) The publisher of any library material that is published in Australia and in which copyright subsists under this Act shall, within one month after the publication, cause a copy of the material to be delivered at his or her own expense to the National Library.

Penalty: $100.

(2) The copy of any library material delivered to the National Library in accordance with this section shall be a copy of the whole material (including any illustrations), be finished and coloured, and bound, sewed, stitched or otherwise fastened together, in the same manner as the best copies of that material are published and be on the best paper on which that material is printed.

(3) When any library material is delivered to the National Library in accordance with this section, the National Librarian shall cause a written receipt for the material to be given to the publisher of the material.

(4) This section is not intended to exclude or limit the operation of any law of a State or Territory (whether made before or after the commencement of this Act) that makes provision for or in relation to the delivery to a specified public or other library in or of the State or Territory of copies of library material published in the State or Territory.

(5) In this section:

"illustrations" includes drawings, engravings and photographs.

"library material" means a book, periodical, newspaper, pamphlet, sheet of letter-press, sheet of music, map, plan, chart or table, being a literary, dramatic, musical or artistic work or an edition of such a work, but does not include a second or later edition of any material unless that edition contains additions or alterations in the letter-press or in the illustrations.

Appendix C

Selected Provisions of Dutch Law

Copyright Act

Article 1

Copyright is the exclusive right of the author of a literary, scientific or artistic work or his successors in title to communicate that work to the public and to reproduce it, subject to the limitations laid down by law.

Article 4

1. Unless there is proof to the contrary, the person who is named as author in or on the work or, where there is no such indication, the person who, when the work is communicated to the public, is named as the author by the party who communicates the work to the public, shall be deemed the author of the work.
2. If the author is not named, the person who delivers a recitation which has not appeared in print shall be deemed the author thereof, unless there is proof to the contrary.

Article 6

If a work has been made according to the draft and under the guidance and supervision of another person, that person shall be deemed the author of the work.

Article 7

Where labor carried out by an employee consists in the making of certain literary, scientific or artistic works, the employer shall be deemed the author thereof, unless otherwise agreed between the parties.

Article 8

A public institution, association, foundation or company which communicates a work to the public as its own, without naming any natural person as the author thereof, shall be rega*rded as the author of that work, unless it is proved that the communication to the public in such manner was unlawful.*

Article 10

1. For the purposes of this Act, literary, scientific or artistic works includes:
   - 1° books, pamphlets, newspapers, periodicals and all other writings;
   - 2° dramatic and dramatic-musical works;

3° recitations;
4° choreographic works and entertainments in dumb show;
5° musical works, with or without words;
6° drawings, paintings, works of architecture and sculpture, lithographs, engravings and the like;
7° geographical maps;
8° drafts, sketches and three-dimensional works relating to architecture, geography, topography or other sciences;
9° photographic works;
10° cinematographic works;
11° works of applied art and industrial designs and models;
12° computer programs and the preparatory material;

and generally any creation in the literary, scientific or artistic areas, whatever the mode or form of its expression. Computer programs do not fall within the category of works referred to in the first sentence sub 1°.

2. Reproductions of a literary, scientific or artistic work in a modified form, such as translations, arrangements of music, cinematographic and other adaptations and collections of different works shall be protected as separate works, without prejudice to the copyright in the original work.

Article 12

1. The communication to the public of a literary, scientific or artistic work includes:
   1° the communication to the public of a reproduction of the whole or part of a work;
   2° the distribution of the whole or part of a work or of a reproduction thereof, as long as the work has not appeared in print;
   3° the rental or lending of the whole or part of a work, with the exception of works of architecture and works of applied art, or of a reproduction thereof which has been brought into circulation by or with the consent of the rightholder;
   4° the recitation, performance or presentation in public of the whole or part of a work or a reproduction thereof;
   5° the broadcasting of a work incorporated in a radio or television programme by satellite or other transmitter or by a closed-circuit system as referred to in article 1 sub g of the Wet op de Telecommunicatievoorzieningen.

2. Rental as referred to in paragraph 1 sub 3° means making available for use for a limited period of time for direct or indirect economic or commercial advantage.

3. Lending as referred to in paragraph 1 sub 3° means making available for use, for a limited period of time, by establishments accessible to the public, for no direct or indirect economic or commercial advantage.

4. A recitation, performance or presentation in public includes that in a restricted circle, except where this is limited to relatives or friends or equivalent persons and no form of payment whatsoever is made for admission to the recitation, performance or presentation. The same shall apply to exhibitions.
5. A recitation, performance or presentation which is exclusively for the purposes of education provided on behalf of the public authorities or a non-profit-making legal person, in so far as such a recitation, performance or presentation forms part of the school work plan or curriculum where applicable, or which exclusively serves a scientific purpose, shall not be deemed public.
6. The simultaneous broadcasting of a work incorporated in a radio or television programme by the organization making the original broadcast shall not be deemed a separate communication to the public.
7. The broadcasting by satellite of a work incorporated in a radio or television programme means the act of introducing, under the control and responsibility of the broadcasting organization, the programme-carrying signals intended for reception by the public into an uninterrupted chain of communication leading to the satellite and back to earth. Where the programme-carrying signals are encrypted, this shall be deemed to constitute the broadcasting by satellite of a work incorporated in a radio or television programme if the means of decrypting the broadcast are provided to the public by or with the consent of the broadcasting organization.

Article 13

The reproduction of a literary, scientific or artistic work includes the translation, arrangement of music, cinematographic adaptation or dramatization and generally any partial or total adaptation or imitation in a modified form, which cannot be regarded as a new, original work.

Article 14

The reproduction of a literary, scientific or artistic work includes the fixation of the whole or part of the work on an object which is intended to play a work or to show it.

Article 16n

1. Reproduction by libraries, museums or archives accessible to the public whose purpose does not include the attainment of a direct or indirect economic or commercial benefit will not be regarded as an infringement of copyright in a literary, scientific or artistic work, provided that the sole purpose of the reproduction is:
   1° the restoration of the specimen of the work;
   2° retention of a reproduction of the work for the in stitution if the specimen is threatening to fall into disrepair;

3° to keep the work in a condition in which it can be consulted if there is no technology available to render it accessible.

2. Reproduction as specified in paragraph 1 shall only be authorized if:
   1° the specimen of the work forms part of the collection held by the library, museum or archive accessible to the public relying on this limitation; and
   2° the provisions in Article 25 are taken into account.

Article 25

1. Even after assignment of his copyright, the author of a work has the following rights:
   a. the right to oppose the communication to the public of the work without acknowledgement of his name or other indication as author, unless such opposition would be unreasonable;
   b. the right to oppose the communication to the public of the work under a name other than his own, and any alteration in the name of the work or the indication of the author, in so far as it appears on or in the work or has been communicated to the public in connection with the work;
   c. the right to oppose any other alteration of the work, unless the nature of the alteration is such that opposition would be unreasonable;
   d. the right to oppose any distortion, mutilation or other impairment of the work that could be prejudicial to the name or reputation of the author or to his dignity as such.
2. Upon the death of the author, the rights referred to in paragraph 1 shall belong, until the expiry of the copyright, to the person designated by the author in his last will and testament or in a codicil thereto.
3. The right referred to in paragraph 1, sub a, may be waived. The rights referred to sub b and c may be waived in so far as alterations to the work or its title are concerned.
4. If the author of the work has assigned his copyright, he shall continue to be entitled to make such alterations to the work as he may make in good faith in accordance with social custom.

   As long as copyright subsists, the same right shall belong to the person designated by the author in his last will and testament or in a codicil thereto, if it may reasonably be assumed that the author would have approved such alterations.

Article 29a

1. Where the phrase 'technical provisions' appears in this Article, it will be taken to mean technology, equipment or components whose normal use would include the prevention or limitation of actions in relation to works and that have not been permitted by the author or his right-holders. Technical provisions will be deemed to be 'purposive' if the use of a work protected by the author or his successors in title is

managed by means of control of access or by application of a protective procedure such as encryption, encoding or some other transformation of the work or a copy protection that achieves the intended protection.

2. Those who circumvent purposive technical provisions knowingly, or who should reasonably know they are doing so, shall be acting unlawfully.
3. Those who provide services or make, import, distribute, sell, hire out, advertise or possess equipment, products or components for commercial purposes will be acting unlawfully if those items are:
   a) offered, recommended, or traded with the intention of circumventing the protected operation of purposive technical provisions, or
   b) of only limited commercial purpose or use, apart from the circumvention of the protected operation of purposive technical provisions, or
   c) primarily designed, manufactured or adapted with the purpose of circumventing the protected operation of purposive technical provisions.
4. Government orders may establish rules obliging the author or his successor in title to provide the user of a literary, scientific or artistic work for purposes specified in Articles 15i, 16, 16b, 16c, 16h, 16n, 17b and 22 of this Act with the means necessary to profit from those limitations, provided that the user has lawful access to the work protected by the technical provisions. The provisions in the previous sentence will not apply to works made available to users under contractual conditions at a time and a place selected by the users individually.

Databases Act 1999

Article 1

1. For the purposes of this Act and provisions laid down pursuant to this act:
   a. database: a collection of independent works, data or other materials arranged in a systematic or methodical way and individually accessible by electronic or other means and for which the acquisition, control or presentation of the contents, evaluated qualitatively or quantitatively, bears witness to a substantial investment;
   b. producer of a database: the person who bears the risk of the investment for creating the database;
   c. extraction: the permanent or temporary transfer of all or a substantial part of the contents of a database to another medium by any means or in any form;

d. re-utilization: any form of making available to the public of all or a part of the contents of a database by the distribution of copies, by renting, by online or other forms of transmission;
e. technical provisions: technology, equipment or components which, in the context of their normal operation, are used to prevent or restrict transactions in relation to databases which are not permitted by the producer of the database or his right-holders; technical provisions will be deemed to be 'efficient' if extraction and re-utilization of a database is managed by the producer of the database or his right-holders by means of an access control or through the application of a method of protection such as encryption, encoding or some other transformation of the database or some copy protection that affords the desired protection;
f. information pertaining to the management of rights: all information supplied by the producer of a database or his right-holders that is linked to a version of the database or which becomes known when a database is re-utilized, and that is used to identify the database, or information concerning the conditions for use of the database, together with the numbers or codes containing that information.

2. The making available by institutions accessible to the public for a limited period and without direct or indirect economic or commercial advantage shall not be regarded as extraction or re-utilisation.
3. The relevant provisions of the Copyright Act shall not apply to computer programs used for the production or operation of databases accessible by electronic means.

Neighbouring Rights Act 2003

Article 1

For the purposes of this Act and provisions laid down pursuant to this Act:

a. performer means an actor, singer, musician, dancer or any other person who acts, sings, delivers or otherwise performs a literary or artistic work, or an artist who performs a variety or circus act or a puppet show . . . .

Article 2

1. A performer shall have the exclusive right to authorize one or more of the following acts:
    a. the recording of a performance;
    b. the reproduction of a recording of a performance;
    c. the sale, rental, lending, supply or otherwise bringing into circulation, or the importing, offering or having in stock for such

purposes of a recording of a performance or a reproduction thereof;

d. the broadcast, repeat broadcast, making available to the public or other form of publication of a performance or a recording of a performance or a reproduction thereof.

Article 6

1. A phonogram producer shall have the exclusive right to authorize:
   a. the reproduction of a phonogram manufactured by him;
   b. the sale, rental, lending, supply or otherwise bringing into circulation, or the importing, offering or having in stock for such purposes, of a phonogram manufactured by him or a reproduction thereof;
   c. the broadcast, repeat broadcast, making available to the public or other form of publication of a phonogram manufactured by him or a reproduction thereof. Article 2, paragraphs 7 to 9, shall apply mutatis mutandis.

Article 10

The following shall not be regarded as infringements of rights as defined in Articles 2, 6, 7a and 8:

. . .

f. reproduction of a recording of a performance, phonogram, first print of a film or recording of a programme or a reproduction thereof, by libraries, educational institutions or museums accessible to the public, or by archives which are not attempting to achieve a direct or indirect economic or commercial benefit, if the reproduction occurs with the sole aim of preserving a recording of a performance, phonogram, first print of a film or recording of a programme or a reproduction thereof in the event of demonstrable threat of falling into disrepair or to keep the work in a condition in which it can be consulted if there is no technology available to render it accessible; Article 16n, paragraph 2, 1o and 2o of the Copyright Act shall apply to this, mutatis mutandis; Article 5 must be observed in relation to a performance;

Appendix D

Selected Provisions of U.K. Law

Copyright, Designs and Patents Act 1988

Copying for preservation purposes by librarians and archivists

42.

(1) The librarian or archivist of a prescribed library or archive may, if the prescribed conditions are complied with, make a copy from any item in the permanent collection of the library or archive—

- in order to preserve or replace that item by placing the copy in its permanent collection in addition to or in place of it, or
- in order to replace in the permanent collection of another prescribed library or archive an item which has been lost, destroyed or damaged,

without infringing the copyright in any literary, dramatic or musical work, in any illustrations accompanying such a work or, in the case of a published edition, in the typographical arrangement.

(2) The prescribed conditions shall include provision for restricting the making of copies to cases where it is not reasonably practicable to purchase a copy of the item in question to fulfill that purpose.

Legal Deposit Libraries Act 2003

S.6 Regulations: Deposit of non-print publications

(1) The Secretary of State may make regulations supplementing sections 1 and 2 as they apply to works published in media other than print.

(2) Regulations under this section may in particular -

(a) make provision about the time at which or the circumstances in which any deposit library becomes or ceases to be entitled to delivery under section 1;

(b) require the person mentioned in section 1(1) to deliver, with the copy of the work, a copy of any computer program and any information necessary in order to access the work, and a copy of any manual and other material that accompanies the work and is made available to the public;

(c) require delivery within a time prescribed by reference to publication or another event;

(d) permit or require delivery by electronic means;

(e) where a work is produced for publication in copies of differing quality, specify the quality of copies to be delivered;

(f) where a work is published or made available to the public in different formats, provide for the format in which any copy is to be delivered to be determined in accordance with requirements specified (generally or in a particular case) by the deposit libraries or any of them;

(g) make provision as to the circumstances in which works published on line are or are not to be treated as published in the United Kingdom;

(h) specify the medium in which a copy of a work published on line is to be delivered.

S.7 Restrictions on activities in relation to non-print publications

(1) Subject to subsection (3), a relevant person may not do any of the activities listed in subsection (2) in relation to relevant material.

(2) The activities are-

(a) using the material (whether or not such use necessarily involves the making of a temporary copy of it);

(b) copying the material (other than by making a temporary copy where this is necessary for the purpose of using the material);

(c) in the case of relevant material comprising or containing a computer program or database, adapting it;

(d) lending the material to a third party (other than lending by a deposit library to a reader for use by the reader on library premises controlled by the library);

(e) transferring the material to a third party;

(f) disposing of the material.

(3) The Secretary of State may by regulations make provision permitting relevant persons to do any of the activities listed in subsection (2) in relation to relevant material, subject to such conditions as may be prescribed.

(4) Regulations under this section may in particular make provision about-

(a) the purposes for which relevant material may be used or copied;

(b) the time at which or the circumstances in which readers may first use relevant material;

(c) the description of readers who may use relevant material;

(d) the limitations on the number of readers who may use relevant material at any one time (whether by limiting the number of terminals in a deposit library from which readers may at any one time access an electronic publication or otherwise).

(5) In this section-

(a) "reader" means a person who, for the purposes of research or study and with the permission of a deposit library, is on library premises controlled by it;

(b) "relevant material" means-

(i) a copy delivered under section 1 of a work published in a medium other than print;

(ii) a copy delivered pursuant to regulations under section 6 of a computer program or material within section 6(2)(b);

(iii) a copy of a work to which section 10(6) applies;

(iv) a copy (at any remove) of anything within any of sub-paragraphs (i) to (iii);

(c) "relevant person" means-

(i) a deposit library or person acting on its behalf;

(ii) a reader;

(d) references to a deposit library include references to the Faculty of Advocates.

(6) A contravention of this section is actionable at the suit of a person who suffers loss as a result of the contravention, subject to the defences and other incidents applying to actions for breach of statutory duty.

S. 8 Activities in relation to non-print publications: copyright etc.

In Chapter 3 of Part 1 of the 1988 Act (acts permitted in relation to copyright works), after section 44 insert-

44A: Legal deposit libraries

(1) Copyright is not infringed by the copying of a work from the internet by a deposit library or person acting on its behalf if-

(a) the work is of a description prescribed by regulations under section 10(5) of the 2003 Act,

(b) its publication on the internet, or a person publishing it there, is connected with the United Kingdom in a manner so prescribed, and

(c) the copying is done in accordance with any conditions so prescribed.

(2) Copyright is not infringed by the doing of anything in relation to relevant material permitted to be done under regulations under section 7 of the 2003 Act.

(3) The Secretary of State may by regulations make provision excluding, in relation to prescribed activities done in relation to relevant material, the application of such of the provisions of this Chapter as are prescribed. (4) Regulations under subsection (3) may in particular make provision prescribing activities-

(a) done for a prescribed purpose,

(b) done by prescribed descriptions of reader,

(c) done in relation to prescribed descriptions of relevant material,

(d) done other than in accordance with prescribed conditions.

(5) Regulations under this section may make different provision for different purposes.

(6) Regulations under this section shall be made by statutory instrument which shall be subject to annulment in pursuance of a resolution of either House of Parliament.

(7) In this section-

(a) "the 2003 Act" means the Legal Deposit Libraries Act 2003;

(b) "deposit library", "reader" and "relevant material" have the same meaning as in section 7 of the 2003 Act;

(c) "prescribed" means prescribed by regulations made by the Secretary of State."

In Part III of the Copyright and Rights in Databases Regulations 1997 (S.I. 1997/3032) (database right), after Regulation 20 insert-

20A: Exceptions to database right: deposit libraries

(1) Database right in a database is not infringed by the copying of a work from the internet by a deposit library or person acting on its behalf if-
- (a) the work is of a description prescribed by regulations under section 10(5) of the 2003 Act,
- (b) its publication on the internet, or a person publishing it there, is connected with the United Kingdom in a manner so prescribed, and
- (c) the copying is done in accordance with any conditions so prescribed.

(2) Database right in a database is not infringed by the doing of anything in relation to relevant material permitted to be done under regulations under section 7 of the 2003 Act.

(3) Regulations under section 44A(3) of the 1988 Act exclude the application of paragraph (2) in relation to prescribed activities in relation to relevant material as (and to the extent that) they exclude the application of section 44A(2) of that Act in relation to those activities.

(4) In this Regulation-
- (a) "the 2003 Act" means the Legal Deposit Libraries Act 2003;
- (b) "deposit library" and "relevant material" have the same meaning as in section 7 of the 2003 Act."

S. 9 Exemption from liability: deposit of publications etc.

(1) The delivery by a person, pursuant to section 1, of a copy of a work is to be taken-
- (a) not to breach any contract relating to any part of the work to which that person is a party, and
- (b) not to infringe copyright, publication right or database right in relation to any part of the work or any patent.

(2) Subsection (1) applies to the delivery, pursuant to regulations under section 6, of a copy of a computer program or material within section 6(2)(b) as it applies to the delivery of a copy of a work pursuant to section 1.

Appendix E

Selected Provisions of U.S. Law

Title 17 of the United States Code

(Title 17 is available at http://www.copyright.gov/title17/.)

Section 101. Definitions

Except as otherwise provided in this title, as used in this title, the following terms and their variant forms mean the following:

. . .

"Copies" are material objects, other than phonorecords, in which a work is fixed by any method now known or later developed, and from which the work can be perceived, reproduced, or otherwise communicated, either directly or with the aid of a machine or device. The term "copies" includes the material object, other than a phonorecord, in which the work is first fixed.

. . .

"Phonorecords" are material objects in which sounds, other than those accompanying a motion picture or other audiovisual work, are fixed by any method now known or later developed, and from which the sounds can be perceived, reproduced, or otherwise communicated, either directly or with the aid of a machine or device. The term "phonorecords" includes the material object in which the sounds are first fixed.

. . .

"Publication" is the distribution of copies or phonorecords of a work to the public by sale or other transfer of ownership, or by rental, lease, or lending. The offering to distribute copies or phonorecords to a group of persons for purposes of further distribution, public performance, or public display, constitutes publication. A public performance or display of a work does not of itself constitute publication.

To perform or display a work "publicly" means —
(1) to perform or display it at a place open to the public or at any place where a substantial number of persons outside of a normal circle of a family and its social acquaintances is gathered; or

(2) to transmit or otherwise communicate a performance or display of the work to a place specified by clause (1) or to the public, by means of any device or process, whether the members of the public capable of receiving the performance or display receive it in the same place or in separate places and at the same time or at different times.

Section 107. Limitations on exclusive rights: Fair use

Notwithstanding the provisions of sections 106 and 106A, the fair use of a copyrighted work, including such use by reproduction in copies or phonorecords or by any other means specified by that section, for purposes such as criticism, comment, news reporting, teaching (including multiple copies for classroom use), scholarship, or research, is not an infringement of copyright. In determining whether the use made of a work in any particular case is a fair use the factors to be considered shall include —

(1) the purpose and character of the use, including whether such use is of a commercial nature or is for nonprofit educational purposes;

(2) the nature of the copyrighted work;

(3) the amount and substantiality of the portion used in relation to the copyrighted work as a whole; and

(4) the effect of the use upon the potential market for or value of the copyrighted work.

The fact that a work is unpublished shall not itself bar a finding of fair use if such finding is made upon consideration of all the above factors.

Section 108. Limitations on exclusive rights: Reproduction by libraries and archives

(a) Except as otherwise provided in this title and notwithstanding the provisions of section 106, it is not an infringement of copyright for a library or archives, or any of its employees acting within the scope of their employment, to reproduce no more than one copy or phonorecord of a work, except as provided in subsections (b) and (c), or to distribute such copy or phonorecord, under the conditions specified by this section, if —

(1) the reproduction or distribution is made without any purpose of direct or indirect commercial advantage;

(2) the collections of the library or archives are (i) open to the public, or (ii) available not only to researchers affiliated with the library or archives or with the institution of which it is a part, but also to other persons doing research in a specialized field; and

(3) the reproduction or distribution of the work includes a notice of copyright that appears on the copy or phonorecord that is reproduced under the provisions of this section, or includes a legend stating that the work may be protected by copyright if no such notice can be found on the copy or phonorecord that is reproduced under the provisions of this section.

(b) The rights of reproduction and distribution under this section apply to three copies or phonorecords of an unpublished work duplicated solely for purposes of preservation and security or for deposit for research use in another library or archives of the type described by clause (2) of subsection (a), if —

(1) the copy or phonorecord reproduced is currently in the collections of the library or archives; and

(2) any such copy or phonorecord that is reproduced in digital format is not otherwise distributed in that format and is not made available to the public in that format outside the premises of the library or archives.

(c) The right of reproduction under this section applies to three copies or phonorecords of a published work duplicated solely for the purpose of replacement of a copy or phonorecord that is damaged, deteriorating, lost, or stolen, or if the existing format in which the work is stored has become obsolete, if —

(1) the library or archives has, after a reasonable effort, determined that an unused replacement cannot be obtained at a fair price; and

(2) any such copy or phonorecord that is reproduced in digital format is not made available to the public in that format outside the premises of the library or archives in lawful possession of such copy.

For purposes of this subsection, a format shall be considered obsolete if the machine or device necessary to render perceptible a work stored in that format is no longer manufactured or is no longer reasonably available in the commercial marketplace.

(d) The rights of reproduction and distribution under this section apply to a copy, made from the collection of a library or archives where the user makes his or her request or from that of another library or archives, of no more than one article or other contribution to a copyrighted collection or periodical issue, or to a copy or phonorecord of a small part of any other copyrighted work, if —

(1) the copy or phonorecord becomes the property of the user, and the library or archives has had no notice that the copy or phonorecord would be used for any purpose other than private study, scholarship, or research; and

(2) the library or archives displays prominently, at the place where orders are accepted, and includes on its order form, a warning of copyright in accordance with requirements that the Register of Copyrights shall prescribe by regulation.

(e) The rights of reproduction and distribution under this section apply to the entire work, or to a substantial part of it, made from the collection of a library or archives where the user makes his or her request or from that of another library or archives, if the library or archives has first determined, on the basis of a reasonable investigation, that a copy or phonorecord of the copyrighted work cannot be obtained at a fair price, if —

(1) the copy or phonorecord becomes the property of the user, and the library or archives has had no notice that the copy or phonorecord would be used for any purpose other than private study, scholarship, or research; and

(2) the library or archives displays prominently, at the place where orders are accepted, and includes on its order form, a warning of copyright in accordance with requirements that the Register of Copyrights shall prescribe by regulation.

(f) Nothing in this section —

(1) shall be construed to impose liability for copyright infringement upon a library or archives or its employees for the unsupervised use of reproducing equipment located on its premises: *Provided,* That such equipment displays a notice that the making of a copy may be subject to the copyright law;

(2) excuses a person who uses such reproducing equipment or who requests a copy or phonorecord under subsection (d) from liability for copyright infringement for any such act, or for any later use of such copy or phonorecord, if it exceeds fair use as provided by section 107;

(3) shall be construed to limit the reproduction and distribution by lending of a limited number of copies and excerpts by a library or archives of

an audiovisual news program, subject to clauses (1), (2), and (3) of subsection (a); or

(4) in any way affects the right of fair use as provided by section 107, or any contractual obligations assumed at any time by the library or archives when it obtained a copy or phonorecord of a work in its collections.

(g) The rights of reproduction and distribution under this section extend to the isolated and unrelated reproduction or distribution of a single copy or phonorecord of the same material on separate occasions, but do not extend to cases where the library or archives, or its employee —

(1) is aware or has substantial reason to believe that it is engaging in the related or concerted reproduction or distribution of multiple copies or phonorecords of the same material, whether made on one occasion or over a period of time, and whether intended for aggregate use by one or more individuals or for separate use by the individual members of a group; or

(2) engages in the systematic reproduction or distribution of single or multiple copies or phonorecords of material described in subsection (d): *Provided,* That nothing in this clause prevents a library or archives from participating in interlibrary arrangements that do not have, as their purpose or effect, that the library or archives receiving such copies or phonorecords for distribution does so in such aggregate quantities as to substitute for a subscription to or purchase of such work.

(h)(1) For purposes of this section, during the last 20 years of any term of copyright of a published work, a library or archives, including a nonprofit educational institution that functions as such, may reproduce, distribute, display, or perform in facsimile or digital form a copy or phonorecord of such work, or portions thereof, for purposes of preservation, scholarship, or research, if such library or archives has first determined, on the basis of a reasonable investigation, that none of the conditions set forth in subparagraphs (A), (B), and (C) of paragraph (2) apply.

(2) No reproduction, distribution, display, or performance is authorized under this subsection if —

(A) the work is subject to normal commercial exploitation;

(B) a copy or phonorecord of the work can be obtained at a reasonable price; or

(C) the copyright owner or its agent provides notice pursuant to regulations promulgated by the Register of Copyrights that either of the conditions set forth in subparagraphs (A) and (B) applies.

(3) The exemption provided in this subsection does not apply to any subsequent uses by users other than such library or archives.

(i) The rights of reproduction and distribution under this section do not apply to a musical work, a pictorial, graphic or sculptural work, or a motion picture or other audiovisual work other than an audiovisual work dealing with news, except that no such limitation shall apply with respect to rights granted by subsections (b), (c), and (h), or with respect to pictorial or graphic works published as illustrations, diagrams, or similar adjuncts to works of which copies are reproduced or distributed in accordance with subsections (d) and (e).

Section 109. Limitations on exclusive rights: Effect of transfer of particular copy or phonorecord

(a) Notwithstanding the provisions of section 106(3), the owner of a particular copy or phonorecord lawfully made under this title, or any person authorized by such owner, is entitled, without the authority of the copyright owner, to sell or otherwise dispose of the possession of that copy or phonorecord. Notwithstanding the preceding sentence, copies or phonorecords of works subject to restored copyright under section 104A that are manufactured before the date of restoration of copyright or, with respect to reliance parties, before publication or service of notice under section 104A(e), may be sold or otherwise disposed of without the authorization of the owner of the restored copyright for purposes of direct or indirect commercial advantage only during the 12-month period beginning on —

(1) the date of the publication in the Federal Register of the notice of intent filed with the Copyright Office under section 104A(d)(2)(A), or

(2) the date of the receipt of actual notice served under section 104A(d)(2)(B), whichever occurs first.

(b)(1)(A) Notwithstanding the provisions of subsection (a), unless authorized by the owners of copyright in the sound recording or the owner of copyright in a computer program (including any tape, disk, or other medium embodying such program), and in the case of a sound recording in the musical works embodied therein, neither the owner of a particular phonorecord nor any person in possession of a particular copy of a computer program (including any tape, disk, or other medium embodying such program), may, for the purposes of direct or indirect commercial advantage, dispose of, or authorize the disposal of, the possession of that phonorecord or computer program (including any tape, disk, or other medium embodying such program) by rental, lease, or lending, or by any other act or practice in the nature of rental, lease, or lending. Nothing in the preceding sentence shall apply to the rental, lease, or lending of a phonorecord for nonprofit purposes by a nonprofit library or nonprofit educational institution. The transfer of possession of a lawfully made copy of a computer program by a nonprofit educational institution to another nonprofit educational institution or to faculty, staff, and students does not constitute rental, lease, or lending for direct or indirect commercial purposes under this subsection.

(B) This subsection does not apply to —

(i) a computer program which is embodied in a machine or product and which cannot be copied during the ordinary operation or use of the machine or product; or

(ii) a computer program embodied in or used in conjunction with a limited purpose computer that is designed for playing video games and may be designed for other purposes.

(C) Nothing in this subsection affects any provision of chapter 9 of this title.

(2)(A) Nothing in this subsection shall apply to the lending of a computer program for nonprofit purposes by a nonprofit library, if each copy of a computer program which is lent by such library has affixed to the packaging containing the program a warning of copyright in accordance with requirements that the Register of Copyrights shall prescribe by regulation.

(B) Not later than three years after the date of the enactment of the Computer Software Rental Amendments Act of 1990, and at such times thereafter as the Register of Copyrights considers appropriate, the Register of Copyrights, after consultation with representatives of copyright owners and librarians, shall submit to the Congress a report stating whether this paragraph has achieved its intended purpose of maintaining the integrity of the copyright system while providing nonprofit libraries the capability to fulfill their function. Such report shall advise the Congress as to any information or recommendations that the Register of Copyrights considers necessary to carry out the purposes of this subsection.

(3) Nothing in this subsection shall affect any provision of the antitrust laws. For purposes of the preceding sentence, “antitrust laws” has the meaning given that term in the first section of the Clayton Act and includes section 5 of the Federal Trade Commission Act to the extent that section relates to unfair methods of competition.

(4) Any person who distributes a phonorecord or a copy of a computer program (including any tape, disk, or other medium embodying such program) in violation of paragraph (1) is an infringer of copyright under section 501 of this title and is subject to the remedies set forth in sections 502, 503, 504, 505, and 509. Such violation shall not be a criminal offense under section 506 or cause such person to be subject to the criminal penalties set forth in section 2319 of title 18.

(c) Notwithstanding the provisions of section 106(5), the owner of a particular copy lawfully made under this title, or any person authorized by such owner, is entitled, without the authority of the copyright owner, to display that copy publicly, either directly or by the projection of no more than one image at a time, to viewers present at the place where the copy is located.

(d) The privileges prescribed by subsections (a) and (c) do not, unless authorized by the copyright owner, extend to any person who has acquired possession of the copy or phonorecord from the copyright owner, by rental, lease, loan, or otherwise, without acquiring ownership of it.

(e) Notwithstanding the provisions of sections 106(4) and 106(5), in the case of an electronic audiovisual game intended for use in coin-operated equipment, the owner of a particular copy of such a game lawfully made under this title, is entitled, without the authority of the copyright owner of the game, to publicly perform or display that game in coin-operated equipment, except that this subsection shall not apply to any work of authorship embodied in the audiovisual game if the copyright owner of the electronic audiovisual game is not also the copyright owner of the work of authorship.

Section 407. Deposit of copies or phonorecords for Library of Congress

(a) Except as provided by subsection (c), and subject to the provisions of subsection (e), the owner of copyright or of the exclusive right of publication in a work published in the United States shall deposit, within three months after the date of such publication —

(1) two complete copies of the best edition; or

(2) if the work is a sound recording, two complete phonorecords of the best edition, together with any printed or other visually perceptible material published with such phonorecords.

Neither the deposit requirements of this subsection nor the acquisition provisions of subsection (e) are conditions of copyright protection.

(b) The required copies or phonorecords shall be deposited in the Copyright Office for the use or disposition of the Library of Congress. The Register of Copyrights shall, when requested by the depositor and upon payment of the fee prescribed by section 708, issue a receipt for the deposit.

(c) The Register of Copyrights may by regulation exempt any categories of material from the deposit requirements of this section, or require deposit of only one copy or phonorecord with respect to any categories. Such regulations shall provide either for complete exemption from the deposit requirements of this section, or for alternative forms of deposit aimed at providing a satisfactory archival record of a work without imposing practical or financial hardships on the depositor, where the individual author is the owner of copyright in a pictorial, graphic, or sculptural work and (i) less than five copies of the work have been published, or (ii) the work has been published in a limited edition consisting of numbered copies, the monetary value of which would make the mandatory deposit of two copies of the best edition of the work burdensome, unfair, or unreasonable.

(d) At any time after publication of a work as provided by subsection(a), the Register of Copyrights may make written demand for the required deposit on any of the persons obligated to make the deposit under subsection (a). Unless deposit is made within three months after the demand is received, the person or persons on whom the demand was made are liable —

(1) to a fine of not more than $250 for each work; and

(2) to pay into a specially designated fund in the Library of Congress the total retail price of the copies or phonorecords demanded, or, if no retail price has been fixed, the reasonable cost to the Library of Congress of acquiring them; and

(3) to pay a fine of $2,500, in addition to any fine or liability imposed under clauses (1) and (2), if such person willfully or repeatedly fails or refuses to comply with such a demand.

(e) With respect to transmission programs that have been fixed and transmitted to the public in the United States but have not been published, the Register of Copyrights shall, after consulting with the Librarian of Congress and other interested organizations and officials, establish regulations governing the acquisition, through deposit or otherwise, of copies or phonorecords of such programs for the collections of the Library of Congress.

(1) The Librarian of Congress shall be permitted, under the standards and conditions set forth in such regulations, to make a fixation of a transmission program directly from a transmission to the public, and to reproduce one copy or phonorecord from such fixation for archival purposes.

(2) Such regulations shall also provide standards and procedures by which the Register of Copyrights may make written demand, upon the owner of the right of transmission in the United States, for the deposit of a copy or phonorecord of a specific transmission program. Such deposit may, at the option of the owner of the right of transmission in the United States, be accomplished by gift, by loan for purposes of reproduction, or by sale at a price not to exceed the cost of reproducing and supplying the copy or phonorecord. The regulations established under this clause shall provide reasonable periods of not less than three months for compliance with a demand, and shall allow for extensions of such periods and adjustments in the scope of the demand or the methods for fulfilling it, as reasonably warranted by the circumstances. Willful failure or refusal to comply with the conditions prescribed by such regulations shall subject the owner of the right of transmission in the United States to liability for an amount, not to exceed the cost of reproducing and supplying the copy or phonorecord in question, to be paid into a specially designated fund in the Library of Congress.

(3) Nothing in this subsection shall be construed to require the making or retention, for purposes of deposit, of any copy or phonorecord of an unpublished transmission program, the transmission of which occurs before the receipt of a specific written demand as provided by clause (2).

(4) No activity undertaken in compliance with regulations prescribed under clauses (1) and (2) of this subsection shall result in liability if intended solely to assist in the acquisition of copies or phonorecords under this subsection.

Section 704. Retention and disposition of articles deposited in Copyright Office

(a) Upon their deposit in the Copyright Office under sections 407 and 408, all copies, phonorecords, and identifying material, including those deposited in connection with claims that have been refused registration, are the property of the United States Government.

(b) In the case of published works, all copies, phonorecords, and identifying material deposited are available to the Library of Congress for its collections, or for exchange or transfer to any other library. In the case of unpublished works, the Library is entitled, under regulations that the Register of Copyrights shall prescribe, to select any deposits for its collections or for transfer to the National Archives of the United States or to a Federal records center, as defined in section 2901 of title 44.

(c) The Register of Copyrights is authorized, for specific or general categories of works, to make a facsimile reproduction of all or any part of the material deposited under section 408, and to make such reproduction a part of the Copyright Office records of the registration, before transferring such material to the Library of Congress as provided by subsection (b), or before destroying or otherwise disposing of such material as provided by subsection (d).

(d) Deposits not selected by the Library under subsection (b), or identifying portions or reproductions of them, shall be retained under the control of the Copyright Office, including retention in Government storage facilities, for the longest period considered practicable and desirable by the Register of Copyrights and the Librarian of Congress. After that period it is within the joint discretion of the Register and the Librarian to order their destruction or other disposition; but, in the case of unpublished works, no deposit shall be knowingly or intentionally destroyed or otherwise disposed of during its term of copyright unless a facsimile reproduction of the entire deposit has been made a part of the Copyright Office records as provided by subsection (c).

(e) The depositor of copies, phonorecords, or identifying material under section 408, or the copyright owner of record, may request retention, under the control of the Copyright Office, of one or more of such articles for the full term of copyright in the work. The Register of Copyrights shall prescribe, by regulation, the conditions under which such requests are to be made and granted, and shall fix the fee to be charged under section 708(a)(10) if the request is granted.